DUSTRIAL MARKET STRUCTURE
ID PERFORMANCE, 1960-1968

ryl N. Winn

chigan Business Studies 1, No. 2

This book reports on a statistical analysis of
relation between market structure and the
ual performance of economic units. It fo-
es on the question: Is the consistent associ-
•n of above-average returns with industrial
rket concentration necessarily a result of
•ct cause and effect (a fundamental assump-
incorporated in current, key recommenda-
is for antitrust policy) or is it the result of
lticollinearity among several phenomena?
additional phenomena whose influence is
estigated are: firm size, capital intensity,
wth, business risk, and distortions arising
n the use of historical costs. In addition
fessor Winn examines the measures of prof-
ility themselves for systematic bias in ob-
/ed measures.

Vorking with a basic panel of 768 firms clas-
d into 132 industries over an eight-year
od of performance, the author uses regres-
analysis to test a set of fundamental
otheses against empirical results.

his study has direct application to public
cy on antitrust measures, as its concise
clusion demonstrates. The reader will find
rofessor Winn's report of his work a valu-
addition to the literature on antitrust
iomics.

aryl N. Winn is associate professor of busi-
economics and public policy at the Col-
of Business and Administration, Univer-
of Colorado, on leave 1975-76 to study the
ndustry's structure and performance as
omist for the Federal Energy
inistration's Office of Economic Impact,
ket Structure and Regulation Impact Divi-

Iany of the numerous articles Dr. Winn has
ten and coauthored and the papers he has
ented at professional meetings have fo-
d on measures of concentration and prof-
ility. His present research concerns the
ct of using replacement costs rather than
orical costs in accounting financial state-
its; managerial behavior and monopoly
ver are among other issues he has investi-
d within his field of major interest — public
cy toward business.

n 1973 Dr. Winn received the Ph.D. from
University of Michigan Graduate School of
iness Administration, where he had also
earned the M.B.A. degree. A native of
Oregon, he was graduated as an accounting
major from Arizona State University. His
career as a student was marked throughout by
many awards and honors; consistent with it has
been the level of his professional activity since
receipt of his doctorate, the dissertation for
which is the basis for *Industrial Market Structure and Performance*.

MICHIGAN BUSINESS STUDIES

Volume I   Number 2

Industrial Market Structure and Performance

1960-1968

Daryl N. Winn

vision of Research • Graduate School of Business Administration • The University of Michigan

ISBN 0–87712–169–9

A Publication of the
Division of Research
Graduate School of Business Administration
The University of Michigan
Ann Arbor, Michigan

CONTENTS

Contents, *continued*

TABLES

TABLE

TABLES, *continued*

FIGURES

PREFACE

In the fall of 1969 I was asked to read President Johnson's Antitrust Task Force Report, known as the Neal Report. Its conclusions and recommendations, which called for the break up of industries with seller concentration ratios of 70 percent or more and the prevention of mergers on the basis of these same seller concentration ratios, impressed me as being quite strong. Its support for the so-called Concentration Industries Act was argued in theory and was drawn from the "correlation of evidence" that high concentration leads to above-average rates of return.

In the belief that these strong recommendations could not be based solely on the existing state of oligopolistic theory, I concluded that they must therefore be based on the existing empirical evidence. After perusing this evidence, it appeared to me that, while high concentration was consistently found to be associated with above-average returns, I was not convinced that their relation was one of cause and effect. In other words, on the basis of the empirical evidence I reviewed, the Neal Report's conclusions seemed unwarranted.

I therefore set out to gather my own evidence. In particular, I attempted to explore several lines of analysis of other influences which, a review of the literature indicated, could possibly account for the collinearity between concentration and profitability. These other influences are firm size, capital intensity, growth, business risk, and the distortions arising from the use of historical costs.

Specifically, this study seeks to answer one fundamental question: Is the frequently observed relation between concentration and profitability one of direct cause and effect or is it a result of multicollinearity among several phenomena?

To answer the question, a basic panel of 768 firms classified into 132 roughly three- and four-digit (SIC) industries is studied for the 1960–68 time period. In addition to four-firm concentration ratios, the other structural factors which are hypothesized to affect observed measures of profitability are: firm size, capital intensity, and rates of growth. Also, the

ix

measures of profitability themselves are explored to determine whether there is systematic bias in observed measures. Regression is the basic method of analysis.

The study of the relations between profitability and the four structural variables involves interindustry analysis using 768 firms as units of observation, intraindustry analysis using 736 firms in 79 industries as units of observation, and finally industry analysis using 79 industries (736 firms) as units of observation. A major portion of the analysis is the determination of how the intraindustry relations between profitability, size, and capital intensity affect the interindustry relations between these variables, including concentration. Another major portion of the analysis is the study of the relation between profitability, size, capital intensity, and growth within six concentration categories used to reflect comparable levels of product market power.

The analysis incorporates the study of two potential biases in these observed measures of performance. First, rates of return are adjusted to reflect risk-comparable returns. Two types of business risk are identified: (1) risk from a firm's uncertainty of (yearly) returns over time (temporal risk) and (2) risk from the uncertainty of the average or level of returns a firm (any potential entrant) would earn were it to enter the various industries (spatial risk). For each type of risk, two components are studied —the standard deviation and the skewness of the appropriate rate-of-return distribution. The relations between these two components of risk and period-average returns are used to estimate firm and industry risk-comparable returns, which are, in turn, used in the analysis.

Second, the study adjusts 339 firm rate-of-return measures to reflect the current costs of plant, machinery, and equipment stocks in use during the 1960–68 period in light of capital expenditure data for the longer period of 1950–68. The adjustments to the current costs of fixed assets and the resultant effects on profits are estimated to compute current-cost rates of return. These returns are then regressed against concentration and the other structural variables.

The results from these analyses are too numerous to summarize here. However, the combined evidence from the study of fifteen hypotheses culminates in the conclusion that there exists considerable doubt as to the validity of the proposition that, after accounting for the independent influences of firm size, capital intensity, growth, business risk, and the distortions arising from the use of historical costs, concentrated industries earn above-average long-run rates of return. In other words, the multicollinearity of the several phenomena analyzed in this study precludes a judgment that it is high product market concentration that causes above-average rates of return.

Acknowledgements

Financial support for this project from the Division of Research, Graduate School of Business Administration, The University of Michigan, is gratefully acknowledged. This support was provided through two grants, entitled "Evolving Competitive Aspects in Major Industries" and "The Analysis of Industry Performance Criteria." Because this study comprises the empirical portion of my dissertation, I wish to thank the members of my committee for their valuable help and time. These members were: Professors Dick A. Leabo, Roger L. Wright, and H. Paul Root of the Graduate School of Business Administration and Michael Klass of the Economic Department, all at The University of Michigan.

I also greatly appreciate the editorial assistance of Henrietta H. Slote, Editor, Division of Research, Graduate School of Business Administration, University of Michigan. A special debt of gratitude is owed to Kathleen Goode for painstakingly programming all the computer analysis. The project could not have been completed without her endurance. And, finally, special thanks to my wife, Elizabeth, whose patience and faith encouraged me to do a better job than I might otherwise have done.

INTRODUCTION

At the time this nation was founded, Adam Smith wrote:

It is the great multiplication of the productions of all the different arts, in consequence of the division of labour, which occasions, in a well-governed society, that universal opulence which extends itself to the lowest ranks of the people.[1]

The essence of this statement underlies many subsequent enunciations of economic principle, although economists' language has changed considerably since Smith wrote. But to speak in terms of competition and monopoly should not be construed as simply extending Smith's argument. Too often it is. Indeed, *competition* and *monopoly* are too often used confusingly. The reader is left to interpret whether a behavioral or a physical concept is intended.[2] Here, clearly, Smith was thinking in terms of physical properties or principles of economic organization, more recently known as market structure. The relation of structure to the behavior or performance of economic units is most complex. Nevertheless much research (both empirical and theoretical) been devoted to establishing the relation, and our legislators and administrators apply the findings in their formulation of antitrust policy.

Nature of the study

The purpose of this study is to seek evidence on the relationship between market structure and the performance of economic units. Average rates of return for 1960–68 are taken to measure the long-run performance of the 768 firms studied. The principal measure of structure is the common measure of monopoly power—seller concentration ratios. While this relation between concentration and profitability, in particular, has received so much attention and is the focus in this study, other physical properties of markets are studied. In addition to concentration

1. *The Wealth of Nations* (Modern Library ed.; New York: Random House, n.d.), p.11.

2. F. M. Scherer adopts the term *rivalry* to distinguish competition in the behavioral sense from competition in the structural sense, because, as he states: "failure to recognize these implied semantic distinctions has often led to confusion in policy discussions." (*Industrial Market Structure and Economic Performance* [Chicago: Rand McNally & Co., 1970], p. 9).

ratios, firm size, capital intensity, and growth rate variables are used to explain differences in profitability among firms. The method of study is regression analysis, where both firms (768) and industries (79) are used as the unit of observation. Because both firm and industry data are used, the relations among these variables are studied not only across industries but within industries as well. It is argued that intraindustry relations among these firm variables may be an important determinant of the interindustry relations. Consequently, in addition to the traditional "horizontal" study across industries (without regard to industry), the effect of intraindustry relations is explored. For example, the following kinds of questions can be addressed: "How does concentration affect the relation between firm size and profitability within industries; or the relation between firm size and capital intensity within industres?"

Another integral part of the study is an attempt to determine whether observed or unadjusted measures of profitability yield biased estimates of the relations between profitability and all or some of the structural variables. Two sources of bias in observed measures of profitability (performance), which could render the measures incomparable, are explored: differences in exposure to business risk and the use of historical costs in the determination of observed rates of return. A second major purpose of this study is to determine whether these distortions are systematically connected to the other relations—in particular, the relation between performance (profitability) and monopoly power (concentration ratios). In sum, this study seeks the answer to one fundamental question: "Is the common empirical finding (supported by theoretical expectations) that monopoly power is associated with above-average rates of return one of direct cause and effect, or can it be explained by the multicollinearity among several phenomena?" The remaining pages of this chapter will demonstrate the importance of the answer to this question.

Antitrust Policy

Today it is the stated policy of the government of the United States to maintain competition and prevent monopoly whenever such action best serves the public interest. Furthermore, the antitrust laws of the government embody and reflect commitment to the belief that the best use of economic resources obtains from competition and capitalism. This belief, of course, presupposes economic freedom, about which Milton Friedman asserts "that the great threat to freedom is the concentration of power."[3] To Adam Smith economic freedom is vital. For with it

3. Milton Friedman, *Capitalism and Freedom* (Phoenix Books; Chicago: University of Chicago Press, 1962), p. 2.

. . . every individual necessarily labours to render the annual revenue of the society as great as he can. He generally, indeed, neither intends to promote the public interest, nor knows how much he is promoting it. . . . [H]e intends only his own gain, and he is in this . . . led by an invisible hand to promote an end which was no part of his intention.[4]

With this often-quoted passage, Smith enunciates his behavioral notion of competition as the "invisible hand." Its relationship to the physical properties of economic organization has not been adequately treated, however. The result is an apparent, and often recognized, contradiction or paradox in antitrust policy, which evolves from attempts to synthesize these behavioral and physical concepts. Criticism that antitrust action protects competitors rather than fosters competition is evidence of this paradox. Indeed, concentration of economic power is defined in physical terms of size or number, while the impact of such concentration is judged in terms of the effects on behavior (often deduced from performance).

In the inability to reconcile these concepts an apparent corollary of economic freedom appears—i.e., that numbers of competitors connotes competition. Furthermore, a large number and wide dispersion of producing entities ensures experimentation, the development of new technology, and the innovation which is so necessary to a viable and dynamic economic system. Thus, a common view seems to be that, to the extent that economic freedom is unobstructed, competition will prevail and with it "the great multiplication of the productions."

However, the record shows that the 500 largest firms (indeed a very small fraction of all producing entities) control over one-half of our economy's nonfarm assets, and the four largest firms of many industries account for more than 70 percent of their industry's output. The question then is this: What is the nature of the forces leading to this condition, if public policy and the basic premises upon which our economic system is predicated oppose this result?

Smith articulated two separate concepts in his discussion of the pin factory and the invisible hand. Both concepts, with some modification, are applicable to current economic theory. The advantages in the division of labor have been extended to the principle of scale economies, both internal and external. The workings of the invisible hand have seen the greatest modifications since the departure from the days of atomistic competition. The former led to the latter, and concepts such as "workable competition" developed. For many years now the trend toward fewer and larger producing entities could be defended as serving the public interest. That is, the public has benefited from the advantages of the

4. Smith, *Wealth of Nations*, p. 423.

physical properties of economic organization more than it has lost in moving away from atomistic competition and the attendant favorable behavioral implications. These two principles are at odds. Arthur Burns makes this point in discussing the applicability of antitrust laws as based on econome theory. He states that:

> . . . Theory is internally contradictory in some circumstances. The lowest cost may be achieved only by firms so large that they are too few to behave competitively. A choice must then be made between (1) firms of the most efficient size but operating under conditions where there is inadequate pressure to compel the firms to continue to be efficient and pass on to the consumer the benefits of efficiency and (2) a system in which the firms are numerous enough to be competitive but too small to be efficient.[5]

In using the term competition, then, policymakers must not look upon it as an end in itself. Originally (supposedly), the attainment of competition—which meant atomostic (competitive) market structures—was thought to serve best the public welfare. How the individual or firm was expected to behave under such "ideal" structural conditions also fell under the label of competition. Thus it could be said that in Adam Smith's time observed structure wrought a behavioral mode or norm. Structure can no longer be viewed in this way. Rather, business must be judged, not in terms of competition, but in terms of its performance in serving the economic interests of its public, whether it be through "competition" or some other means. And furthermore, the goal of antitrust policy should be to establish public welfare, not competition. It is this goal of public welfare that is enunciated in the Neal Report,[6] a report of the White House Task Force on Antitrust Policy appointed by President Johnson to study and make recommendations on the nation's antitrust policy.

While the above goal of antitrust policy is not debated, the methods used to pursue this goal can be, should be, and are, hotly debated.[7] It

---

5. Thurman Arnold, Arthur R. Burns, *et al.*, "The Effectiveness of the Antitrust Laws," in *Monopoly Power and Economic Performance,* ed. by Edwin Mansfield (New York: W. W. Norton & Co., 1964), p. 129.

6. U.S., Congress, Senate, Phil C. Neal, Chairman, White House Task Force on Antitrust Policy, "Task Force Report on Antitrust Policy," *Congressional Record,* May 27, 1969, pp. S5642–S5659 (hereafter cited as the *Neal Report*).

7. This debate has culminated in the contrasting views of two Presidential task forces charged by two different Presidents to make recommendations on the means to effect antitrust policy. While President Johnson's task force, in the Neal Report, recommends breaking up concentrated industries, President Nixon's task force, in the Stigler Report, concludes that existing knowledge calls for no such action. Instead, the Stigler Report (issued shortly after the Neal Report) calls for antitrust action to be directed against uncompetitive pricing activities. (U.S., Congress, Senate,

is one thing to affirm a noble goal; it is another to effect successful policy to attain that goal. In a capsule, the issue in antitrust policy today lies in the following widely held view expressed in the Neal Report.

> Effective antitrust laws must bring about both competitive behavior and competitive industry structure. *In the long run, competitive structure is the more important since it creates conditions conducive to competitive behavior.*[8] [Emphasis supplied.]

This statement is almost incomprehensible to even the trained economist. The *italicized* words contain the crux of the issue; they represent an inextricable web of a priori economic theory, empirical observation, ideology, and philosophy. There is no question that business behavior must be judged on the basis of its impact on economic freedom and consumer-public welfare. But it is a far more complex task to adduce market structure as "the" force in the determination of this behavior, which is at issue here. In familiar terms, *this study seeks empirical evidence on the relationship between market structure and market performance.*

Market structure and market performance

Before further discussion, a short digression on what economists mean by market structure and performance would seem useful. Performance refers to the end result of business activity or conduct in serving the economic interests of the public. It is often judged by quantitative criteria such as prices, profits, output, and costs; and by qualitative criteria such as innovation, product design and quality. Some include the facilitation of stable, full employment and equity of income distribution in their definition of performance.[9] In other words, performance encompasses the complex adjustments to changes in conditions of demand and supply in related markets.

Market structure, on the other hand, refers to various physical properties of relations among firms in associated markets. Among these economists include the number and size distribution of firms (sellers and buyers), product differentiation, barriers to entry, ratio of fixed costs to total costs, vertical integration, and product diversification.

George J. Stigler, Chairman, "White House Task Force on Productivity and Competition," *Congressional Record,* June 12, 1969, pp. 15654–15657 [hereafter cited as the *Stigler Report*].)

8. *Neal Report*, p. S5642.

9. For a good discussion of the dimensions of performance and its relation to market structure and conduct (soon to be discussed) see Scherer, *Industrial Market Structure and Economic Performance,* chap. 1.

Bain suggests, not one, but two determinants of business performance:

> First, the organization or structure of an industry (or group of competing enterprises) exercises a strong influence on the performance of the industry. That is, *market structure* constrains and canalizes enterprise activities and their results; and variations in structure may lead to associated variations in performance. Second, the *market conduct* of enterprise— . . . politics, practices, and devices they employ in arriving at adjustments to the markets in which they participate—also influences performance.[10]

Too often, studies of the relation between performance and structure fail to recognize and appreciate the intervening variable—conduct—which may alter "predictable" relationships between performance and market structure. The task, then, is to establish a relationship between structure and conduct on one hand, and structure and performance on the other. To do this it is first necessary to find if cause-and-effect relations between the structure, conduct, and performance variables exist.

Structure-performance relationship

Before cause and effect can be discussed, however, one must seek to determine why a certain structure exists in a particular market. Too often, it seems, market structure is taken as a given, and with this as a point of departure, economists begin to analyze its good or bad features. In doing so, they fail as scientists. As Scherer illustrates, there may be underlying forces which may lead to (cause) the observed patterns of structure in markets. Thus a fourth element, which Scherer calls "basic conditions," enters the framework of this analysis. Both supply and demand factors are seen to influence the emergence of a market structure. On the supply side Scherer lists: raw material location and ownership, technology, product durability, the ratio of product value to its weight, business attitudes, and unionization. On the demand side he lists: price elasticity, rate of growth, availability of substitutes, purchasing habits of buyers and the product's marketing characteristics, and the cyclical and seasonal character of the product.[11] Generally, this broad framework of analysis allows one to draw informed conclusions—in terms of the aforementioned goals of antitrust policy—about various patterns of structure and conduct which severally and jointly may be conducive to "good" performance.

It has long been recognized that pure and perfect competition does

---

10. Joe S. Bain, *Industrial Organization* (2d ed.; New York: John Wiley & Sons, 1968), p. 3.

11. Scherer, *Industrial Market Structure and Economic Performance*, pp. 4–5.

not exist in the United States. Thus theory has evolved which attempts to replace the classical models of competition and monopoly and their assumptions about market structure.[12] Just as economic theory adjusts to changes in atomistic market structures, so it has adjusted to changes in ideas about market conduct. Profit maximization no longer is the fundamental premise of business conduct but, instead, is being replaced or modified by theories of revenue maximization, profit satisficing, managerial emoluments, and, more generally, a "behavioral" theory of the firm.[13] While these refinements in theory advance our knowledge and perspective of the subject at hand, they also complicate the task tremendously and render empirical analysis of the structure-performance relationship too involved to be undertaken as a single study. Thus we will not be directly or immediately concerned with such refinements here. Instead, as is common in many other empirical studies, this study, to a certain extent, ignores or assumes away differences in motivation and its matrix of possible influences on a structure-performance relationship. This does not imply that conduct is unimportant. In fact, it could be argued that conduct not only becomes an intervening variable which may explain or cause failure to find universal structure-performance relationships, but that conduct—generally the host of possible intervening variables—could also aid in assessing whether the direction of causation was from structure to performance or from performance to structure.

In this study relations are not sought for their "predictive" ability, but for their usefulness in indicating cause and effect. This follows because public policy should not be concerned with removing symptoms, but rather should be concerned with causes and their effects.

A quotation from the Neal Report summarizes a commonly held view of the importance of market structure to conduct and performance in the attainment of the economic goals of our society.

> Market structure is an important concern of antitrust laws for two reasons. *First,* the more competitive a market structure (the larger the number of competitors and the smaller their market shares) the greater the difficulty of maintaining collusive behavior and the more easily such behavior can be detected.

---

12. The two most notable examples are Edward Chamberlin, *The Theory of Monopolistic Competition* (7th ed.; Cambridge, Mass.: Harvard University Press, 1956), and Joan Robinson, *The Economics of Imperfect Competition* (London: Macmillan & Co., 1933).

13. See for example: William J. Baumol, *Business Behavior, Value and Growth* (rev. ed.; New York: Harcourt, Brace & World, 1967); Oliver Williamson, *The Economics of Discretionary Behavior:Managerial Objectives in a Theory of the Firm* (Englewood Cliffs, N.J.: Prentice-Hall, 1964); R. M. Cyert and J. G. March, *A Behavioral Theory of the Firm* (Englewood Cliffs, N.J.: Prentice-Hall, 1963). For a good summary of many of these revisions see Williamson, chap. 2.

Second, in markets with a very few firms effects equivalent to those of collusion may occur even in the absence of collusion. In a market with numerous firms, each having a small share, no single firm by its action alone can exert a significant influence over price and thus output will be carried to the point where each seller's marginal cost equals the market price. This level of output is optimal from the point of view of the economy as a whole.

Under conditions of monopoly—with only a single seller in a market—the monopolist can increase his profits by restricting output and thus raising his price; accordingly, prices will tend to be above, and output correspondingly below, the optimum point. In an oligopoly market—one in which there is a small number of dominant sellers, each with a large market share—each must consider the effect of his output on the total market and the probable reactions of the other sellers to his decisions; the results of their combined decisions may approximate the profit-maximizing decisions of a monopolist. Not only does the small number of sellers facilitate agreement, but agreement in the ordinary sense may be unnecessary. Thus, phrases such as "price leadership" or "administered pricing" often do no more than describe behavior which is the inevitable result of structure.[14]

The assessment of the cause and the effect here is all too clear. The key concepts or assertions, of course, are that structure affects performance via behavior, which seemingly results from the existence of a few decision-making units.

This long quotation is presented for several reasons. First, it summarizes the basic arguments showing how structure influences conduct and performance. Second, it enunciates the premises of the governmental task force which was charged to make specific recommendations to the President concerning legislation to effect antitrust policy. Third, it embodies many of the complex and various assumptions about relationships of structure and performance (which have been subjected to numerous empirical studies). Fourth, and not least important, the test of these arguments or hypotheses, as embodied in the Neal Report, serves as the motivating force behind this study.

On the basis of their theoretical framework, the Neal Report concludes:

The alternatives, other than accepting the undesirable economic consequences, are either regulation of price (and other decisions) or improving the competitive structure of the market.

We believe that the goals of antitrust policy require a choice wherever possible in favor of attempting to *perfect the self-regulating* mechanism of the market [the "invisible hand"] before turning to public control. It is for this reason that we favor steps that will increase the effectiveness of the antitrust laws in promoting competitive market structure. Such steps are desirable, not only because the problem of concentrated industries is significant in economic

14. *Neal Report*, p. S5643.

terms, but because the existence of such concentration is a continuing (and perhaps increasing) temptation for political intervention.[15]

It is this assumed association between market structure and performance that must be carefully determined. Otherwise, should policy be based on erroneous analysis and conclusions, the warning about the "temptation for political intervention" may result in poetic justice and nothing more.

Profitability—criterion of performance

Economic literature is replete with theory which relates structure and performance, and it has been so for many years. Perhaps partly because it is the most observable index, profitability seems to be the performance measure in many of the empirical studies. And likewise it is in this study. It is also argued, however, that long-run rates of return as a simple index most meaningfully summarize the results of the interaction of many, if not all, performance criteria cited earlier. Furthermore, it should be noted that profitability is not only a criterion of performance that can be used in analyzing the workings of markets, but it is also the most important decision variable in those markets. George Stigler asserts: "There is no more important proposition in economic theory than that, under competition, the rate of return on investments tends toward equality in all industries."[16] In this proposition, profitability is not only an index which tests the nature of the competition in the economy, but it is the very decision variable that makes such a proposition operational. Discrepancies in the rates of return show themselves first, before the movement of capital (economic resources) can exert its debilitating effect on them and result in the equilibrium condition, i.e., equality of rates of return.

It is the above proposition that provides the general framework of analysis. That rates of return, under competition, tend toward equality "has been taken by some economists as a *definition* of competition; persistently high profits in an industry would be proof that the industry is not competitive."[17] The authors of the Neal Report incorporate this type of analysis into their thinking by asserting that

> . . . above-average profits in a particular industry signal the need and provide the incentive for additional resources and expanded output in the industry, which in due time should return profits to a normal level. It is the persistence

---

15. *Ibid.*, p. S5643.

16. George J. Stigler, *Capital and Rates of Return in Manufacturing Industries* (Princeton, N.J.: Princeton University Press, 1963), p. 54.

17. *Ibid.*, p. 55.

of high profits over extended time periods and over whole industries rather than in individual firms that suggests *artificial restraints on output and the absence of fully effective competition. The correlation of evidence of this kind with the existence of very high levels of concentration appears to be significant.*[18] [Emphasis supplied.]

Above all, the Neal Report recommends that a "Concentrated Industries Act" be enacted. In essence, the proposed act would "deconcentrate" any industry in which four (or fewer) firms had an aggregate market share of 70 percent or more of the industry output.

In March of 1973, Senator Philip A. Hart submitted his "Industrial Reorganization Act" (S. 1167) calling for such divestiture and deconcentration. The possession of "monopoly power" in any line of commerce in any section of the country was declared to be unlawful. Following the reasoning of the Neal Report, "monopoly power" was said to be possessed

(1) by any corporation if the average rate of return on net worth after taxes is in excess of 15 per centum over a period of five consecutive years out of the most recent seven years preceding the filing of the complaint, or

. . . .

(3) if any four or fewer corporations account for 50 per centum (or more) of sales in any line of commerce in any section of the country in any year out of the most recent three years preceding the filing of the complaint.[19]

The extreme to which the arguments and conclusions of the Neal Report can be carried is clear. However, it is this conclusion of the Neal Report (which, in part, is the basis for the Hart Bill) that is vehemently debated in the Stigler Report.

Concern with oligopoly has led to proposals to use antitrust laws (perhaps amended) to deconcentrate highly oligopolistic industries by dissolving their leading firms. We cannot endorse these proposals on the basis of existing knowledge. As indicated, the correlation between concentration and profitability is weak, and many factors besides the number of firms in a market appear to be relevant to the competitiveness of their behavior . . . A flat condemnation of oligopoly thus seems to us unwise. . . .[20]

Purpose and Objectives of Study

The place in economic theory held by measures of profitability is clear. Profitability is central to economic theory upon which the essence of

18. *Neal Report,* p. S5644.
19. U.S., Congress, Senate, "A Bill to Supplement the Antitrust Laws, and to Protect Trade and Commerce against Oligopoly Power or Monopoly Powers and, for Other Purposes," S. 1167, 93d Cong., 1st sess., 1973, *Congressional Record,* Mar. 12, 1973, p. S4362.
20. *Stigler Report,* p. 15655.

antitrust laws is based and behind which theories of industrial organization rest. Under the assumption of profit maximization the relationship between structure and profitability follows easily from the theory of perfect competition and a single-seller monopoly. But, since neither of these forms is observed in the "real world," the relationship can only be found by empirical analysis. The difficulties of forming deterministic models which are of any practical significance are well known in the theory of oligopoly. However, on the basis of empirical analysis, powerful conclusions are drawn and incorporated into the development of economic policy. *The purpose and objectives of this study are to test the hypothesis that an association exists between industrial structure and performance where performance is represented by profitability and—borrowing from the precedent established by previous empirical analysis and the singular importance attached to it by the Neal Report, Stigler Report,[21] and the Hart bill—structure, e.g., monopoly power, is represented by concentration ratios.*

In particular, the purpose of this study is to test the validity of the proposition that high concentration leads to above-average profits. While the Neal Report attaches cause and effect to this proposition, this writer believes that this strong conclusion (though it may be true) is not warranted by the "correlation of evidence."[22] Reviews of the literature indicate several possible explanations other than cause and effect for the correlation between concentration and profitability. The validity of the inferences from previous studies is questioned for two fundamental reasons. First, the basic methodology often seems inadequate because the hypothesis and, therefore, the scope of the study are too narrowly delimited. Second, this writer believes that previous research does not deal adequately with difficulties in the measurement of profitability.

Methodology

The first objection is implicit in several studies of concentration which suggest that one might specify concentration as the dependent variable and other variables, including profit, as independent variables. With this

---

21. The Stigler Report recommends use of "the effective number of rivals" instead of a direct use of four-firm concentration ratios. "The effective number may be roughly estimated at twice the number there would be if all firms were as large as the largest in the industry." (*Stigler Report,* p. 15655.)

22. The writer is not alone in this opinion. Armen A. Alchian and William R. Allen assert that the "evidence does not support that common contention, nor does economic analysis." (*Exchange and Production; Theory in Use* [Belmont, Calif.: Wadsworth, 1969], p. 391.) After surveying the literature, John M. Vernon states:

suggestion some recognize that perhaps variables other than profitability "explain" concentration, or, alternatively, that there are variables other than concentration which "explain" profitability yet are correlated with concentration.

In this study, observed profitability measures are retained as the dependent variable, yet the scope of the analysis is broadened by extending the number of independent variables to include nonstructural as well as structural variables. That is, this is a study of profitability. Primarily it seeks to explain the observed inequality of profitability among firms and therefore among industries. It follows then, that the basic unit of analysis is the firm, not the industry. Though concentration is the prime explanatory variable, others should obviously be considered. The writer believes that much of the inadequacy of previous methodology results from emphasis upon monopoly power rather than upon profitability. The definition of monopoly power, and therefore its measure, is an industry concept. So in the use of concentration ratios one's primary orientation is toward the industry, its structure, and its profitabilty. In the study of firm profitability the concentration variable becomes the concentration ratio for the industry in which each firm functions. More important, however, is determining whether this concentration ratio is related to the other variables that may explain differences in observed profitability measures in firms.

One of the most glaring inadequacies of many concentration-profitability studies is the use of industry-aggregated profit measures. By using only aggregated data, it is difficult to include many potentially important variables which may explain differences in observed profitability between firms, and therefore between industries. That is, many hypotheses which may explain differences in firm profitability can only be tested by using the firm as the unit of observation. The use of industry-aggregated data confounds several important hypotheses explaining differences in rates of return. For example, industry average rates of return are frequently a weighted average of member firm returns rather than a simple average.[23]

"The overwhelming conclusion would appear to be that solid, factual support for public policy in this area [link between structure and performance] does not exist." (*Market Structure and Industrial Performance: A Review of Statistical Findings* [Boston: Allyn & Bacon, 1972], p. 117.)

23. A simple average is arrived at by simply averaging the rate-of-return measures for all firms in the industry. However, these data are frequently not available in many sources. Rather, total industry profits and industry assets (or stockholders' equity) are available. The industry rate-of-return measure as total profits divided by total assets (stockholders' equity) is then a weighed-average return—weighted by the numerator of the fraction.

If there exists a positive relation between firm size and profitability within an industry (scale economies), then the weighted-average rate of return will exceed the simple average. Thus, the use of weighted-average returns confounds the relation between profitability and firm size and the relation between profitability and concentration.

Because of the use of firm data, two structural variables (in addition to concentration) can be employed in the analysis. These variables are firm size (measured in assets) and capital/output ratios. Previous research indicates that firm profitability is associated with firm size, and that, in turn, firm size is associated with capital/output ratios. Although growth can be used as either an industry variable or a firm variable, for purposes of compatability with the other variables, growth is defined for the firm and included in the analysis.

The second fundamental objection to previous research is the inadequate attention given to the observed rate of return as a measure (proxy) for economic performance. It is the writer's opinion that the only relevant profit concept for the study of concentration follows directly from the nature of economists' ultimate concern—resource allocation, i.e., real asset employment. The income concept, therefore must measure total income on assets regardless of the fact that its components may be labeled profits, dividends, or interest.[24] Naturally, then, total assets are the investment base for rate-of-return calculations.

The appropriate concepts having been defined, the measurement process becomes critical.[25] Two important problems in the measurement of profits must be faced. Many concentration-profitability studies recognize that observed rates of return lack comparability insofar as they are earned under different exposures to risk. To this writer's knowledge, only a few researchers have attempted to correct for this distortion The results are, however, as Stigler terms them, "not heartening."[26] This study seeks to analyze the effects differing exposures to risk have on risk premiums included in observed rates of return. Furthermore, it seeks to determine the relations of these risk premiums and risk-adjusted rates of return (rates of return after allowing for differences in risk exposure) to the structural variables.

The second problem in the measurement of profit, one long bemoaned by economists, is the use of historical costs in accounting when deter-

---

24. The total profit measure must therefore include the imputed interest on "non-interest-bearing" liabilities.

25. Profits (as well as assets), as defined and measured for tax purposes, are deemed inappropriate for studies of concentration.

26. *Capital and Rates of Return*, p. 63.

mining the rate of return.[27] Stigler states that "inflation makes historical costs, and depreciation based on historical costs, obsolete. The returns in industries which have relatively durable assets, and in industries with relatively old assets, will be overstated relative to industries with the opposite characteristics."[28] Though this is a rather simple observation, the importance of its implications is overlooked or excluded in almost all studies of profitability and concentration.

If adjusting observed rates of return to reflect current costs of assets would leave the relative performance of industries unchanged, there would be no point in pursuing this problem any further. However, two items suggest that the pattern of rates of return would not remain unchanged. First, growth rates are observed to be slower in concentrated industries,[29] and second, capital intensity increases with the size of the firm.[30] The degree of capital intensity indicates the relative importance of durable assets to a firm's operations. The purpose of adjusting observed rates of return to reflect current costs is to determine whether these adjustments are somehow related to the basic structural variables, in particular to the concentration ratio.

In summary, this study tests the validity of the proposition that high concentration leads to above-average profits. In doing so, the firm becomes the basic unit of observation, for which three other structural variables are defined—firm size, capital intensity, and growth—and included in the analysis. A purpose of this study is to determine the relation between all four structural variables. Finally, the study seeks to quantify two frequently recognized distortions in observed rates of return and adjust the rates accordingly. These distortions are caused by profits being earned under different exposures to risk and by the use of historical costs in determining observed rates of return.

Before the methodology for these undertakings was developed, the foundation for the basic analysis was built on a review of the major empirical works related to the structure-performance hypotheses—the "correlation of evidence."

27. For a good theoretical discussion of the many inadequacies of using accounting profits as a proxy for economic performance see: Joe S. Bain, "The Profit Rate as a Measure of Monopoly Power," *Quarterly Journal of Economics*, 55 (Feb. 1941): 271–93.

28. *The Organization of Industry* (Homewood, Ill.: Richard D. Irwin, 1968), p. 143.

29. For example, see Ralph L. Nelson, *Concentration in the Manufacturing Industries in the United States*, Economic Census Studies No. 2 (New Haven, Conn.: Yale University Press, 1963), pp. 48–58.

30. For example, see John R. Moroney and Jan W. Duggar, "Size of Firm and Capital-Output Ratios; A Comparative Study in U.S. Manufacturing," *MSU Business Topics* 15 (Summer 1967): 16–23.

1

THE GENERAL HYPOTHESES AND THE MEASUREMENT OF PROFITABILITY AND CONCENTRATION

The primary purpose of this study is to test whether the exercise of market power enables firms in concentrated industries to enjoy above-average profitability. The question is one of causality, not one of mere association or correlation. There is reason to believe that an industry which is highly concentrated possesses other structural characteristics which may account for its above-average rates of return, as well as for its being concentrated. A brief review of the evidence provides the basis for a set of interrelated hypotheses on the relations between these structural variables and their relation to performance.

The fourteen hypotheses which follow are used both to summarize the previous research[1] and to give direction to the present undertaking. They are grouped according to the variable used to explain the variation of average rates of return among firms. However, because primary attention is given to concentration as an explanatory variable, the relation between concentration and each of the other variables is explored in some detail.

The Initial Hypothesis

The initial hypothesis to be tested is:

I. Firms in concentrated industries earn above-average long-run rates of return.

The first major study on the relation between concentration and profitability must be credited to Bain,[2] who, in 1951, found a dichotomous

---

1. For a detailed review of these studies and most all of those referred to in this chapter and others, see the author's review of the structure-performance literature forthcoming from the Division of Research, Graduate School of Business Administration, University of Michigan, Ann Arbor, Michigan.

2. Joe S. Bain, "Relation of Profit Rate to Industry Concentration: American Manufacturing, 1936–1940," *Quarterly Journal of Economics* 65 (Aug. 1951): 293–324.

rather than continuous relation. With one notable exception,[3] subsequent studies for different levels of aggregation have found the relation to be positive though sometimes best described as continuous (linear and nonlinear) and other times as discontinuous. From the review of many studies[4] the following conclusions seem warranted:

1. Concentration ratios, computed in quite divergent fashions and not always intended to reflect comparable economically meaningful markets, are with few exceptions positively correlated with most measures of profitability.

2. The results are not overly sensitive to which measure of profitability is used. There is however, evidence that after-tax rates of return produce better results and that rates of return defined for stockholders frequently produce better results than rates of return to all suppliers of capital.

3. Although the relations between concentration and profitability are usually statistically significant, the marginal effect of increases in concentration on rates of return is generally moderate.[5]

4. The relation between concentration and profitability is stronger the more highly aggregated are the data. That is, the size of the regression coefficient for concentration and the percentage of variation in profitability explained by concentration ratios seem to fall in going from the two-digit industry to four-digit industry aggregation.

3. George J. Stigler, *Capital and Rates of Return in Manufacturing Industries* (Princeton, N.J.: Princeton University Press, 1963).

4. Norman R. Collins and Lee E. Preston, *Concentration and Price-Cost Margins in Manufacturing Industries* (Berkeley, Calif.: University of California Press, 1970); Harold M. Levinson, *Postwar Movement of Prices and Wages in Manufacturing Industries*, Study Paper No. 21, U.S., Congress, Joint Economic Committee (Washington, D.C.: Jan. 1960); Leonard W. Weiss, "Average Concentration Ratios and Industrial Performance," *Journal of Industrial Economics* 11 (July 1963): 237–54; Howard J. Sherman, *Profits in the United States* (Ithaca, N.Y.: Cornell University Press, 1968); Richard A. Miller, "Market Structure and Industrial Performance: Relation of Profit Rates to Concentration, Advertising Intensity and Diversity," *Journal of Industrial Economics* 27 (Apr. 1969): 104–18; George J. Stigler, "A Theory of Oligopoly," *Journal of Political Economy* 72 (Feb. 1964): 44–61; U.S., Federal Trade Commission, *Economic Report on the Influences of Market Structure on the Profit Performance of Food Manufacturing Companies* (Washington, D.C.: Superintendent of Documents, Sept. 1969); W. G. Shepherd, "The Elements of Market Structure," *Review of Economics and Statistics* (Feb. 1972): 25–37; Joe S. Bain, *Barriers to New Competition* (Cambridge, Mass.: Harvard University Press, 1956); and H. Michael Mann, "Seller Concentration, Barriers to Entry, and Rates of Return in Thirty Industries, 1950–1960," *Review of Economics and Statistics* 48 (Aug. 1966): 296–307.

5. A regression coefficient for concentration is roughly .2 on before-tax returns and .1 on after-tax returns. In other words, for every 10-point increase in the concentration ratio, rates of return increase by 2 percentage points before taxes and by 1 percentage point after taxes. Frequently the increase in returns is found to be considerably less.

5. The form of the functional relationship remains ambiguous. The various studies reviewed here individually indicated the relation is best described as dichotomous, linear, logarithmic, or parabolic.

6. No obvious generalization about the cyclical nature of the concentration-profitability relationship has emerged.[6]

7. Reasons other than cause-and-effect may explain some or all of the association between concentration and profitability. On the one hand, sample bias may provide a correlation. On the other hand, other structural variables (captured in a barrier-to-entry variable) are correlated with both concentration and profitability and, therefore, the multicollinearity among these may result in an association between concentration and profitability.

8. There is evidence suggesting that above-average rates of return in highly concentrated industries deteriorate over time and that the frequently observed relations between concentration and profitability over various segments of time result from conditions of "disequilibrium."

The importance of this last observation cannot be stressed too heavily. Yale Brozen (perhaps following the lead of Stigler[7]) must receive primary credit for initiating the upsurge of concern for the persistence of the relationship between high profitability and high concentration over extended periods of time.[8] In 1969 Brozen began publishing his finding with supporting arguments to the effect that previously determined relations between concentration and profitability might be "simply a manifestation of a disequilibrium situation."[9] Briefly, he finds that the high returns in the selected highly concentrated industries observed by Bain, Mann, and Stigler converge toward all-industry rates of return when the analysis is extended to the future. Conclusion: the high returns in these industries at one time (when originally studied) were not the long-run rates of return for those industries. While primary concern in

6. The studies reviewed are judged too diverse in methodology to warrant good comparisons for this purpose. Elsewhere Collins and Preston have noted "that a number of investigations have indicated a tendency for the association between concentration and profitability to be stronger in the two observed years of recession (1954 and 1958) than in the previously observed year of prosperity (1947)." However, after comparing their 1958 results with new 1963 results they conclude that "there is no evidence here to support the view . . . that the concentration margins relationship might be [a] cyclical phenomenon. . . ." Collins and Preston, "Price-Cost Margins and Industry Structure," *Review of Economics and Statistics* 51 (Aug. 1969): 284.

7. In *Capital and Rates of Return.*

8. Yale Brozen, "Significance of Profit Rate Data for Antitrust Policy," *Public Policy toward Mergers*, ed. by J. Fred Weston and Sam Peltzman (Pacific Palisades, Calif.: Goodyear Publishing Co., 1969): 110–27; "Concentration and Structural and Market Disequilibria," *Antitrust Bulletin* 16 (Summer 1971): 241–48; "The Antitrust Task Force Deconcentration Recommendation," *Journal of Law and Economics* 13 (Oct. 1970): 279–92; and "The Persistence of 'High Rates of Return' in High-Stable Concentration Industries," *Journal of Law and Economics* 14 (Oct. 1971): 501–12.

9. Brozen, "Significance of Profit Rate Data for Antitrust Policy," p. 119.

the present study is to observe the relation between rates of return and concentration for a given period (1960–68), the deficiency in this approach is noted and an attempt is made to explore the validity of Brozen's objections.

Firm Size

The study of the relation between firm size and profitability has more historical precedent than does the study of the relation between concentration and profitability. Two studies, one by Stekler and one by Sherman,[10] are particularly useful in establishing the general nature of the relationships between size and profitability.

For *all* manufacturing corporations they point out, there is a positive association between size and rate of return (on assets) from the lowest size class up to about the 10- or 20-million-dollar class. At this point it appears a plateau is reached, with no observable further trend. The positive association is most clearly observed when after-tax profits to stockholders' equity is the measure for the rate of return.

From this empirical evidence and on the basis of Baumol's a priori arguments,[11] it is hypothesized:

II. Large firms earn higher rates of return than small firms.

Difficulties in testing this hypothesis arise for several reasons. First, excess salary withdrawals in small firms (less than $500,000 in assets) are seen to understate their profitability and therefore to bias the findings.[12] Adjustment for this problem, however, although it weakens the relationship, leaves the positive association intact. Separating corporations into income and no-income corporations makes a strong case for the contention that the frequently observed positive relation results from a negative relation between firm size and the rate of loss for no-income corporations.[13] In other words, the association between firm size and

10. Howard J. Sherman, *Profits in the United States;* H. O. Stekler, *Profitability and Size of Firm* (Berkeley, Calif.: Institute of Business and Economic Research, University of California, 1963).

11. Baumol's argument can be summarized as follows: Large firms have all the same investment opportunities that small firms have, plus those opportunities unattainable by the small firms. Therefore, one would expect that the greater the absolute size of the firm the higher the long-run rates of return. See Baumol, *Business Behavior, Value and Growth* (rev. ed; New York: Harcourt, Brace, and World, 1967).

12. Stekler, *Profitability and Size of Firm;* Stigler, *Capital and Rates of Return;* Robert W. Kilpatrick, "Stigler on the Relationship between Industry Profit Rates and Market Concentration," *Journal of Political Economy* 76 (Mar.–June, 1968): 479–88.

13. Stekler, *Profitability and Size of Firm;* Richard C. Osborn, "Concentration and Profitability of Small Manufacturing Corporations," *Quarterly Review of Economics and Business* 10 (Summer 1970): 15–26.

rates of return is either negative or it is not apparent when only corporations showing profits (income corporations) are examined. Because the current study includes only large, publicly held corporations, the excess salary withdrawals associated with the use of small firms in the sample is avoided. Any probable income–no-income distortion is minimal, because for the larger corporations the percentage of no-income corporations appears to be quite small.[14]

The concern in this study is not so much that large firms earn high returns, but that previous research may have confounded the relations among concentration, firm size, and profitability. A classical argument is that the presence of economies of scale in certain industries leads to a few large firms in those industries. It is, therefore, best to distinguish between Baumol's "absolute-size" hypothesis and a more classical "relative-size" hypothesis.

Marcus challenges the general validity of the size-profitability hypothesis when he finds that firm size is associated with profitability within only 44 of the 118 IRS industries.[15] This finding suggests that the size-profitability relationship varies from industry to industry, depending, perhaps, upon certain industry characteristics. As a result, in addition to the test of the absolute-size hypothesis, the possibility that the size-profitability relationship within industries is related to structural factors gives rise to what is referred to as the relative-size hypothesis. That is, not only may advantage of absolute size increase profitability, but a firm's size relative to other firms within its industry (though on an absolute basis the firm is small) may also confer advantages. Furthermore, this relative-size relationship may distort the observed absolute-size relationship.

Previous research (especially of Hall and Weiss,[16] and Osborn) has presented evidence which indicates that size and concentration are inextricably related. One could argue that the study of profitability and size within industries is, in part, measuring the degree to which economies of scale are present. Because economies of scale is a structural variable considered as a barrier to entry, which may be associated with concentration, the following hypothesis is tested:

III. The positive effect of firm size on firm rates of return is greater within concentrated industries than within unconcentrated industries.

14. Osborn, "Concentration and Profitability," Table 6, p. 19.
15. Matityahu Marcus, "Profitability and Size of Firm: Some Further Evidence," *Review of Economics and Statistics* 51 (Feb. 1969): 104–7.
16. Marshall Hall and Leonard Weiss, "Firm Size and Profitability," *Review of Economics and Statistics* 49 (Aug. 1967): 327.

Finally, the possibility that the absolute-size–profitability relationship confounds the relationship between profitability and concentration must be explicitly considered. In studies of profitability, the accumulated evidence strongly suggest that rates of return increase as firm size (used by some as a capital requirement barrier to entry) increases and as concentration increases. A difficulty arises because concentrated industries are, on the average, composed of larger firms.[17] The question then is whether, and to what extent, either structural variable—size or concentration—has an independent influence on profitability. That is, may each structural variable simply be a proxy for (correlated with) the other structural variable? In more pragmatic terms for public policy purposes, the question is: Is it bigness *and/or* market power that is associated with (leads to) high rates of return? The answer to this question is of the utmost importance. In part, this is the question Hall and Weiss raise in their study, and they conclude that "concentration would seem to be less important than [the] capital requirements barrier [firm size] as a determinant of profitability."[18] Their policy recommendation, therefore, is to direct more effort "toward an attack on capital market imperfections than to anti-trust programs oriented toward divestiture, dissolution, and merger."[19]

In order to determine the magnitude of the collinearity between these two structural variables, the following hypothesis is tested (although the ultimate purpose is to determine the independent association of each with profitability):

IV. Concentrated industries are composed of larger firms than are unconcentrated industries.

Capital/Output Ratios

Two elements of market structure identified by Scherer are the ratio of fixed costs to total costs and the degree of vertical integration.[20] It is expected, therefore, that capital/output ratios would serve as a proxy

---

17. For a clear tabular presentation of the collinearity of firm size, concentration, and profitability, see Osborn, "Concentration and Profitability."

18. Hall and Weiss, "Firm Size and Profitability," p. 327.

19. *Ibid.*, p. 330.

20. F. M. Scherer, *Industrial Market Structure and Economic Performance* (Chicago: Rand McNally and Co., 1970), pp. 4–5.

for an absolute-capital requirement barrier-to-entry variable,[21] the degree of vertical integration, and the ratio of fixed costs to total costs.[22] It has been found that capital/output ratios are positively correlated with firm size across industries[23] as well as within industries.[24] It is therefore hypothesized:

V. Large firms have higher capital/output ratios than do small firms.

Because size is found to be positively associated with both concentration and capital/output ratios, and because capital/output ratios may be a proxy (along with size) for other structural variables (degree of vertical integration, ratio of fixed costs to total costs, and capital requirements), it is hypothesized that:

VI. Concentrated industries have higher capital/output ratios than do unconcentrated industries.

The testing of this hypothesis is a step toward determining if it is concentration that causes higher returns or if, alternatively, it is capital/output ratios (a proxy for other structural characteristics of markets) that cause higher returns. To this end, the following hypothesis is tested:

VII. Firms with high capital/output ratios earn above-average rates of return.

In a review of previous studies on the size-profitability hypothesis, I find that the combined evidence of Sherman and Stekler[25] suggests a positive relation of the variability of returns to firm size over time. Because size and capital/output ratios are positively correlated, profit

---

21. The ratio of total assets or depreciable assets to total sales is a measure of the amount of capital required to generate a dollar of sales, or, alternatively, the amount of capital required to attain a given market share of industry output.

22. William S. Comanor and Thomas A. Wilson, "On Advertising and Profitability," *Review of Economics and Statistics* 53 (Nov. 1971): 408–10.

23. See, for example, Walter A. Chudson, *The Pattern of Corporate Financial Structure* (New York: National Bureau of Economic Research, 1945); Joseph Steindl, *Small and Big Business: Economic Problems of the Size of Firms* (Oxford: Basil Blackwell, 1947); Stanley S. Schor, "The Capital-Product Ratio and Size of Establishment for Manufacturing Industries," unpublished Ph.D. dissertation, University of Pennsylvania, 1952; Matityahu Marcus, "Size of Establishment and the Capital-Output Ratio: An Empirical Investigation," *Southern Economic Journal* 32 (July 1965): 53–62; and John R. Moroney and Jan W. Duggar, "Size of Firm and Capital-Output Ratios," *MSU Business Topics* 15 (Summer 1967): 16–23.

24. Hiram S. Davis, "Relation of Capital-Output Ratio to Firm Size in American Manufacturing: Some Additional Evidence," *Review of Economics and Statistics* 38 (Aug. 1956): 286–93.

25. Sherman, *Profits in the United States;* Stekler, *Profitability and Size of Firm;* and H. O. Stekler, "The Variability of Profitability with Size of Firm, 1947–1958," *Journal of the American Statistical Association* 59 (Dec. 1964): 1183–93.

variability also may be associated with capital/output ratios. Furthermore, it would appear that the higher the capital/output ratio, the higher the ratio of fixed to total costs. Consequently, it would seem that large, capital-intensive firms, when subjected to demand fluctuations similiar to those experienced by smaller firms, would be subject to greater profit variability than the small firms are.[26] The following hypothesis is therefore tested:

> **VIII. The higher the firm's capital/output ratio, the greater the variability in rates of return over time.**

This hypothesis is ultimately designed to serve as a link with the next set of hypotheses on the variability of returns, or risk.

Business Risk

The variability (distribution) of returns is taken to represent profit risk. Cootner and Holland conducted the first major study of business risk (distribution of firm profits, as opposed to the returns in stock and bond markets—financial risk).[27] They identified two quite distinct concepts of risk, although subsequent analysis of business risk has, unfortunately, tended to blur their differences. The first type is associated with a firm's temporal rate-of-return distribution. It is argued that the greater the variance (or standard deviation) and the less the skewness, the higher the expected returns, if firms are averse to risk.[28] The empirical evidence supports these expectations[29] with one notable exception.[30] To the extent that observed rates of return are affected by different exposures to risk, these returns are not comparable. As a consequence, use of

26. Roger Sherman and Robert Tollison, "Technology, Profit Risk, and Assessments of Market Performance," *Quarterly Journal of Economics* 86 (Aug. 1972): 449–62. Also see, Comanor and Wilson, "On Advertising and Profitability."

27. The original study is: Paul H. Cootner and Daniel M. Holland, "Risk and Rate of Return," Massachusetts Institute of Technology, DSR Project 9565, Mar. 1963, revised Feb. 1964. (Mimeographed.) Its major results are summarized in the same authors' "Rate of Return and Business Risk." *Bell Journal of Economics and Management Science* 1 (Autumn 1970): 211–26.

28. Fred Arditti, "Risk and the Required Return on Equity," *Journal of Finance* 22 (Mar. 1967): 19–36; I. N. Fisher and G. R. Hall, "Risk and Corporate Rates of Return," *Quarterly Journal of Economics* 83 (Feb. 1969): 79–92.

29. Fisher and Hall, "Risk and Corporate Rates of Return"; "Risk and Corporate Rates of Return: Reply," *Quarterly Journal of Economics* 85 (Aug. 1971): 518–22; Cootner and Holland, "Rate of Return and Business Risk"; Gordon R. Conrad and Irving H. Plotkin, "Risk/Return: U.S. Industry Pattern," *Harvard Business Review* 46 (Mar.–Apr., 1968): 90–99.

30. Stigler, *Capital and Rates of Return*.

reported profitability as the measure of performance in studies of profitability and concentration or size may result in the finding of a relation between the variables studied which is spurious. This is, indeed, a probability because profit variability (risk) has been found to be associated with firm size (by Sherman and by Stekler), and it, therefore, might also be associated with concentration. Therefore, while most previous performance-structure studies do not consider risk, it appears necessary to include a study of risk if one is to study the structure-performance hypothesis in its proper context.[31] That is, performance measured by rates of return becomes an operational dependent variable because, in Stigler's words, "there is no more important proposition in economic theory than that, under competition, the rate of return on investment tends toward equality in all industries."[32] The rate of return Stigler is speaking of is a risk-comparable rate of return.

The following hypothesis is tested:

IX. **The greater the risk associated with a firm's ability to predict its rate of return over time, the higher are its rates of return.**

The second type of business risk is labeled spatial risk and relates to the dispersion of firm period-average rates of return around their respective industry average returns. It must be emphasized that this measurement of risk captures an altogether different concept or type of risk (though the measures may be correlated).[33] This spatial approach to risk treats it as an industry characteristic tantamount to an entry barrier. It is found that the greater the dispersion and the less the skewness of the distribution of firm returns around their respective industry returns, the higher the industry average returns.[34] Accordingly, it is hypothesized:

X. **Average rates of returns of an industry are higher the greater is the risk associated with a firm's ability to predict its average rate of return upon**

31. Quite recently this concern has been expressed in the literature. See Samuel H. Baker, "Risk, Leverage and Profitability: An Industry Analysis," *Review of Economics and Statistics* 55 (Nov. 1973): 503–7 and Sherman and Tollison, "Technology, Risk and Market Performance."

32. *Capital and Rates of Return*, p. 55.

33. Probably the greatest reason that these two types of risk, distinguished by Cootner and Holland, have been blurred in subsequent analysis is the finding by Fisher and Hall (for their 11-industry sample) that risk premiums calculated for temporal risk and spatial risk are quite similar. That the two concepts of risk have been blurred is an understatement. For example, in a study which clearly should involve temporal risk, Sherman and Tollison employ spatial risk as a proxy. (Sherman and Tollison, "Technology, Profit Risk, and Assessments.")

34. Conrad and Plotkin, "Risk/Return: U.S. Industry Pattern"; and Fisher and Hall, "Risk and Corporate Rates of Return."

entering the industry (because firms in that industry earn different rates of return).

It is a natural concomitant of market power that highly concentrated industries are in a position not only to earn high average rates of return but also, first, to minimize the impact of cyclical fluctuations on year-to-year profitability and, second, to maintain a floor below which yearly rates of return will not fall.[35] Accordingly, the greater the degree of concentration, the less the temporal risk ought to be. In addition, because one could argue that the market power of an industry, measured by its concentration ratio, is a power that extends to all firms in that industry, the spatial dispersion of firm rates of return within concentrated industries ought to be less than that within competitive industries. Indeed, that firms in concentrated industries are less likely to have a negatively skewed distribution than are firms in competitive industries follows from Osborn's hypothesis that "large firms hold a sufficient price umbrella over the [concentrated] industries in which they are dominant to shield the small companies from the rigors of competition which prevail in the less concentrated industries."[36] The following hypothesis is tested:

XI. Both temporal risk and spatial risk are less in concentrated than in unconcentrated industries.

Growth

Growth rates are important to this study for three reasons First, evidence indicates that concentration and growth are related. Second, profitability and growth ought to be positively related. There is evidence that these two propositions combined may bear on the observed relation between concentration and profitability. Third, the distortion in observed rates of return which is caused by the use of historical costs depends in large part on the age of assets—i.e., the growth of firms.

Several studies suggest that changes in concentration and market growth are negatively related. A priori, it is argued that a rapidly growing industry tends to become less concentrated because small firms already in the industry find it easier to expand their market share only at the expense of a reduced rate of increase in sales for the large firms. In no-growth

---

35. For a contrary view and resulting debate see R. E. Caves and B. S. Yamey, "Risk and Corporate Rates of Return: Comment," *Quarterly Journal of Economics* 85 (Aug. 1971): 513–17, and Fisher and Hall, "Risk and Corporate Rates of Return: Reply."

36. Osborn, "Concentration and Profitability," p. 15.

industries, increased market shares, of course, could be obtained only at the expense of a sales *decrease* by the dominant firms. Furthermore, it is argued that, *ceteris paribus,* new firms can enter rapidly growing industries more easily for much the same reason.[37] On the basis of the foregoing, the following is hypothesized:

XII. Firms in concentrated industries grow more slowly than firms in unconcentrated industries.[38]

It seems rather obvious that profitable firms would expand more rapidly than less profitable firms, other things being equal. Consequently, it is hypothesized that:

XIII. Above-average growth firms (industries) earn above-average rates of return.

The question arises, however, whether this general relationship is affected by the degree of concentration. That is, do profitable concentrated industries grow as rapidly as do equally profitable unconcentrated industries? Accordingly, the following hypothesis is tested:

XIV. The general relationship between growth and profitability is affected by concentration.

This last hypothesis is the lever to open the analysis of Brozen's "disequilibrium hypothesis" and Wenders's extension.[39] Briefly, the thesis is that rates of return in concentrated and unconcentrated industries are systematically distorted in a way that produces a correlation between concentration and profitability.[40]

37. For example see Ralph L. Nelson, "Market Growth, Company Diversification and Product Concentration, 1947–1954," *Journal of the American Statistical Association* 55 (Dec. 1960): 640–49; and William G. Shepherd, "Trends of Concentration in American Manufacturing Industries, 1947–1958," *Review of Economics and Statistics* 66 (May 1964): 200–12. David R. Kamerschen, however, tests this hypothesis for the longer period 1947–63 and concludes: ". . . that market growth leads to lower levels of industry concentration does not receive positive support." ("Market Growth and Industry Concentration," *Journal of the American Statistical Association* 63 [Mar. 1968]: 241.)

38. The reader may note that this hypothesis is only implied by, and does not necessarily directly follow from, the hypothesis concerning growth and changes in concentration. Also note that the hypothesis is in terms of *firm* growth (in assets or total sales) rather than in terms of market growth. The hypothesis is put in this form as a link to the hypothesis on historical-cost accounting distortions.

39. John T. Wenders, "Profits and Antitrust Policy: The Question of Disequilibrium," *Antitrust Bulletin* 16 (Summer 1971): 249–56.

40. See Brozen, "Significance of Profit Rate Data"; "Barriers Facilitate Entry," *Antitrust Bulletin* 14 (Winter 1969): 851–54; "Concentration and Disequilibria"; De-

Current-Cost Rates of Return

There is reason to believe that the distortions of economic performance caused by historical-cost accounting techniques may be systematically related to concentration. First, it is hypothesized above (Hypothesis VI) that concentrated industries are more capital intensive. Second, it has just been hypothesized that concentrated industries grow more slowly than do unconcentrated industries. The greatest distortion from using historical costs arises in the accounting for long-lived assets. The difference between historical-cost rates of return and current-cost rates of return is, in large part, a function of the difference between the historical cost of fixed assets and their current or replacement costs, and the importance of depreciation in determining profits. In times of inflation the difference between these asset values is, in turn, directly related to the age of those assets. Therefore, because there is reason to believe that the fixed assets in concentrated industries are older (since these industries grow more slowly), and because depreciation may be a more significant cost in concentrated industries (because of their greater capital intensity), there may be a systematic bias in the (reported) profitability-concentration relationship. On the basis of this brief line of reasoning, the following is hypothesized and tested:

> XV. **The ratio of observed rates of return to current-cost rates of return is higher in concentrated industries than in unconcentrated industries. Alternatively stated, the adjustment to current-cost rates of return affects concentrated industries' rates of return more than it affects unconcentrated industries' rates of return.**

The purpose of this hypothesis is to determine whether observed rates of return for concentrated industries are systematically overstated as compared to those of unconcentrated industries.

Fundamental hypothesis restated

The essence of the foregoing hypotheses, taken as a whole, is that the several variables—profitability, concentration, size, capital/output ratios, and risk—may be interrelated in such a way that the commonly observed relation between profitability and concentration is attributable to multi-

concentration Recommendation"; "Bain's Concentration and Rates of Return Revisited," *Journal of Law and Economics* 14 (Oct. 1971): 351–69; and "The Persistence of 'High Rates of Return.'" Also see Wenders, "Profits and Antitrust Policy: The Question of Disequilibrium"; and Daryl Winn and Dick A. Leabo, "Rates of Return, Concentration and Growth—Question of Disequilibrium," *Journal of Law and Economics* 17 (Apr. 1974): 97–115.

collinearity rather than to direct cause and effect. The foregoing hypotheses are presented in a manner which, by interrelating them, suggests a restatement of the original fundamental hypothesis. From the tests of these individual hypotheses taken together, the following hypothesis is tested:

XVI. After the independent influences of size, capital intensity, growth, risk, and the distortions arising from historical-cost accounting are accounted for, firms in concentrated industries can be shown to earn above-average long-run rates of return.

The purpose of this study is to test this hypothesis.

The Measurement of Profitability and Concentration

Earlier, objections were raised about the apparent lack of concern for the problems associated with the measurement of profitability. With any attempt to determine the relationship between performance and the various structural variables, I see two major and formidable problems to be confronted. First, proper definition of the variables must be consistent with the theory upon which the analysis rests. Once the theory to be subjected to empirical examination is fully formulated, the theoretical definition of the variables should likewise be clear. With what to measure clearly in mind, the second problem is how to measure it.

Unfortunately, theories and their testable hypotheses are notoriously lacking in their specification of the variables. For example, take Bain's hypothesis "that the average profit rate of firms in oligopolistic industries of a high concentration will tend to be significantly larger than that of firms in less concentrated oligopolies or in industries of atomistic structure."[41] It is hypothesized that two variables are related, but the form of the relationship is not specified. As a result, through the years it has been found to be continuous—linear and nonlinear—and discrete. The determination of the form, however, could be left to empirical examination. In fact, the nature of the form may be a function of the defiinitions of the two variables.

To me, at least, the theoretical notion of "oligopolistic industries of a high concentration" is more precise than the "average profit rate of firms." Theoretically, "oligopolistic industries of a high concentration" refers to how a particular market's product sales are distributed among the firms selling in that market. Though in theory the notion is clear, the problems of quantification are large. The difficulties come from the necessity of combining into one variable the notions of a product market and the

41. Bain, "Relation of Profit Rate," p. 294.

distribution of sales among firms. As a result, of course, a large variety in the measurement occurs. The disagreement in the notion of market power has been not so much with the theory as with how best to capture it by measurement.

On the other hand, "average profit rate of firms" is far less precise. Because of this, a large variety of schemes for the measurement of profitability have arisen to test this hypothesis. For example, is "the average profit rate of firms" intended to mean a simple or weighted average; of all firms or only dominant firms; before or after taxes, on total assets, stockholders' equity, or sales; or, before or after interest?

I maintain very emphatically that, were the theory (hypothesis) to be tested fully stated, these questions would not need to be answered. With these questions one is not quibling with the practical problems of measurement; one is, in fact, changing the theory underlying the analysis. For example, whether the original hypothesis intended profitability to mean the total earnings on total assets employed (or total stockholders' equity) as opposed to the average of firm profit rates leaves it unclear as to whether the "average" should be a weighted average or simple average. This is a theoretical question, not one of measurement. What many researchers do not seem to realize is that alternative profitability measurement schemes change the hypothesis being tested. For these reasons we must examine the empirical definitions of "profit rates" and "concentration."

Profitability—A Measure of Economic Performance

It is my view that the only relevant concept of profitability in the study of performance and structure follows directly from the nature of the economists's ultimate concern—the allocation of economic resources. This concern occasions a leading economist to assert: "There is no more important proposition in economic theory than that, under competition, the rate of return on investment tends toward equality in all industries,"[42] for when this equilibrium is achieved, the optimal allocation of society's resources is obtained. Now what *is* this "rate of return on investment"? Because it is a rate, two variables are involved—a numerator and denominator. In my opinion, "investment" can only mean the assets committed to the production of goods and services. Therefore, the denominator must be total assets, i.e., the scarce economic resources to be allocated efficiently among alternative uses.

---

42. Stigler, *Capital and Rates of Return*, p. 55.

With assets as the denominator, the next step is to determine the measure of profits derived from those assets. In considering the numerator, it would be helpful to digress briefly and consider the accountant's traditional balance sheet. On the left-hand side are recorded the economic resources (assets), whose total must equal the total of the claims on those resources (equities) shown on the right-hand side. Although income is earned by using the economic resources, it is claimed (distributed or accrued) by the various equities. Hence, because of the accounting conventions of reporting, income earned on those assets is usually separated according to its claimants—common and preferred stockholders, and explicit-interest-bearing debt holders. Needless to say, from the point of view of the profitability of the *assets,* this division is purely arbitrary and without meaning. It becomes meaningful if, and only if, one should be concerned with a rate of return on a particular class of *financial* investment. As a consequence, because the structure-performance hypothesis concerns the allocation of real assets as opposed to financial assets, the use of profitability on stockholders' equity (or any other specific class of financial investment) is wholly inappropriate.

Despite the fact that accounting convention is designed to compute profits to stockholders, the analyst must not let those procedures interfere with the computation of total income to all sources of capital. The appropriate definition of profit, then, includes the earnings to all suppliers of financial capital. First, it includes income to stockholders or suppliers of "risk capital." Second, it includes the earnings to creditors. Income earned on long-term debt is usually fairly easily determined. It is simply the interest "expense" (so labeled because the statement is prepared from the point of view of the stockholders) appearing on the income statement. While the earnings to stockholders and long-term creditors are explicitly recognized in financial reports, earnings to all short-term creditors are not. For a complete and consistent concept of profits, earnings to these suppliers of capital must, then, be imputed. Earnings to these creditors can be estimated by first averaging the amount of short-term capital supplied throughout the year and then multiplying this by an appropriate interest rate.[43] This figure is then added to stockholders' profits plus interest to obtain total income.

Two lines of criticism might be leveled against the imputation of income to short-term credit. First, one might suggest that short-term

---

43. The interest rate used is the 40–60 day commercial paper rate for each of the nine years of this study. Average short-term credit is determined by taking an average of beginning-of-year and end-of-year non-interest-bearing short-term liabilities. The great bulk of this liability is short-term credit of trade suppliers.

credit is free and therefore, quite naturally, not disclosed in the income statement. There is, however, no such thing as a "free lunch." It is not disclosed on the income statement, because it cannot be "objectively" computed. As a consequence, the cost of short-term credit is pooled with the cost of purchases from trade suppliers. I contend that the selling price of goods and services bought from others includes the cost of extending credit. Thus this element of income is included as a cost of sales which is deducted from revenues. The second argument against this imputation might be, What difference does it make? It would make little difference if all firms used short-term sources of credit to a comparable extent. However, should there be a greater usage of short-term credit by unconcentrated industries, for example, then their rates of return would be systematically understated compared to those of concentrated industries.[44]

In summary, all the elements of income to be included in the numerator for the rate of return on assets are now identified. The next step is to construct the measure for the rate of return. A rate of return is a ratio of the sum of these flow variables (income elements) to a stock variable (assets). Frequently, in the final construction of this rate, the nature of these variables as stocks and flows has been ignored. As a result, many have computed the rate of return by dividing the income (which was earned on the assets over the entire period) by beginning-of-year or end-of-year assets. Clearly this is inappropriate since income is earned on assets employed throughout the year. Accordingly, the simple average of beginning total assets and ending total assets is taken as a proxy for the assets actually in use during the year. It should be pointed out, however, that the use of year-end assets as the denominator distorts a comparison of firm rates of return, because rates of asset growth differ. Rapidly growing firms' (industries') rates of return are understated compared to slow-growth or declining firms' (industries') rates of return. To use this rate of return in establishing a relationship with, say, concentration results in a bias, if growth and concentration are related.[45]

Having determined all the elements of income to be included in the numerator of the rate of return measure, the analyst must decide whether

44. There is little evidence of this from empirical research. However, Manak C. Gupta, in "The Effect of Size, Growth, and Industry on the Financial Structure of Manufacturing Companies," *Journal of Finance* 24 (June 1969): 517–29, finds that the ratio of accounts payable to total assets falls as firm size increases. Since others find size and concentration positively related, this possibility is at least suggested.

45. A hypothesis tested in this study is that concentrated industries grow (in terms of assets) more slowly than unconcentrated ones. If this is true, the rates of return for rapidly growing unconcentrated industries are understated if the denominator is year-end assets.

to include taxes and/or extraordinary profits and losses as a part of this income.

Extraordinary profits and losses

In this study the appropriate profit figure is that figure which indicates the results of the normal operations of a firm. The gain or loss of sale or discontinuance of a plant in a particular year does not reflect the results of that year's operating decisions and therefore should be excluded from that year's measure of performance. Indeed, such a gain or loss is a result of a past decision or an inadequate allocation of costs over previous periods. The results of each year's operations are best reflected by excluding these extraordinary or nonoperating gains and losses.[46]

Another reason for excluding extraordinary gains and losses is that in the analysis of temporal variability of rates of return (risk) one should not introduce artificial fluctuations which are due to inadequacies of the accounting techniques.

The problem of taxation

One must realize that the selection of the source of data in fact defines the data. The two basic sources of profit data are (1) tax returns, and (2) stockholders' financial reports. Profits are treated as cardinal measures. Though this is as it should be, it must be recognized that these measures result from some arbitrary definitions, procedures, and principles of financial and tax accounting. Recognizing this fact, many researchers have believed it more defensible to use Internal Revenue Service data (tax returns) than stockholders' financial reports, because tax law is consistently *applied* across all firms. It is believed that profit measures reported for tax purposes are more comparable for interfirm and interindustry analysis. Others contend that it makes little difference which source is used because both measures will be about the same if a lengthy time period is used. I contend, however, that neither of these arguments is valid.

First, the concepts of profit involved in these two data sources are totally different, primarily because of the IRS definitions of revenues and ex-

46. A year is just an arbitrary period of time selected by convention. A true measure of performance can be determined only after a firm has concluded a particular venture and completely liquidated the assets employed. The accuracy of a performance measure for any period shorter than this necessarily decreases as the length of the period diminishes. The accountant's tools of measurement are difficult to calibrate to short time periods—even a year.

penses in arriving at profits and because of management's desire to defer the payment of taxes.[47] For example, in 1966 profits reported to stockholders (all manufacturing corporations) were $25.3 billion, and profits reported to the IRS were almost 10 percent less, at $22.9 billion. For the percentage of these differences as distributed among two-digit industries, see Table 1.

Second, it is not necessarily true that over a considerable time period the two definitions of profits will result in comparable measures, especially if profits are expressed as ratios in the form of rates of return on an annual basis. A rapidly growing industry, ceteris paribus, would tend to show lower IRS profits than a stable or declining one simply because of the continual deferral of taxable income and taxes. Complicating this

TABLE 1

COMPARISON OF IRS INCOME WITH BOOK INCOME FOR TWO-DIGIT SIC MANUFACTURING INDUSTRIES, 1966

SIC INDUSTRY GROUP	IRS INCOME (MILLIONS OF DOLLARS)	BOOK INCOME (MILLIONS OF DOLLARS)	DIFFERENCE AS PERCENTAGE OF IRS INCOME
20 Food	1,997	2,062	3.2
21 Tobacco	. . .	. . .	. . .
22 Textiles	629	676	7.5
23 Apparel	475	497	4.6
24 Lumber	334	346	3.4
25 Furniture and fixtures	249	267	7.0
27 Printing and publishing	987	1,021	3.5
28 Chemicals	2,152	2,278	5.9
29 Petroleum	1,533	3,103	102.4
30 Rubber	479	514	7.4
31 Leather	148	151	1.8
32 Stone, glass, clay	476	567	19.0
33 Primary metals	1,848	2,011	8.8
34 Fabricated metals	1,400	1,441	2.9
35 Machinery, nonelectrical	2,800	2,814	.5
36 Electrical machinery	1,763	1,773	.6
37 Transportation	3,390	3,423	1.0
38 Instruments	715	756	5.7
39 Miscellaneous	337	342	1.5
All manufacturing	22,853	25,294	10.7

Source: U.S., Treasury Department, Internal Revenue Service, *Statistics of Income—1966, Corporation Income Tax Returns* (Washington, D.C.: Government Printing Office, 1970), Table 7, p. 112.

47. For some of the differences see, for example, U.S., Treasury Department, Internal Revenue Service, *Statistics of Income—1966, Corporation Income Tax Returns* (Washington, D.C.,: Government Printing Office, 1970), pp. 107–13.

factor is the attendant impact on the denominator in rate-of-return measure. Obviously—when accelerated depreciation of assets is being considered—the investment base is different under tax procedures and financial reporting procedures. Because of the basic differences in the timing of revenues and expenses under tax and financial reporting, the temporal pattern of profitability is also affected. This is crucial to the analysis, particularly when risk is considered. For a comparison of the temporal variability of the IRS and book profits, see Table 2. The question, then, is what definition most nearly corresponds to a profit concept as developed and used in economy theory? Without supporting the assertion with a lengthy discussion here, the writer contends that profit in financial reports to stockholders best conforms to economic profits, and that the measure of such profit is *more* appropriate for interindustry analysis and comparison.

TABLE 2

COMPARISON OF IRS INCOME WITH BOOK INCOME, ALL
CORPORATIONS
1964–66

	TOTAL INCOME LESS DEFICIT		
YEAR	IRS INCOME (MILLIONS OF DOLLARS)	BOOK INCOME (MILLIONS OF DOLLARS)	DIFFERENCE AS A PERCENTAGE OF IRS INCOME
1964	34,350	46,099	34.2
1965	41,374	50,423	21.9
1966	41,390	48,213	16.5

Source: Internal Revenue Service, *Statistics of Income—1966, Corporation Income Tax Returns* (Washington, D.C., Government Printing Office, 1970), Table 4.1, p. 107.

Note: Includes only those corporations which show income or deficit per books. The reader should note that these are highly aggregated data and therefore grossly understate the potential differences between firms for these years.

For publicly held firms of the sizes that are used in this study, conformity in the application of accounting principles is not as serious a problem as it would be in a study of both small, privately held companies and large, publicly held corporations. One of the major goals of the Securities and Exchange Commission (SEC) and the American Institute of Certified Public Accountants (AICPA) is to present financial information to investors from which they can accurately assess the past, present, and future performance of a firm. The standards, procedures, and principles applied by accountants under the guidance of the SEC and the AICPA result in a better statement of profit with which to measure performance and on which to base decisions. Recalling that the fundamental propositions of this study are predicated on the behavioral aspects of firms in various conditions of competitive and concentrated market structures, then the *data* used in decision making seem the most appropriate.

Financial reports are used by both of the two primary decision units around which this study and its hypotheses are centered—the investor and the manager. Neither party uses tax-return data as the primary information source. Equilibrium rates of return on alternative investment opportunities only result if these decision makers base their actions on predicted or expected profits. The best source for predicting profitability (performance) rests with the financial reports, not tax returns. One need only trace the underlying motives in designing the procedures and principles of financial reporting and tax law (and tax reporting) to see the overwhelming appropriateness of financial reports for measures of profitability as they are to be used in this study.[48]

Although intentionally there has been no lengthy and detailed discussion of the propriety of using profits as determined (and defined) by financial reports, one item needs further amplification. When financial reports are accepted as the best source for the profit measures, the problem of tax accounting still remains. Unless it is decided to use profits before taxes, the tax figures reported to stockholders distort after-tax profits. Before 1968, it was not uncommon for corporations to carry the tax charges determined by IRS definitions of revenues and expenses directly to the financial reports.[49] As a result, reported profits after taxes is a hybrid figure, resulting from a mix of tax and financial reporting techniques.

For this and other reasons given below, profits before taxes are deemed the most appropriate measure. One could argue that taxes are simply an allocation of income to social overhead, i.e., government. Thus, profits before taxes might be viewed as a mix of social and private profits.

48. For example, the Accounting Principles Board of the AICPA states the objectives of financial accounting as follows: "The basic purpose of financial accounting and financial statements is to provide financial information about individual business enterprises that is useful in making economic decisions. . . . General and qualitative objectives aid in fulfilling this basic purpose and provide means for evaluating present and proposed accounting principles." (Accounting Principles Board, *Basic Concepts and Accounting Principles Underlying Financial Statements of Business Enterprises*, Statement No. 4 [New York: American Institute of Certified Public Accountants, Oct. 1970], p. 9.)

49. In 1967, the Accounting Principles Board expressed an opinion (to become effective for all fiscal periods that began after December 31, 1967) that firms allocate taxes, thereby removing much of this objection. (Accounting Principles Board, *Accounting for Income Taxes*, Opinion No. 11 [New York: American Institute of Certified Public Accountants, Dec. 1967].)

Furthermore, one could argue that the tax policy of government is not primarily aimed at efficient allocation of resources through a policy of maintaining effective market structures (in this regard, tax law could be said to be neutral), but rather it is a means of generating public revenues and, in some cases, of allocating resources to specific products or production, independent of attempts to effect competitive markets.[50] Many studies have used both measures of profits, and generally they conclude that the definition does not significantly alter the results. In this study taxes are included in the numerator of the primary rate-of-return measure, i.e., before-tax profits are used.

Now that I have briefly presented a few reasons why the rate of return should be calculated as a ratio of all income elements to total assets, I offer a few additional comments in defense of the selection. In this study, not only is the selection of the rate of return important to the test of the structure-performance hypothesis, but it must be consistent with the hypotheses on business risk and distortions from historical-cost accounting. A comment or two on each of these hypotheses follows.

The concept of business risk

Earlier a brief yet careful distinction was made between business risk and financial risk—business risk being considered to be that risk associated with the employment of productive assets, and financial risk, on the other hand, considered to be that risk associated with financial investments (stocks and bonds). Business risk, then, relates to the variability of profits earned from productive assets, and financial risk concerns the variability of profits earned on investments in stocks and bonds. The two types of risk are not unrelated.

Briefly, "risk" is argued to be a rather complex combination of behavior and structure in which there are several distinguishable elements. First, the variability of returns on a firm's assets is labeled, here, business risk. Risk aversity (for business risk) is a behavioral characteristic ascribable to a firm's management, as opposed to its stockholders. Though the greater effort has been devoted to the risk aversity of stockholders in the financial markets, some observers have argued that quite apart from these phenomena, business managers, too, are risk averse. For example, Baumol summarizes this case.

---

50. It should also be pointed out that during the 1960s there were substantial changes in taxation, e.g., off and on usage of the investment tax credit, 1964 tax reduction, surcharge on and off, liberalization of depreciation guidelines. The temporal impact of these (on after-tax profits) should not be assumed to be equal among industries.

. . . With the development of the corporate form of organization the vast body of stockholders have lost effective control over the organizations of which they are the legal proprietors. As has often been observed, absentee ownership increases management's reluctance to undertake risks. Reasons are not hard to find.

The remuneration of the top executive is fairly sticky. If his gamble turns out well the executive is likely to receive little permanent addition to his income stream, though profit-sharing schemes may result in his getting something out of it. Failure, on the other hand, can have serious consequences. At best, it is only embarrassing. At worst, the management group will be turned out of office.

Moreover, the executive who gambles successfully may find that his reward is worse than meager—sometimes he will suffer an indirect penalty. In fact, extraordinary but unrepeatable success may cost him almost as dear as failure.[51]

This relation between a manager's risk aversity and the variability of returns on assets across many firms and industries has seen the least empirical illumination.

The next distinguishable link in the risk chain is that of the variability of firm rates of return on particular classes of financial capital. Here considerably more research, across firms, has been done. This type of risk must be considered a hybrid of two general types of risk labeled above. "Business-financial" risk is the type of risk studied by Fisher and Hall, though they call it business risk. As previously argued, the variability of returns on, say, stockholders' equity (Fisher and Hall) is a function of the variability of returns on assets and the managerial prerogatives with regard to the firm's capital structure (debt-equity ratio). What factors influence managers in this optimal capital structure decision? Among other things, it is the variability of returns on assets and managerial perceptions of how stockholders and creditors react to risk. Quite simply, increased leverage increases the level of average returns as well as the variability of returns to stockholders (for a given variance of returns on assets). At the same time, greater leverage increases the risk of creditors and they, accordingly, will require higher yields. That "times interest earned" is often computed as a measure of creditor's risk illustrates these phenomena. Thus, the debt-equity ratio is in part, first, a function of the variability of returns on assets employed[52] and, second, a function of how managers perceive the way each class of investors reacts

---

51. Baumol, *Business Behavior, Value and Growth*, pp. 101–2.

52. One must be careful in the definition of business risk. That managers are risk averse and will trade variability against expected returns affects the investment decision process and explains why certain productive investments are preferred to others.

to the variability of returns on its respective investments. Indeed, should management perceive a change in the attitudes of any one class of investors, all other things being equal, a change in the debt-equity ratio would be in order.

The last link is the financial risk of investors from the variability of returns on investment in financial assets—stocks and bonds. Considerable effort has been expended on empirical study of this subject. Unfortunately less study has been devoted to the entire risk-return chain. This chain, because it starts with business risk and ends with financial risk, should not be construed as implying flows of causation. Indeed, management's attitudes and reaction to risk must be influenced by their perceptions of how investors view risk. In other words, a firm's choice among all productive investment possibilities is influenced by managerial attitudes (which are, in part, influenced by perceived investor attitudes). Next, given the *chosen* (committed) investments, again based on perceptions of investors' attitudes, management chooses among the several means of financing those assets. These are distinguishable managerial decision processes. Both affect the "realized" or financial risk to investors in financial assets. In a behavior sense, there is no unidirectional line of causation. However, in a sequence of a time, it is, first, management's choice among all the productive investment alternatives and, second, among the financing alternatives that determine the risk to investors.

The problem of historical cost

Finally, the primary performance measure as the ratio of all income to assets, in addition to being the most appropriate for business risk, is also that measure most appropriate for determining an estimate of rates of return adjusted to reflect current costs rather than historical costs. The fundamental difference between these two rates of return stems from the revaluation of assets recorded in the accounts. Therefore, in order to adjust rates of return to reflect current values of assets, it is most appropriate to define the rate of return as that return on those assets.

Before we leave this section on the measures of profitability, it should be stated that, although I argue rather strongly for one particular definition of the rate of return, six different measures are used in the study. Before- and after-tax profits are computed for three basic measures. First, a rate of return is calculated as suggested in this chapter—profit to stockholders, plus explicit interest, plus imputed interest on short-term credit, divided by assets. The second measure is the same as the first except the imputed interest is dropped from the numerator. Finally, the third basic measure is the ratio of stockholders' profits to stockholders' equity.

The Concentration Ratio—A Measure of Monopoly Power

In the Introduction several reasons are given for the choice of the concentration ratio as the measure of monopoly power. Among these are the wide usage of the ratio in empirical research and the apparent importance attached to this index in the Neal Report. Its popular usage is attested to by the exclusive reliance on it by many studies when it comes to measuring the structure in product markets. Though there are differences in the construction of the index, the basic measure is the percentage of an industry's sales accounted for by the leading four or eight firms. The most fundamental criticism of this type of measure is that it summarizes only one point on the distribution of an industry's sales among firms. For example, a four-firm concentration ratio of 80 percent reveals nothing about the individual share distributions of the individual firms.

In attempts to get a better index which encompasses the entire distribution of individual firm shares, many alternative measures are advocated.[53] To date, a better measure for use in empirical analysis has not been found, and generally the various measures are highly correlated.[54] Scherer summarizes the state of the arts in the measurement of market concentration as follows:

> With such a rich menu of alternative market structure measures, which should the analyst use? The most common choice criterion is a pragmatic one: use the best index possible, given data constraints. In a majority of cases, this means the humble four-firm concentration ratio. Fortunately, the chances of making a grievous analytic error in the choice of a market structure measure are slender, for the principal concentration indicators all display similar patterns. . . . For most interindustry comparison purposes, then, it is senseless to spend sleepless nights worrying about choosing the right concentration measure.[55]

53. For example, see: Gideon Rosenbluth, "Measures of Concentration," in National Bureau of Economic Research, *Business Concentration and Price Policy* (Princeton, N.J.: Princeton University Press, 1955), pp. 57–95; Marshall Hall and Nicolaus Tideman, "Measures of Concentration," *Journal of the American Statistical Association* 62 (Mar. 1967): 162–68; Robert W. Kilpatrick, "The Choice among Alternative Measures of Industrial Concentration," *Review of Economics and Statistics* 49 (May 1967): 258–60; M. A. Adelman, "The Measurement of Industrial Concentration," *Review of Economics and Statistics* 33 (Nov. 1951): 269–96.

54. Duncan Bailey and Stanley E. Boyle, in "The Optimal Measure of Concentration," *Journal of the American Statistical Association* 46 (Dec. 1971): 702–6, study these various measures. They conclude that no one measure "appears superior to any other," and "that on grounds of economic efficiency alone, the use of CR4 [four-firm] concentration estimates seems to be called for in most studies which require a structure variable" (p. 706).

55. Scherer, *Industrial Market Structure and Economic Performance*, p. 52.

Though the alternatives to using the concentration ratio appear to offer little empirical refinement, refinements are still needed in the concentration ratio itself. Unfortunately, concentration ratios as determined by the Census Bureau do not always conform to the economist's concept of economically meaningful products and markets.[56] Two major problems arise. First, the Census Bureau constructs its primary tables by defining a market to encompass the United States geographically. To the extent that an industry's firms sell only in local or regional markets, the concentration ratio constructed for national markets understates the effective monopoly power. The other problem lies with the product (industry) definition. Industries are often defined too narrowly and, therefore, do not include reasonable alternative products (substitutes) available to the buyer. In this case, the concentration ratio overstates the degree of effective monopoly power. On the other hand, other industries and products are defined too broadly and, therefore, include products which are not reasonable alternatives for the buyer, leading to understatement in the concentration ratio of the degree of effective monopoly power.

Many studies recognize these problems, but the solutions they offer vary a good deal. At the one extreme, Bain deals with the problem by essentially eliminating those industries where the Census concentration ratio was not considered meaningful. While some essentially ignore the problem, others (especially Weiss) face it squarely and rather than eliminating any industries adjust the Census concentration ratios to reflect economically meaningful markets, the approach also taken in this study. Specifically, this study follows the approach to these adjustments taken by Hall and Weiss.[57] Census four-firm, 1963, concentration ratios are adjusted for over- and under-aggregation and nonnational markets. Four-firm ratios are used because data for some of the adjustments are only available on a four-firm basis.[58] In addition to the use of these adjusted Census ratios, this study makes use of another set of ratios constructed from Shepherd's subjective estimates of 1966 four-firm, four-digit industry ratios.[59] The details of the procedures and the resulting concentration ratios, for both sets, are given in Appendix A.

56. U.S., Congress, Senate, Committee on the Judiciary, Subcommittee on Antitrust and Monopoly, Report prepared by the Bureau of the Census, *Concentration Ratios in Manufacturing Industry 1963*, Part I (1966) and Part II (1967) (Washington, D.C.: Government Printing Office). For an authoritative discussion of these points see *ibid.*, Part I, pp. v–viii and xi–xvii.
57. In, "Firm Size and Profitability."
58. There is little evidence (theoretical or empirical) which suggests the preferability of an eight-firm ratio over a four-ratio, or vice versa.
59. Shepherd, *Market Power and Economic Welfare*, Appendix Table 8.

2

THE STUDY—RESULTS AND ANALYSIS

The primary purpose of this study is to scrutinize rigorously the inference that high concentration causes high long-run average rates of return. To accomplish this end, we attempt to explain, first, differences in rates of return among firms and, second, differences in rates of return among industries. In addition to monopoly power (measured by concentration ratios), five other factors which are hypothesized to influence reported measures of profitability are studied. These factors are: asset size, capital intensity, growth, business risk, and historical-cost accounting procedures.

The Panel

The use of both firms and industries as units of observation is a distinguishing feature of this study. Because of this approach the analysis rests upon two basic sets of data. The time period studied is 1960–68 and the primary source for all financial data is Standard and Poor's Compustat Annual Industrial Tapes.

After firms are eliminated for the lack of data and other miscellaneous reasons, the original list of 1,253 firms is reduced to a panel of 768 firms.[1] These 768 firms are then taken as units of observation for regression analysis. Next, these firms are classified into roughly three- and four-digit homogeneous industries. Eliminating those industries with fewer than three firms, the industry panel is reduced to 736 firms in 79 industries.[2] The panel in this study is intended to be a census of publicly held (large) manufacturing firms which can be considered to produce a reasonably homogenous product line. Thus, the panel does not include firms which

1. See Appendix B for the reason for eliminating firms.
2. See Appendix B for the procedures used here.

40

are primarily nonmanufacturing, diversified, and private. There are many firms for which data were not available for the 1960–68 time period that otherwise would have been included. Because this is intended to be a census, regression analysis is used as a descriptive and analytical tool rather than as a method for drawing inferences. That is, significance tests are irrelevant because the relationships established are based on a census and not on a probability sample. However, one may wish to treat this panel as a sample of all economic units, including small firms, private firms, firms for which information is not publicly available, nonmanufacturing firms, divisions of conglomerates, firms in other time periods, and firms in international markets. For this reason, the t ratios of the regression coefficients are given in the following tables. However, further use of significance tests is avoided.

The Basic Variables

To identify the influences of the six basic factors on profitability, many variables have been generated and incorporated into various parts of the study.[3] The discussion of many of these variables will be deferred to accompany that part of the analysis where they are incorporated. This chapter begins with a discussion of the five basic variables, the presentation of the results, and an analysis of multivariate regressions using 768 firms as units of observation.

Measure of profitability

As discussed in the previous chapter, for research which ultimately concerns the allocation of real resources, the average of beginning-of-year and end-of-year total assets should be the investment base in the rate-of-return performance measure. Profits, accordingly, should be defined broadly to include all income earned (regardless of how it is labeled) on the employment of these assets. This primary performance measure is called the implicit operating return before taxes and is denoted throughout the study as IORB. Three other measures of firm performance are used at various points in the analysis that follows. The first is simply the after-tax counterpart to the primary measure. This is denoted IORA. The other two measures are before- and after-tax returns to stockholders.[4]

---

3. See Appendix C for details of the computations of the basic variables. All industry variables are simple (unweighted) averages of each industry's member-firms' period averages used in firm analysis. Where the writer may be ambiguous, industry variables are denoted by the subscript j. The subscript i denotes a firm variable.

4. It is most important to note the distinction between return to stockholders (used almost universally in the literature) and returns to common equity. In this study,

Profits reported for stockholders (after interest) are divided by the average of beginning-of-year and end-of-year stockholders' equity.[5]. These two profitability measures are called the stockholders' return before and after taxes and are respectively denoted SRB and SRA. For each firm, the simple 1960–68 period average of these yearly rates of return is taken to represent the long-run performance in the analysis that follows.

Measure of concentration

Also discussed in Chapter 1 are the two sets of concentration ratios used in this study. First, Census 1963, four-firm concentration ratios are adjusted to reflect economically meaningful markets. The other set of four-firm ratios is constructed from W. G. Shepherd's subjective estimates of 1966 concentration ratios for economically meaningful markets.[6] In the following analysis, the Census concentration ratios and the Shepherd concentration ratios are denoted as CCR and SCR respectively.

Measure of size

When the relationship between size and profitability is studied by firms without regard to industry classification, we analyze the absolute-size profitability hypothesis advanced by Baumol. Size of firm is measured by total assets, which is taken as a proxy for Baumol's size concept of the "amount of owned and borrowed money capital."[7] Though Baumol himself does not specify the exact functional form of the relation, Hall and Weiss in a later study argue that size is best measured as the reciprocal of the logarithm (base 10) of firm assets, denoted here as $R \mathrm{Log} A$.

---

the return is to common equity (as opposed to preferred stock) only, though for brevity, it is just labeled stockholders' rates of return. In other words, in this study preferred stock is treated like a bond with fixed "interest" payments—a leveraging instrument.

5. Roughly half of those who have empirically studied profitability and structure argue that the return to stockholders is the best measure of performance. In addition to the arguments given earlier against this measure of performance, there exists one other rather compelling reason for its inappropriateness. In the original panel of 787 firms, it was found that about a dozen firms had a negative stockholders' equity in one or more years in the period from 1960–68. This, however, is only the top of the iceberg. This fact suggests the high probability that for many firms stockholders' equity is near zero. Firms with profits or losses, which in absolute terms may be quite small, when divided by a denominator that approaches zero may indicate tremendously large rates of return. In fact, one firm had a nine-year average rate of return of over 1300 percent. This and similar firms were subsequently deleted from the analysis.

6. See Appendix A for a full discussion of these measures.

7. William J. Baumol, *Business Behavior, Value and Growth* (rev. ed.; New York: Harcourt, Brace, and World, Inc., 1967), p. 5.

We used the logarithmic form of asset size for the argument that the difficulty of raising another one per cent in assets is more nearly comparable between General Motors and, say, American Motors than is the difficulty of raising another million dollars for each firm. We used the reciprocal form because we anticipated that another percentage addition to assets might, in fact, be easier for General Motors to raise than for a smaller firm.[8]

Although only the results using the reciprocal of the logarithm are given in the following analysis, the simple linear functional form and the simple logarithmic form are also regressed against profitability. A higher percentage of the variance in rates of return (no matter how defined) always results in the model expressing size as the reciprocal of the logarithm.

In the rate-of-return measure, each year's average assets are taken as the investment base. For the firm-size measure, a simple average of these nine yearly values is computed. Hence, firm size is taken to be the average size of the firm over the entire time period and the logarithms are then taken on this value.

Measure of capital intensity

Two common measures of capital intensity are the ratios of total assets to sales and fixed assets to sales. Because these measures are highly correlated, one of them needs to be chosen as the more appropriate measure. The measure chosen is the ratio of total assets to sales—labeled the asset/output ratio, and denoted A/Q.[9] Because capital intensity in this study is employed as a market structure variable representing another aspect of the barrier to entry presented by absolute-capital requirements, the broader definition of capital appears more appropriate. The capital required to generate a dollar in sales in the various industries should not

8. Marshall Hall and Leonard Weiss, "Firm Size and Profitability," Appendix to *Review of Economics and Statistics* 49 (Aug. 1967): 322. The result of expressing firm size as the reciprocal of the logarithm of assets is that for proportional or equal percentage increases in firm size, rates of return rise but at a decreasing rate. If the relationship is expressed as $R = a + b\log A$, then equal percentage increases in A give rise to *equal absolute* increases in rates of return (and, therefore, rates of return rise but at a decreasing rate). If the relationship is expressed as $R = a - b/\log A$ (the sign of the regression coefficient becomes negative if there is a positive association between firm size and profitability), then for equal percentage increases in A, $1/\log A$ decreases by decreasing absolute amounts. Therefore, rates of return increase, but by *decreasing absolute* amounts, as well as by decreasing percentage amounts.

9. The ratio of fixed assets to sales, called fixed capital/output ratio (denoted K/Q) is also employed in the analysis. In the following analysis, these findings are given when the two measures produce materially different results. Generally, however, the results are not particularly sensitive to the definition of capital intensity.

be restricted to the dollar commitment for depreciable fixed assets. For example, the investment necessary upon entering an industry also includes working capital.

For firm size, the period average of assets is computed. This figure becomes the numerator in the asset/output ratio. The denominator, average sales, is computed as the simple average of the nine annual sales figures.

Measure of growth

The two obvious measures of growth are sales and assets, which would be, of course, highly correlated. Because assets are used as the measure of firm size and as the denominator in the primary rate-of-return measure, asset growth is used as the primary measure of firm growth.[10] For each firm, growth is measured as the ratio of the difference between 1960 and 1968 year-end assets (sales) to the 1960 year-end assets (sales). Again, when the alternative use of sales growth and asset growth produces materially different results, both findings are presented.[11]

Table 3 summarizes these variables by their descriptive measures.

Empirical Results for 768 Firms

The four fundamental structural variables are employed to explain the variance in each of the four firm rate-of-return measures, and the results are presented in Table 4. The coefficients of determination (R^2) are relatively low, ranging from .130 for profitability definied as the implicit operating return before taxes (IORB) to .194 for profitability defined as stockholders' return before taxes (SRB). Consistent with previous research is the finding that the structural variables are more highly correlated with returns on stockholders' equity than with returns on assets. However, little difference is found between before- and after-tax returns.

Concentration

The initial hypothesis that concentrated industries earn above-average long-run rates of return (Hypothesis I) is confirmed. While the results

---

10. It is hypothesized that the reported rates of return of older, more slowly growing industries (in terms of assets) are overstated relative to young, fast growing industries' rates of return because of the reliance on historical-cost accounting procedures.

11. Generally, when both sales and asset growth variables are used in regression analysis, sales growth contributes very little to explaining the variance of rates of return.

TABLE 3

DESCRIPTIVE MEASURES OF BASIC FIRM VARIABLES FOR 768 FIRMS, 1960–68 AVERAGES

VARIABLE	NOTATION	MEAN	STANDARD DEVIATION	RANGE	
				MINIMUM	MAXIMUM
Rate of return					
Implicit operating return before taxes	IORB	.1437	.0790	−.1237	.5073
Implicit operating return after taxes	IORA	.0803	.0395	−.1171	.2585
Stockholders' return before taxes	SRB	.2231	.1385	−.4008	.9575
Stockholders' return after taxes	SRA	.1152	.0719	−.3706	.4523
Concentration ratios					
Census concentration ratio	CCR	.4666	.1585	.1000	.9900
Shepherd concentration ratio	SCR	.5963	.1722	.1600	.9600
Firm size					
Total assets (millions of dollars)	A	272.5	841.2	1.611	12,608.
Reciprocal of log of assets (base 10)	RLogA	.6710	.4089	.2439	4.828
Capital intensity					
Asset/output ratio	A/Q	.7626	.3307	.0724	3.503
Fixed capital/output ratio	K/Q	.2825	.2429	.0054	1.485
Growth					
Asset growth	AG	2.052	4.043	−.8286	56.17
Sales growth	SG	1.966	4.918	−.9893	97.58

Note: See Appendix C for the definitions and calculations of variables.

TABLE 4

ANALYSIS OF PROFITABILITY AND STRUCTURE FOR 768 FIRMS, 1960–68

Equation	Rate of Return*	Constant	Regression Coefficients—Independent Variables†					R^2
			Concentration (CCR)	Size (RLogA)	Capital Intensity (A/Q)	Growth (AG)		
1	IORB	.1725	.0656 (3.77) *.132*	−.0265 (3.95) *−.137*	−.0617 (7.74) *−.271*	.0038 (5.67) *.193*		.130
2	IORA	.0939	.0271 (3.11) *.109*	−.0152 (4.53) *−.157*	−.0273 (6.54) *−.228*	.0023 (7.03) *.239*		.133
3	SRB	.2774	.1060 (3.60) *.121*	−.0585 (5.16) *−.173*	−.1127 (7.99) *−.269*	.0104 (9.29) *.304*		.194
4	SRA	.1418	.0475 (3.08) *.105*	−.0371 (6.24) *−.211*	−.0458 (6.18) *−.211*	.0054 (9.11) *.302*		.176

* Notations are: implicit operating returns before taxes, IORB; implicit operating returns after taxes, IORA: stockholders' returns before taxes, SRB; stockholders' returns after taxes, SRA.

† Absolute value of t ratios in parentheses. beta coefficients in italics.

in Table 4 are only for Census concentration ratios (CCR), these models are also fitted for Shepherd concentration ratios (SCR). These results, however, are practically identical in all respects and therefore are not given or discussed.

If all other independent variables are held at their mean values, the marginal effect of concentration can be assessed. When this procedure is followed for the first regression for implicit operating returns (Equation 1), a firm in an industry with a concentration ratio of .10 would earn a return of 12.0 percent (IORB) in contrast to a return of 17.2 percent for a firm with a ratio of .90—a 44 percent increase in profitability. Equation 3 suggests a 46 percent greater return on stockholders' equity for the firm in the highly concentrated industry. These comparisons suggest that concentration does confer a rather marked advantage in profitability. However, it is precisely this hasty inference which is subjected to closer scrutiny throughout much of the remainder of this chapter.

Firm size

The hypothesis that larger firms earn higher long-run rates of return (Hypothesis II) is also supported by the results given in Table 4. Much of the previous research on the absolute-size profitability hypothesis did not study the relationship between the very large firms (above $250 million in assets).[12] Generally, these studies find a plateau in earnings around the $10–$20 million asset size range, with the implication that beyond that point further advantage is not evident. Hall and Weiss, however, who conducted one of the first studies among the largest firms, conclude that the advantages of absolute size extend beyond this range to the very largest of firms.[13] It would appear that support for the Hall and Weiss result is found here.[14]

The marginal effect of size on profitability in the case of these large firms may be assessed by again holding the other independent variables at their mean values. Using this procedure in Equation 1, a firm with $2 billion in assets would earn better than twice the before-tax return on those assets (15.4 percent) that a firm with $2 million in assets would earn (7.4 percent). In comparison to the marginal effect of concentration, the

---

12. Most previous research uses IRS data where data are categorized by size. The upper size class is $250 million and up.

13. Hall and Weiss, "Firm Size and Profitability."

14. In the panel of 768 firms, the average firm size is $272 million with 87 firms above the $500 million mark.

influence of size on rates of return (over the extreme ranges) is consider-ably greater. However, the determined relation between absolute size and profitability is curvilinear and, therefore, the inference of significant advantages for the largest of large firms is unwarranted. The following tabular presentation gives the relation between size and profitability for select sizes.

FIRM SIZE (IN MILLIONS OF DOLLARS)	RATE OF RETURN (IN PERCENTAGE)
2	7.35
5	12.36
10	13.50
20	14.22
50	14.59
100	14.83
500	15.17
1,000	15.27
2,000	15.35

It is quite clear that, for this fitted model, absolute size has very little influence on rates of return above the $100 million asset size. In fact, this result supports the conclusion that a plateau *is* reached at about the $10–20 million range.[15] More on the absolute-size profitability hy-pothesis later.

Capital intensity

It is hypothesized that the capital-intensive firms earn above-average long-run rates of return (Hypothesis VII). We expected that capital/out-put ratios would be positively correlated with profitability, because, in part, they serve as a proxy for an absolute-capital-requirement barrier-to-entry variable and the degree of vertical integration. However, these expectations are consistently and strongly contradicted by the results.[16] (See Table 4, column 5.) In other words, the results suggest that profit

15. Studies subsequent to that of Hall and Weiss have found negative size-profitability relations. Shepherd consistently finds a negative relation; however, his average firm size is very large. (The mean natural logarithm translates to a size of $3 billion.) W. G. Shepherd, "The Elements of Market Structure," *Review of Economics and Statistics* 54 (Feb. 1972): 25–37.

16. As in previous research, two measures of capital/output ratios, alternatively defining capital as total assets and fixed assets, are employed. The results are not sensitive to the measure of capital. Therefore, the results of capital/output ratios with capital defined as fixed assets are not given or discussed here.

margins do not increase proportionally as asset/turnover ratios decrease.[17] Full discussion of this finding is deferred to later analysis, but at this time one obvious explanation is noted. For a certain degree of capital intensity, given the requirements of efficient production, one would expect the observed measure to be higher or lower depending upon the marketing success of the firm. The higher the sales volume, given the capital investment, the lower the capital/output ratio and the higher the profit rate. In other words, capital/output ratios, instead of being considered a structural variable, might be viewed as a performance variable.

In fact, Schor's explanation for the positive association between size and capital intensity is similarly reasoned. "He thought that larger firms would tend to be under less competitive pressure to economize on the use of capital than smaller firms, especially in an oligopolistic situation."[18] This explanation would account for the observed relation between capital intensity and size on the one hand, and, on the other hand, it would explain the negative association between capital intensity and profitability.

Growth

The results in Table 4 support the hypothesis that across all firms growth is positively associated with profitability (Hypothesis XIII). Although results are presented only for growth measured by assets, the sales-growth measure is also used. As expected, these results are very similar.

Relative importance of each independent variable

Because it is difficult to judge the comparative importance of the four independent variables by direct comparison of the regression coefficients,

---

17. The asset/turnover ratio is the reciprocal of the asset/output ratio. Its usefulness comes from the following identitity, linking rates of returns with profit margins:

$$\frac{\text{Profit}}{\text{Assets}} = \frac{\text{Profit}}{\text{Sales}} \times \frac{\text{Sales}}{\text{Assets}}$$

Norman R. Collins and Lee E. Preston have used the profit margin extensively as the performance measure and have found it positively related to concentration. See especially *Concentration and Price-Cost Margins in Manufacturing Industries* (Berkeley, Calif.: University of California Press, 1970).

18. Hiram S. Davis, "Relation of Capital/Output Ratio to Firm Size in American Manufacturing," *Review of Economics and Statistics* 38 (Aug. 1956): 287.

the beta coefficients are given below t ratios of each coefficient.[19] On the basis of these beta coefficients, concentration ratios are indicated to be the *least* important variable regardless of the profitability measure. Size of firm, however, follows closely except for stockholders' return after taxes (SRA), where size is considerably more important than concentration. Generally, the beta coefficients for growth and asset/output ratios are twice as large as those for size and concentration.

Weighted regressions

One of the assumptions in linear regression analysis is that the variance of residuals is constant.[20] It has been found, however, that among larger firms profit rates vary less than they do for smaller firms.[21] The diversification of larger firms is the primary reason given. First, large firms simply operate more plants in the same line of production. Second, these plants are geographically diversified. And third, larger firms may be more diversified among lines of production. Many argue that basically for these reasons large firms should, and do, evidence smaller variances in rates of return.[22]

Either a theoretical or empirical approach can be taken to determine the relationship between firm size and the variance of profit rate residuals. The theoretical approach begins with the assumption that large firms are composed of a greater number of plants or units of operation which are randomly distributed among large and small firms. The variance of the larger firms is then $1/N$ times the variance of the smaller firms, where N is the ratio of the size of the larger to the smaller firms. That is, the

19. The beta coefficient is computed by multiplying each independent variable's regression coefficient by the ratio of the standard deviation of the independent variable to the standard deviation of the dependent variable. The beta coefficient then becomes an indication of the importance of the individual regressors according to their contributions to the predicted value of the dependent variable. That is, the importance of a predictor is judged by the effect of a "standard" change in each predictor. See Arthur S. Goldberger, *Econometric Theory* (New York: John Wiley & Sons, 1964), pp. 197–98.

20. J. Johnston, *Econometric Methods* (New York: McGraw-Hill Book Co., 1963), p. 107. Because this panel is intended to be a census, the problem of bias in predictors due to heteroscedasticity changes. Predictors estimated from sample data might, under these circumstances, be biased estimates of the true regressor. However, in a census the (unweighted) regressor is the true regressor.

21. H. O. Stekler, "The Variability of Profitability with Size of Firm, 1947–1958," *Journal of the American Statistical Association* 59 (Dec. 1964): 44–61.

22. It is noted, however, that these arguments go for temporal variance as well and may be summarized by simply observing that larger firms can lessen business risk through diversification. We return to this point when risk is discussed.

large firm is composed of N smaller firms. Empirically, it has been found that the variance does not fall off as rapidly as the theoretical model would suggest.[23]

Because this is an empirical study, the empirical approach is taken. From the previous (unweighted) regressions, the sum of the squares of the residuals for successive groups of 32 firms (ordered by size) is calculated. These 24 (768/32) sums of squares are then plotted against each group's mean of the logarithm of firm size.[24] Figure 1 is the plot using Equation 3 of Table 4 to compute the residuals. Inspection indicates that the curve could be reasonably approximated by the equation

$$\text{Sum of Squares} = \frac{k}{\text{Log } A}$$

where k is an arbitrary constant given the value of .65. The encircled four points are outliers because of only two or three very extreme firms. These four points would all fall reasonably close to the fitted curve of the residuals if the two or three most extreme firms (of the 32) were eliminated from the computation of the sum of the squares for their groups. Accepting this relationship between size and the variance of the residuals, the appropriate correction for heteroscedasticity is to weight the constant term and all observations of each variable in the regression equations by the square root of the logarithm of each firm's asset $(\text{Log} A)^{1/2}$.[25]

Generally, the results of weighted regressions (Table 5) are not materially different from the unweighted results. The marginal effect of size on rates of return is roughly doubled for the model using implicit operating return before taxes (IORB) as the rate-of-return variable.

23. See, for example, Stephen Hymer and P. Pashigian, "Firm Size and Rate of Growth," *Journal of Political Economy* 70 (Dec. 1962): 556–69; Sidney S. Alexander, "The Effect of Size of Manufacturing Corporation on the Distribution of the Rate of Return," *Review of Economics and Statistics* 31 (Aug. 1949): 229–35. T. R. Dyckman and H. O. Stekler, in "Firm Size and Variability," *Journal of Industrial Economics* 13 (June 1965): 214–18, show that with different assumptions the variance would fall off less rapidly than in this procedure.

24. The typical procedure for testing for heteroscedasticity is to plot the residuals against size. Heteroscedasticity would show up, in this case, as a funnel with the large end at the lower size ranges. This method, however, does not help in determining the appropriate correction for heteroscedasticity.

25. See Johnston, *Econometric Methods*, pp. 207–11. The nature of the relationship between size and the square of the residuals does not seem to change significantly among the various profitability and concentration measures.

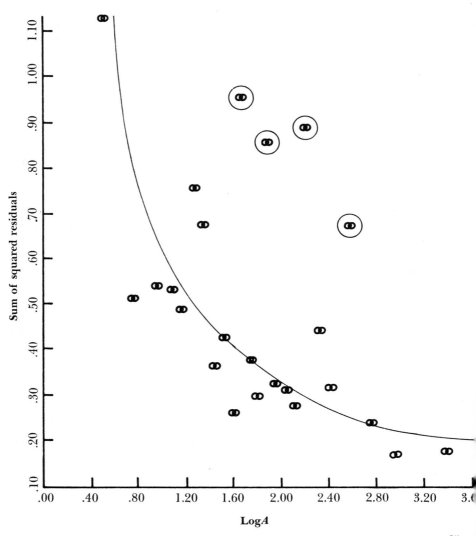

Fig. 1.   Plot of sum of squared residuals and sum of squared residuals $= \dfrac{.65}{\mathrm{Log}A}$
(Equation 3, Table 4).

TABLE 5

ANALYSIS OF PROFITABILITY AND STRUCTURE FOR 768 FIRMS, 1960–68, WEIGHTED REGRESSIONS
(ABSOLUTE VALUE OF t RATIOS IN PARENTHESES)

EQUATION	RATE OF RETURN	REGRESSION COEFFICIENTS—INDEPENDENT VARIABLE						
		CONSTANT	CONCENTRATION (CCR)	SIZE (RLogA)	CAPITAL INTENSITY (A/Q)	GROWTH (AG)	WEIGHT	R^2
Regressions weighted by $(LogA)^{1/2}$								
1	IORB*	.0574 (0.62)	.0737 (4.36)	−.0595 (1.15)	−.0627 (8.02)	.0039 (5.21)	.1433 (3.28)	.257
2	SRB†	.0062 (0.04)	.1143 (4.07)	−.0676 (0.79)	−.1093 (8.42)	.0116 (9.33)	.2698 (3.72)	.300
Regressions weighted by $(A)^{1/4}$								
3	IORB*	.0513 (0.96)	.0873 (5.63)	−.0433 (1.58)	−.0631 (8.92)	.0041 (4.76)	.1528 (11.05)	.479
4	SRB†	.0293 (0.33)	.1352 (5.31)	−.0693 (1.54)	−.1099 (9.47)	.0126 (8.85)	.2540 (11.21)	.492
Regressions weighted by $(A)^{1/2}$								
5	IORB*	.7197 (2.33)	.1211 (9.76)	−.2857 (2.39)	−.0694 (11.42)	.0040 (3.39)	.2050 (6.36)	.784
6	SRB†	.8628 (1.76)	.1826 (9.31)	−.3854 (2.04)	−.1192 (12.41)	.0142 (7.52)	.3150 (6.19)	.786

* Implicit operating return before taxes.
† Stockholders' return before taxes.

In the model for stockholders' return before taxes (SRB), the marginal effect of size increases about 10 percent. The only other difference worth mentioning between the unweighted and weighted regressions is that for all profitability measures, the marginal effect of concentration increases by roughly 10 percent (see Table 5).

The results of another possible empirical weight, the fourth root of firm assets $(A^{1/4})$ are presented.[26] As would be expected—because $(\log A)^{1/2}$ and $A^{1/4}$ would move in similar fashion—these results are very similar. For comparison, the weighted regressions using the theoretical weights, the square root of assets $(A^{1/2})$, are presented. These results indicate that this is not a good correction for these models. One would expect the constant term in the weighted regressions to be zero if the correction for heteroscedasticity were perfect for these models. That is, the constant terms in these equations would be zero if the sum of the squared residuals were proportional to $1/\log A$, $1/A^2$, and $1/A$ respectively for the three weights. For the first two sets of weights the constant is, in fact, statistically not "significantly" different from zero. For the theoretical weights, the constants are quite large and "signicantly" different from zero. For this reason, the regression coefficients for size are also large and misleading.[27]

Current-Cost Rates of Return

Many economists have for several reasons argued that accounting rates of return are poor proxies for economic rates of return,[28] one important reason being that historical rather than current costs are used in accounting statements. Economic returns, in and of themselves, are not the focus in this study. Rather, the focus here is on the question of whether the use of accounting returns distorts the relation between economic returns and concentration.

26. This weight is used in another similar study. See U.S., Federal Trade Commission, *Economic Report on the Influences of Market Structure on the Profit Performance of Food Manufacturing Companies* (Washington, D.C.: Superintendent of Documents, Sept. 1969), p. 19.

27. Because of the introduction of improper weights, it is possible that spurious correlation is introduced. Note that for the $A^{1/2}$ weight the models explain more than 78 percent of the variance in the dependent variables.

28. For example, see Joe S. Bain, "The Profit Rate as a Measure of Monopoly Power," *Quarterly Journal of Economics* 65 (Aug. 1951): 293–324; Yale Brozen, "Significance of Profit Data for Antitrust Policy," in *Public Policy toward Mergers,* ed. by J. Fred Weston and Sam Peltzman (Pacific Palisades, Calif.: Goodyear Publishing Co., 1969), pp. 110–27; George J. Stigler, *Capital and Rates of Return in Manufacturing Industries* (Princeton, N.J.: Princeton University Press, 1963).

Measurement of income

In my opinion, the best practical definition of income is that it is the change in purchasing power between two points in time.[29] In practice, the measurement of income is accomplished by the measurement and proper matching of revenues and expenses. Difficulties are encountered in the matching of expenses and revenues when physical resources (assets) are employed to generate revenues over several time (income) periods. These resources produce rather easily identifiable revenues in each time period; however, the expenses are not as easily identified. For example, various methods of depreciation are used to spread the costs of an acquired asset over its revenue-producing life. Though one might quibble with the use of depreciation as a method to *match* expenses with revenues in the determination of a period's income, as defined here, another and stronger objection to accounting practice is made. While the purpose of depreciation is to allocate the "costs" among the periods, it in no way attempts to determine the loss in the purchasing power through the use of the assets over the periods.

The dollar cost of acquiring an asset represents a dollar amount of purchasing power only at the time it is acquired unless, of course, there is no change in purchasing power in general over time. One dollar in 1950 was not worth the same (in purchasing power) as a dollar in 1970. Thus the adjustment of the accountant's historical costs involves the restatement of the costs of long-lived assets in terms of current purchasing power, hereafter labeled current costs, and the restatement of depreciation in terms of decreases in current purchasing power. Although income distortions result implicitly from the accounting of any asset with a life of longer than one year, only adjustments for fixed assets are attempted in this study.[30]

29. J. R. Hicks defines an individual's income as "what he can consume during the week and still expect to be as well off at the end of the week as he was at the beginning." *Value and Capital* (2d ed.; Oxford: Clarendon Press, 1946). p. 176. Although a better definition in theory, this definition is empirically unmanageable because it is oriented to the future rather than historically. Based on Hicks' definition, business income would involve the discounting of future (expected) income. The defiinition given in the text is, however, a function of past events and not expectations about future events.

30. The two major classes of assets affected by these considerations are long-term or fixed assets and inventories. Because requisite data for inventories are not available, they are excluded from these current-cost calculations. However, the distortions arising from inventories would be far less important than those arising from fixed assets.

Problems in measurement

The methodology to adjust historical costs to current costs[31] borrows heavily from the underlying concepts developed by Edwards and Bell in *The Theory and Measurement of Business Income.*[32] The following paragraphs discuss a few fundamental concepts briefly, using the language of Edwards and Bell whenever practical.

First, these theoreticians discuss the problem that arises when assets are held for two or more time (income) periods. They identify the attendant difficulties by distinguishing between two types of flows.

> The first, the vertical or production flow, relates to the movement of inputs from their acquisition to their sale as outputs, that is, to the movement of inputs through the various stages of production within the business firm. The second flow, the horizontal or holding flow, relates to the movement of inputs (and "inputs" is used here in the broad sense of including all the assets of the business firm) from one moment in time to another, that is, over the period of time for which a measurement is attempted.[33]

It is important to distinguish between these two flows because each is a source of two equally distinguishable types of income.

> . . . Any gains which accrue to the firm as a result of horizontal movements, or *holding activities,* are *capital gains.* Any gains made by the firm as a result of vertical movements, or *operating activities,* are *operating profits.*
>
> These two kinds of gains are often the result of quite different sets of decisions. . . . The difference between the forces motivating the business firm to make profit by one means rather than by another and the difference between the events on which the two methods of making profit depend require that the two kinds of gain be careful separated if the two types of decision involved are to be meaningfully evaluated.[34]

Ordinary accounting profits combine holding and operating gains and do not distinguish between them. Briefly, the reason for this stems from the depreciation expense (based on historical cost) taken each year. The amount of holding gain included in accounting income each year is equal to the difference between the amount of depreciation which would be based on the current cost of the asset and the amount based on historical cost.[35]

To the extent that accounting profits serve as a basis for investment

---

31. See Appendix D for the details of the methodology used.
32. Edgar O. Edwards and Philip W. Bell, *The Theory and Measurement of Business Income* (Berkeley, Calif.: University of California Press, 1970).
33. *Ibid.,* p. 71.
34. *Ibid.,* p. 73.
35. By convention, accountants do not typically recognize gains until an asset (which has increased in value) has been sold. However, a depreciable asset *is* "sold" each year to the extent that a depreciation expense is taken.

decisions, it is very likely that the wrong decisions are made, with the results that society misallocates its resources. That income came from holding or current operating activities is of the utmost importance. Again, Edwards and Bell are lucid and succinct in covering this point.

> But to call the [holding] gain (more accurately the cost saving achieved by buying when prices were low) an operating profit is simply not an accurate representation of the facts. The confusion may even tempt management into unsound decisions and is almost certain to perform this disservice for outsiders. Consider the following situation. A wise management enters an industry at a time when the necessary assets can be purchased at exceedingly favorable prices. As time passes, other firms enter the industry purchasing their assets at substantially higher prices. If all firms now in the industry are equally efficient in their operating activities, the first firm will record a substantially larger "operating profit" than the other firms in the industry. After all, the depreciation charges of the first firm are substantially lower in terms of historic cost than are those for the newer firms in the industry. But this excess does not result from the wisdom with which the management operates its assets; it is the result of the wisdom which the management displayed at the time it purchased the assets and in its many subsequent (perhaps passive) decisions to hold the asset.[36]

The implications of these observations for this study are clear. If holding gains are higher among concentrated industries (older assets), then observed rates of return are more overstated. However, the argument about new firms entering the industry may be turned around slightly. Suppose that while observed rates of return are attractively high, potential entrants (after careful analysis) do not decide to enter the industry. For example, it might not be too unreasonable to assume that, knowing the current cost of fixed assets, and after carefully analyzing the direct costs (raw materials, labor, etc.) and the profit prospects given current prices, the potential entrant might decide that entrance was, in fact, unattractive. With fewer entrants (and competitors) in the industry than might otherwise be expected, given the observed rates of return, hasty analysis might conclude that the oligopolistic structure resulted from limit pricing or barriers to entry.

The proper measure of profits for which Edwards and Bell argue they label "current operating profit,"[37] i.e., "the excess of the current purchasing power represented by the current value of output over the current purchasing power represented by the current value of input."[38]

36. *Business Income*, p. 224.

37. Several other concepts of income are developed by Edwards and Bell, e.g., realized business profit (current operating income plus realized holding gains) and realizable business profits (realized business profits plus realizable holding gains).

38. *Business Income*, p. 124.

In this section, current operating rates of return are calculated and regressed against the structural variables. Very briefly, the following paragraphs outline the methodology used in calculating the current operating rates of return.[39]

Methodology

Before discussing the methodology, it is important to state explicitly a previous implication. The adjustment of historical costs to current costs of fixed assets results from changes in specific prices rather than in general prices. Corrections are not being made to reflect changes in the general purchasing power of the dollar (i.e., consumer price index or GNP implicit deflator). Corrections are being made because the replacement costs of specific assets change over time, irrespective of the movement of prices in general.[40]

It would be a rather straightforward (though tedious) procedure to adjust historical costs to current costs if the detailed records of each firm were available to the analyst. Basically, the procedure would be to determine the date of acquisition, the original cost, and the useful life of each asset currently in use. The next step would entail getting estimates of the replacement cost of each asset according to, perhaps, current price indexes for the particular type of equipment or buildings in question. The restatement of a firm's fixed assets and their appropriate depreciation would then be matter of arithmetic.

These data are not generally available, however, and methodology must be developed to estimate them. Very briefly, the dates of acquisition of the current stock are estimated by assuming a first-in, first-out flow of capital assets and backwards accumulating capital expenditures from the current period until the total equals the current gross plant account. Because the period studied begins with 1960, the process begins with estimating the dates of acquisition of the stock of fixed assets on January 1, 1960. To do so, each firm's capital expenditure series from 1950 to 1959 are utilized. These data are available on the Compustat tapes for 339 of the original 768 firms. After the average dates of the acquisition of these asset bundles (yearly capital expenditures) are esti-

---

39. For a detailed discussion of the methodology see Appendix D.

40. If rates of return are also adjusted for the changes in general purchasing power, they are typically called real rates of return. However, because current operating profits are automatically in current dollars, no adjustment is necessary for changes in general purchasing power. Other measures of profitability (not discussed here) do need adjustment however. See Edwards and Bell, *Business Income,* chap. 13, for a discussion of these points.

mated, the next step is to estimate their respective current costs. For these purposes, a price index for machinery, equipment, and structures is used. For example, if a firm's 1960 fixed-asset stock is determined to include $10,000 of capital expenditures in 1952, then the current cost of these assets is calculated by multiplying the $10,000 by the ratio of the 1960 to 1952 price index.[41]

The final piece of data needed for computation of current operating profit is that of useful life. In each industry useful life is a weighted average of 1964 IRS useful-life guidelines for specific assets for specific industries.[42] The estimated useful life is used to estimate current-cost depreciation expense by assuming straight-line depreciation.[43]

In the following analysis, three rate-of-return measures are used. First, an implicit operating return (on assets) before taxes is calculated for each of the 339 firms (labeled, as previously, IORB). The second rate of return is the implicit current operating rate of return, labeled ICOR. This rate of return is identical to IORB except that in its calculation the current instead of historical costs of fixed assets are used to determine profits (the numerator) and total assets (the denominator). The third rate of return is called the implicit historical operating rate of return, labeled IHOR. This rate of return, which like IORB is based on historical costs, is identical to IORB except that instead of being based on actual depreciation expenses and actual net asset values (gross plant, less accumulated depreciation), its values are calculated according to the estimates of useful life and average age and according to the straight-line procedures used to generate ICOR. The use of IHOR is to determine whether there exists a systematic bias in these procedures that may alter the relations between profitability and the structural variables. Whether it is the adjustment to current costs or the adjustment to comparable depreciation procedures that may alter these relations is of great importance.

Results of analysis

Table 6 provides the descriptive measures of the variables used in the analysis of current-cost rates of return. First, a comparison of the means for the 339 firms with those given in Table 3 for 768 firms indicates the

41. Actually, price indexes for each year are computed separately for each industry according to an estimated ratio of equipment (and machinery) to structures. (See Appendix D.)

42. See Appendix D.

43. Actual depreciation expenses are not used in these calculations because methods vary by industry—comparability would not be attained.

TABLE 6

DESCRIPTIVE MEASURES FOR FIRM CURRENT-COST VARIABLES FOR 339 FIRMS, 1960 AVERAGES

VARIABLE	NOTATION	MEAN	STANDARD DEVIATION	MINIMUM	MAXIMUM
Rate of return					
Implicit current operating return before taxes	ICOR	.1250	.0813	−.0579	.4942
Implicit historical operating return before taxes	IHOR	.1480	.0806	−.0348	.5174
Implicit operating return before taxes	IORB	.1501	.0793	−.0067	.5073
Concentration ratios					
Census concentration ratio	CCR	.5104	.1646	.1000	.9900
Shepherd concentration ratio	SCR	.6427	.1724	.1600	.9600
Firm size					
Reciprocal of log of assets (base 10)	RLogA	.4674	.1281	.2439	1.020
Capital intensity					
Asset/output ratio	A/Q	.8188	.3534	.1713	2.504
Fixed-capital/output ratio	K/Q	.3528	.2837	.0445	1.485
Growth					
Asset growth	AG	1.293	1.398	−4.331	14.14
Sales growth	SG	1.242	1.640	−4.379	23.16

following: The 339 firms are on the average smaller (average assets of $218 million versus $272 million), more concentrated (ratios approximately five percentage points higher), and more capital intensive. The greatest difference between the two panels is found in their growth rates. For the larger panel, asset- and sales-growth variables average about 2.0, but for the 339-firm panel these variables average only about 1.25. As one might expect, firms with complete data back to 1950 are older, more capital intensive, and more concentrated. The 339 firms earn an average implicit operating rate of return before taxes (IORB) of .1501 compared to the 768-firm average of .1437.

Relation between alternative measures of performance. When observed rates of return are "standardized" for depreciation policy by assuming straight-line depreciation and IRS useful-life guidelines, average rates of return are slightly reduced from .1501 (IORB) to .1480 (IHOR). However, the greatest discrepancy in observed rates of return results from the use of historical rather than current costs. Current-cost rates of return average 12.5 percent versus observed returns of 15.0 percent.[44] Furthermore, it is noted, the absolute dispersion of current-cost returns is greater than that of historical-cost returns. In other words, historical costs tend to reduce the absolute variances of rates of return among firms.

Regression results. The results of the regressions between each of these three rates of return and the structural variables are given in Table 7.[45]

To obtain a proper perspective on the results, it seems necessary to contrast the results (IORB) between the 339-firm panel and the 768-firm panel. Several differences are noteworthy. First, the degree of explanatory power is moderately increased, as would be expected because of the reduction in the number of observations. Second, in the 339-firm panel, size of firm is found to be negatively associated with profitability; however, size is found to have very little influence on returns.[46] Third, in the

44. Recall, however, that absolute levels of current-cost returns are not the object of this analysis.

45. In this section both measures of capital intensity and both measures of growth rates are included in the regressions. The reasons for this are the dual roles that growth and capital intensity each have in influencing rates of return. Here, in addition to the structural relation, there is a tautological relation, because it is the adjustments in fixed-asset values that give rise to the discrepancy between historical- and current-cost rates of return. It should also be noted that in order to obtain the greatest degree of comparability among the results, all structural variables using asset figures are stated in terms of historical costs rather than current costs. Further analysis should adjust the measures of structure (e.g., asset size, capital intensity, and asset growth) to reflect current costs.

46. This negative relation is found in a similar study with a comparable-sized panel. W. G. Shepherd, "The Elements of Market Structure," *Review of Economics and Statistics* 54 (Feb. 1972): 25–37.

TABLE 7

ANALYSIS OF PROFITABILITY MEASUREMENT AND STRUCTURE FOR 339 FIRMS, 1960–68

EQUATION*	RATE OF RETURN	CONSTANT	CONCENTRATION		SIZE	CAPITAL INTENSITY		GROWTH		R^2
			(CCR)	(SCR)	(RLogA)	(A/Q)	(K/Q)	(AG)	(SG)	
1	IORB	.1160	.1097	…	.0066	−.0081	−.0742	.0058	.0038	.162
			(4.37)	…	(0.21)	(0.41)	(3.03)	(0.94)	(0.73)	
			.228		*.011*	*−.036*	*−.266*	*.102*	*.079*	
2	IHOR	.1070	.1100	…	.0051	−.0049	−.0790	.0059	.0533	.175
			(4.34)	…	(0.15)	(0.24)	(3.20)	(0.96)	(1.01)	
			.210		*.008*	*−.020*	*−.259*	*.010*	*.101*	
3	ICOR	.0879	.1047	…	.0028	.0057	−.1109	.0084	.0048	.232
			(4.25)	…	(0.09)	(0.29)	(4.62)	(1.39)	(0.97)	
			.212		*.004*	*.025*	*−.387*	*.144*	*.097*	
4	IORB	.0702	…	.1493	.0249	−.0120	−.0810	.0028	.0057	.208
			…	(6.28)	(0.78)	(0.62)	(3.40)	(0.47)	(1.14)	
				.325	*.040*	*−.054*	*−.290*	*.049*	*.119*	
5	IHOR	.0662	…	.1487	.0231	−.0098	−.0857	.0029	.0073	.218
			…	(6.18)	(0.72)	(0.45)	(3.56)	(0.48)	(1.43)	
				.297	*.034*	*−.036*	*−.281*	*.047*	*.138*	
6	ICOR	.0449	…	.1479	.0215	.0015	−.1177	.0055	.0066	.278
			…	(6.34)	(0.69)	(0.08)	(5.04)	(0.94)	(1.34)	
				.314	*.034*	*.006*	*−.411*	*.094*	*.134*	

REGRESSION COEFFICIENTS—INDEPENDENT VARIABLES†

* Notations are as follows: CCR, census concentration ratio; SCR, Shepherd concentration ratio; RlogA, reciprocal of log of assets (base 10); A/Q, asset/output ratio; K/Q, fixed-capital/output ratio; AG, asset growth; SG, sales growth; IORB, implicit operating return before taxes; IHOR, implicit historical operating return before taxes; ICOR, implicit current operating return before taxes. Precise definitions of variables (except IHOR and ICOR) are given in Appendix C. Definitions of IHOR and ICOR are found in Appendix D. See Table 6 for description of variables.

† Absolute value of *t* ratios in parentheses, beta coefficients in italics.

339-firm panel, asset growth is found to have less positive influence on rates of return, and sales growth is found to be positively, rather than negatively, associated with performance. Fourth, in the 339-firm panel the influence of concentration on rates of return (judging from the beta coefficients) is roughly double its influence in the 768-firm panel.

Comparing the results of the three alternative measures of performance reveals that neither the adjustments to comparable depreciation policies (reflected in IHOR) nor the adjustments to current costs (reflected in ICOR) materially affect the observed relationship between performance and the structural variables (seen in IORB). In other words, the distortions in observed profitability measures generally do not appear to result in biased structure-performance relationships. In particular, the influence of concentration on performance is only ever so slightly greater for observed rates-of-return than for current-cost rates-of-return.[47]

The conclusion that the discrepancies between measures using observed performance and measures using adjusted performance are not materially and systematically related to the structural variables is confirmed by further analysis. Here the ratios of the observed-profitability measures to the adjusted measures are regressed against these structural variables. Table 8 gives the results. If the ratios of the observed- to the adjusted-performance measures are taken to represent the relative amount of distortion, then the very small coefficients of determination (ranging from .105 to .043) confirm this conclusion.

These results also support, although weakly, the following conclusions. Concentrated industries tend to understate rates of return through departures from straight-line depreciation and IRS useful-life guidelines. (The ratios of IORB to IHOR are negatively associated with concentration ratios.) However, the opposite occurs for large firms—i.e., larger firms tend to overstate performance measures by their depreciation policies. Finally, firms which are more capital intensive understate rates of return, and fast-growing firms overstate returns by their depreciation policies.

With regard to distortions caused by using historical instead of current costs (indicated by the ratios of IORB to ICOR), the following conclusions are indicated: Performance measures are overstated in the highly concentrated and capital-intensive industries and understated for large and fast-growing firms. In particular and in summary, the hypothesis that the adjustment to current-cost rates of return affects concentrated in-

47. A result that should not go unnoticed is the substantial increase in the coefficient of determination for ICOR over those for IORB. Table 7 shows that R^2 increases from .162 to .232 for Census ratios and that R^2 increases from .208 to .278 for Shepherd ratios.

TABLE 8

ANALYSIS OF DISTORTIONS IN OBSERVED-PROFITABILITY MEASURES AND STRUCTURE FOR 339 FIRMS, 1960–68

MEASURES OF RELATIVE DISTORTION	CONSTANT	REGRESSION COEFFICIENTS—INDEPENDENT VARIABLES*					
		CONCENTRATION		SIZE (RLogA)	CAPITAL INTENSITY (A/Q)	GROWTH (AG)	R^2
		(CCR)	(SCR)				
IORB/IHOR	2.088	−.2571 (0.68) −.038	. . .	−1.6409 (3.36) −.186	−.3807 (2.11) −.119	.0435 (1.00) .054	.043
IORB/IHOR	1.968	. . .	−.1830 (0.05) .002	−1.6042 (3.25) −.120	−.3995 (2.19) −.125	.0425 (0.97) .053	.042
IORB/ICOR	1.288	.5416 (0.72) .040	. . .	−.7798 (0.80) −.045	.1562 (0.44) .025	−.1473 (1.70) −.093	.015
IORB/ICOR	1.025	. . .	.8268 (1.12) .064	−.6613 (0.67) −.038	.1078 (0.29) .017	−.1531 (1.76) −.197	.018

Note: The following notations are used: IORB, implicit operating return before taxes; IHOR, implicit historical operating return before taxes; CCR, census concentration ratios; SCR, Shepherd concentration ratios; RLogA, reciprocal of log of assets (base 10); A/Q, assets/output ratio; AG, asset growth; ICOR, implicit current operating return before taxes.

* Absolute value of t ratios in parentheses, beta coefficients in italics.

dustries' rates of return more than it does those of unconcentrated industries (Hypothesis XV) is supported. Though the indicated distortion is small, it should be recalled that the purpose of this section is not to determine the true relation between economic performance and concentration, but rather to determine the direction of the distortions from using historical data. In other words, though it is unlikely that the use of historical costs in observed-return measures results in the association between performance and concentration, the possibility cannot be completely ruled out. Only complete and full adjustment would decide the question.[48]

48. No doubt actual current-cost rates of return based on complete adjustment for fixed assets as well as for inventories would be lower than those obtained here.

3

EMPIRICAL RESULTS—A FURTHER EXPLORATION

In terms of general results, firm profitability, concentration, size, capital intensity, and growth have shown most of the expected relations. In particular, concentration is found to be a statistically significant determinant of profitability, though the least important according to the beta coefficients. However, because the explanatory variables are correlated and because they are theoretically interrelated in complex fashion, further exploration of the positive association between profitability and concentration is called for. In addition to the more latent features of the interrelation of the above explanatory variables, distortion in these measures of profitability arising because of risk is explored in an attempt to determine whether the distortion is systematically related to concentration and therefore, in part, explains some of the observed relation.

Absolute Size, Concentration, and Profitability

In the review of the literature evidence is cited which rather strongly indicates the collinearity between size and concentration. In fact, Osborn goes so far as to assert that the reason for the common finding of a positive association between concentration and profitability is this collinearity. Evidence is even offered which suggests that concentration is negatively associated with profitability once this collinearity is accounted for. That concentration and size are correlated is confirmed in this study by the results of first order correlation coefficients. For 768 firms as units of observation, the correlation coefficient between Census ratios and the logarithms of firm size is .30; for 79 industries, the correlation coefficient is .59.

Size-adjusted rates-of-return

A rather direct method of testing Osborn's hypothesis is to incorporate the use of dummy variables in a bi-variate absolute-size profitability

66

model. Again, the influence of size is assumed to be correctly represented by the reciprocal of the logarithm (base 10) of firm assets. The absolute-size profitability hypothesis states that larger firms earn higher long-run rates of return than do smaller firms for a set of specific reasons. However, there are a myriad of reasons other than those explicitly considered in this study that may account for large firms' earning of higher rates of return. Several of these reasons may be common to whole industries. That is, characteristics peculiar to the industry affect observed firm rates of return. Therefore, industry dummy variables are used to capture these combined industry influences. The fitted models for the two (before-tax) rate-of-return measures are (t ratios in parentheses):

$$IORB_{ij} = S_j - .0247RLogA_{ij} \qquad R^2 = .292; \quad N = 736$$
$$(3.47)$$

$$SRB_{ij} = S_j - .0528RLogA_{ij} \qquad R^2 = .281; \quad N = 736.$$
$$(4.21)$$

The S_j's are the industry dummy variables. In the previous analysis 768 firms were analyzed. However, for this analysis and subsequent analyses where the concept of industry (groupings of firms) is employed, 32 firms are dropped, leaving 736 firms.[1] Compared to the results of similar bi-variate analysis without the use of dummy variables, the explanatory power of these two models is far superior. These simple bi-variate results for the 768 firms are (t ratios in parentheses):

$$IORB_i = .157 - .0197RLogA_i \qquad R^2 = .010; \quad N = 768$$
$$(2.83)$$

$$SRB_i = .252 - .0434RLogA_i \qquad R^2 = .016; \quad N = 768.$$
$$(3.58)$$

It is interesting to note that the marginal effect of size on profitability from both of these two procedures is quite comparable (though somewhat smaller) to those in the full model.[2]

Use of the dummy variables has, in part, minimized the confounding of relationships. This is illustrated graphically in Figure 2. Quite simply what is illustrated is that firm size may be collinear with other variables

---

1. The 768 firms are grouped into relatively homogeneous industries. Only those industries with three or more firms are analyzed. Consequently, this left 736 firms classified into 79 industries. See Appendix B.

2. The regression coefficients in the multivariate models given in Table 4, Chapter 2, —.0265 and —.0585 for IORB and SRB respectively.

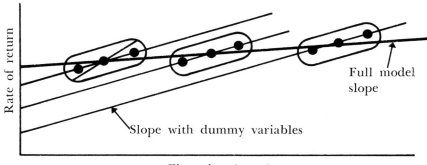

Fig. 2. Size and profitability—intraindustry and interindustry.

Note: The firms which are grouped together are assumed to belong to the same industries.

which may not be fully captured by the full model and are, therefore,
attributed to size.

Size-adjusted rates of return and concentration. From Figure 2, it
is clear that the differences in the intercepts represent the combined
influences of all other factors which affect firms' rates of return common to all firms in each industry. These intercepts, which are in
fact the dummy variable values, can be interpreted as each industry's
average rate of return after the rate of return of each member firm has
been adjusted for the influence of absolute size. In this model it is
assumed that the effect of size on the firms' rate of return within each
industry is independent of other industry characteristics. As a consequence, the dummy variable is what the industry-average rate of return
would be if there were no general relationship between firm size (absolute) and profitability across all industries. Because concentrations and
size are collinear, these industry-average adjusted rates of return (S_j) are
regressed against concentration ratios. The results for the two principal
rate-of-return measures using Census ratios (CCR) are, t ratios in parentheses:

$$IORB{:}S.Ad_j = .158 + .00968CCR_j \qquad R^2 = .001; \ N = 79$$
$$(0.32)$$
$$\text{beta coefficient} = .036$$

$$SRB{:}S.Ad_j = .252 + .0172CCR_j \qquad R^2 = .001; \ N = 79$$
$$(0.34)$$
$$\text{beta coefficient} = .039$$

The regression coefficients for concentration are considerably smaller than those found in the bi-variate regression between unadjusted rates of return and concentration.[3] These results are (*t* ratios in parentheses):

$$IORB_i = .123 + .0439CCR_i \qquad R^2 = .008; \ N = 768$$
$$(2.45)$$
$$\text{beta coefficient} = .088$$

$$SRB_i = .192 + .0670CCR_i \qquad R^2 = .006; \ N = 768$$
$$(2.13)$$
$$\text{beta coefficient} = .077.$$

Though these results are not strictly comparable (one obvious reason for this being the difference in N), they do suggest that the collinearity between size and rates of return is such that it might affect the concentration-profitability findings and attribute more importance to concentration than it deserves. The relative importance of concentration on adjusted and unadjusted rates of return can also be assessed by observing that the beta coefficients fall roughly in half for the adjusted returns.

Intraindustry Analysis of Size and Capital Intensity

It has been implicitly assumed that the relations between the variables, when studied across industries and without regard to industry, are unaffected by the characteristics peculiar to industries. However, in the last section of analysis, the possible impropriety of this approach has been suggested. In this section, evidence is sought which might reveal the potential difficulties of previous analysis where profitability is related to size, capital intensity, and concentration without regard to how relative size and relative capital intensity within each industry may affect these across-industry relations. Obviously, this is not a problem with concentration, because concentration is an industry variable in this study and does not vary within an industry.

Profitability and firm size—intraindustry analysis

Marcus has previously taken exception to the inference that the absolute-size hypothesis is valid across all industries. On the basis of his findings that firm size and profitability are significantly positively related

---

3. The regression coefficients for concentration in the multivariate analysis are +.0656 and +.1060 for rates-of-return defined as IORB and SRB respectively (Table 4, Chapter 2).

within only 35 of 118 IRS industries, he concludes that the absolute-size hypothesis does not have general validity.[4] I take an altogether different view, which is that if size and profitability are not correlated within any particular industry it may be because certain industry characteristics conceal the presence of correlation. For example, small firms in concentrated industries may earn a higher rate of return than their counterparts in unconcentrated industries, while concentration confers little or no additional advantage to the large firms in the concentrated industry. Or, to take another example, economies of scale or diseconomies of scale within a particular industry may add to the absolute-size effect or may negate it. There then arises the question, which Marcus could have addressed himself to but did not, as to whether these 35 industries have factors in common. Answering that question is the purpose of this section. In this study, however, the analysis is seriously impaired because for many industries only a few firms are included. Though regressions are run within each of the 79 industries, the following analysis is somewhat tenuous and simply suggestive of the possibilities.

Intraindustry regressions by concentration categories. Within each of the 79 industries (736 firms), the absolute-size profitability models are fitted for each of the two profitability measures, implicit operating return before taxes (IORB) and stockholders' return before taxes (SRB). In only 47 of 79 industries is a positive relation found between firm size and profitability. To repeat the question implicit in Hypothesis III (see Chapter 1): Is the degree of concentration associated with intraindustry size-profitability relations? Two major and opposing hypotheses are frequently offered on this count. First, it is argued that excessive market power results in or is accompanied by "X-inefficiency.[5] Hence, one might expect to find size of firm and profitability negatively correlated within highly concentrated industries. On the other hand, the classical argument would be that it is economies of scale which first give rise to above-average returns for the industry's larger firms and/or, secondly, which lead to the elimination of smaller firms. As a result, a highly concentrated industry with a few large firms might obtain. If one observes an industry where economies of scale are present, as evidenced by this positive size-profit-

4. Matityahu Marcus, "Profitability and Size of Firm: Some Further Evidence," *Review of Economics and Statistics* 51 (Feb. 1969): 104–7. Comanor and Wilson find firm size and profitability to be positively related in only 29 of 41 consumer goods industries. (William S. Comanor and Thomas A. Wilson, "Advertising and the Advantages of Size," *American Economic Review* 59 [May 1969]: 87–98.)

5. H. Leibenstein, "Allocative Efficiency and 'X-Efficiency,'" *American Economic Review* 56 (June 1966): 392–415.

abilty association, then he probably observes a concentrated industry.[6] On the other hand, however, the failure to find a positive size-profitability association would not necessarily indicate an unconcentrated industry.

These influences can be studied by stratifying the panel into six concentration categories and analyzing the intraindustry size-profitability relations by these categories. Each of the 79 industries (and their firms) is classified into one of six concentration categories, first according to Census concentration ratios and finally according to Shepherd ratios. The six concentration categories are arbitrarily established as follows:

Category   I .... Ratios (as percentages):   0– 29
Category II .... Ratios (as percentages): 30– 39
Category III .... Ratios (as percentages): 40– 49
Category IV .... Ratios (as percentages): 50– 59
Category V .... Ratios (as percentages): 60– 69
Category VI .... Ratios (as percentages): 70–100

After firm size is regressed against profitability within each industry, the industries are then grouped by these six concentration categories. Table 9 summarizes the number of positive and negative relations found for the industries in each category. No clear pattern emerges. In other words, economies of scale and/or the greater market power of each industry's larger firms do not appear to confer a consistent advantage to those firms in concentrated industries.[7]

Generally, these results indicate that the larger firms in Category II (ratios from 30 to 39) and in the highest concentration category are most frequently at the disadvantage. Large firms in the second highest concentration category, however, generally have the advantage. By successively grouping Categories I and II, III and IV, and V and VI, perhaps a clearer pattern emerges. For the least concentrated industries (0–39), there appears to be no consistent advantage to relative size. For what might be considered the moderate concentration ranges (40–59), the larger firms

6. One obvious problem of this simplistic approach is that at any time, even in an industry where the optimal size firm is small relative to the total market, there will be yet smaller less-profitable firms. That is, at a given point in time, all firms may not have reached optimal size. The reader should note Brozen's disequilibrium hypothesis as set forth in "Bain's Concentration and Rates of Return Revisited," *Journal of Law and Economics* 14 (Oct. 1971): 351–69.

7. Although a regression is run within each of the the 79 industries, use of the regression coefficients themselves does not seem warranted in this analysis. Initially, it was thought that averages of the sizes of the regression coefficients could be used to indicate the average strengths of the relations in the six concentration categories. However, it is found that the averages for several categories are greatly distorted by one or two very extreme industries which often have only three firms (observations).

TABLE 9

INTRAINDUSTRY SIZE-PROFITABILITY ANALYSIS FOR 736 FIRMS IN 79 INDUSTRIES BY SIX CONCENTRATION CATEGORIES, 1960–68

ITEM	CONCENTRATION CATEGORIES*						TOTALS
	I (0–29)	II (30–39)	III (40–49)	IV (50–59)	V (60–69)	VI (70–100)	
Census ratios							
Number of industries	11	17	18	16	8	9	79
Number of positive relations	7	8	13	10	6	4	48
Positive as percentage of total	64	47	72	63	75	44	61
Grouped percentages	I–II 54		III–IV 68		V–VI 59		
Shepherd ratios							
Number of industries	4	6	16	13	18	22	79
Number of positive relations	3	2	10	8	13	12	48
Positive as percentage of total	75	33	63	62	72	55	61
Grouped percentages	I–II 50		III–IV 62		V–VI 63		

* The concentration ratio range for each category in percentages is set forth in parentheses below the category designation.

in these industries are most frequently more profitable. It is for this range of concentration ratios that monopoly power is frequently thought to begin emerging. Finally, for the most concentrated industries, the chances of finding an industry's larger firms being more profitable than its smaller firms remain high, although falling off considerably for Census ratios. Thus, there is the slightest support for the conclusion that relative size of firm confers a greater advantage to the larger firms in concentrated industries; however, there is also evidence that X-inefficiency may obtain for those firms in the most concentrated industries.

Intraindustry analysis across industries. The difficulty of analyzing the size-profitability relationship by analysis within each industry can be partially overcome by taking an altogether different approach. If the largest firms in each industry generally earn the highest rates of return in those industries, this indicates the existence of a relation between relative size and profitability. In this section, the deviation of each firm's rate of return from its industry-average return expressed as a ratio to the industry-average return is computed. This measure is called the relative rate of return and is denoted, for example, as REL:IORB. This relative return is then regressed against the firm's similarly computed deviation in terms of size (REL:A). In other words, the hypothesis being tested is that a firm which is, say, 20 percent above the industry average in terms of size will earn a proportionately greater rate of return than the average-firm rate of return, regardless of the absolute sizes and returns of firms. The fitted model for REL:IORB suggests that a firm which is three times as large as the average firm in its industry would earn only a 6 percent greater rate of return than the average—a very small difference indeed. (See Table 10.)

By repeating this regression within each of the six concentration categories, the relationship between concentration and the effect of size on rates of return within industries can be estimated. The results of this analysis, presented in Table 11, indicate that relative size has its strongest influence within the highest concentration category and in the categories which generally are considered to include those industries where effective market power is beginning to emerge. (However, the explanatory power of this model is very low in all cases.) For the Census ratios this would be roughly in the 30–49 range (Categories II and III) and for Shepherd ratios this range would be from 40–59. (Shepherd ratios are on the average 14 percentage points higher than the Census ratios.) In the competitive industries (Census ratios from 0–29, and Shepherd ratios from 0–39), relative size is seen to have little or a negative influence on relative

TABLE 10

ANALYSIS OF RELATIVE PROFITABILITY AND RELATIVE SIZE
FOR 736 FIRMS IN 79 INDUSTRIES BY SIX CONCENTRATION
CATEGORIES, 1960–68

CONCENTRATION		NUMBER OF FIRMS	DEPENDENT VARIABLE (REL: IORB)	CONSTANT	COEFFICIENT OF INDEPENDENT VARIABLE* (REL:A)	R^2†
CATEGORY	RATIO					
All firms		736	. . .	1.6×10^{-6}	.0301 (2.31)	.006
Census ratios						
I	0– 29	71	. . .	2.8×10^{-7}	.0005 (0.01)	.000
II	30– 39	175	. . .	1.8×10^{-6}	.0670 (2.29)	.023
III	40– 46	166	. . .	1.5×10^{-6}	.0380 (1.16)	.002
IV	50– 59	201	. . .	2.4×10^{-6}	.0020 (0.11)	.000
V	60– 69	71	. . .	1.5×10^{-6}	.0581 (1.36)	.012
VI	70–100	52	. . .	3.0×10^{-7}	.1121 (1.90)	.048
Shepherd ratios						
I	0– 29	23	. . .	4.8×10^{-7}	—.0357 (0.31)	.000
II	30– 39	49	. . .	8.6×10^{-7}	—.0389 (0.59)	.000
III	40– 49	149	. . .	1.1×10^{-6}	.0697 (2.08)	.022
IV	50– 59	128	. . .	2.3×10^{-6}	.0221 (0.92)	.000
V	60– 69	191	. . .	1.4×10^{-6}	.0188 (0.81)	.000
VI	70–100	196	. . .	1.3×10^{-6}	.0393 (2.54)	.004

* Absolute value of t ratios in parentheses.
† Coefficient of determination adjusted for degrees of freedom.

TABLE 11

INTRAINDUSTRY ANALYSIS OF SIZE AND CAPITAL INTENSITY FOR 736 FIRMS IN 79 INDUSTRIES BY SIX CONCENTRATION CATEGORIES, 1960–68

ITEM	CONCENTRATION CATEGORIES*						TOTALS
	I (0–29)	II (30–39)	III (40–49)	IV (50–59)	V (60–69)	VI (70–100)	
Census ratios							
Number of industries	11	17	18	16	8	9	79
Number of positive relations	8	10	11	9	4	8	50
Positive as percentage of total	73	59	61	56	50	89	63
Grouped percentages	I–II 64		III–IV 59		V–VI 71		
Shepherd ratios							
Number of industries	4	6	16	13	18	22	79
Number of positive relations	3	5	10	6	12	14	50
Positive as percentage of total	75	83	63	46	67	64	63
Grouped percentages	I–II 80		III–IV 55		V–VI 65		

* The concentration ratio range for each category is in parentheses, below the category designation.

returns. The results are not materially different when profitability is defined as return on stockholders' equity.

Size, capital intensity, and profitability—intraindustry analysis

The hypothesis that large firms are more capital intensive can be viewed in much the same way as the size-profitability hypothesis. The absolute-size hypothesis is founded upon the notion that, first, large firms have an advantage in the imperfect markets for capital; and, second, large firms have more investment alternatives from which to choose because the size of required investment is less of an obstacle or barrier to entry for them.

As with the relation between profitability and size, the relation, first between asset/output ratios and size, and, in turn, between profitability and asset/output ratios has its interindustry (absolute) effects and its intraindustry (relative) effects. Davis argues that size of firm enables larger firms "to undertake activities requiring more capital than those commonly undertaken by the small operators."[8] It follows that the larger firms in any particular industry (in relative, not absolute, terms) may be in a position to produce the more capital-intensive products within the same product-line definition or may be in a position to enjoy any cost or other advantages from vertical integration. This suggests the study of the relations between capital intensity and size and between capital intensity and profitability within industries.

Intraindustry regressions by concentration categories: capital intensity and firm size. Within each of the 79 industries, each firm's asset/output ratio is regressed first against the logarithm of the firm's assets, and finally against each firm's implicit operating rate of return before taxes (IORB). The hypothesis that large firms have higher output ratios than small firms (Hypothesis V) is found to hold among firms within the same industry. These results are presented in Table 11. Fifty of the 79 industries exhibit a positive relation, and only 29 show a negative relation. When industries are classified by their concentration ratios, no obvious pattern emerges (see Table 11). For Census ratios, though, the results for the most concentrated industries (Category VI—concentration from 70 to 100) indicate that the positive relation between size and and capital intensity is more consistently observed within those industries. This is not, however, the case for Shepherd ratios. What is clear from this analysis is that

8. Hiram S. Davis, "Relation of Capital-Output Ratio to Firm Size in American Manufacturing: Some Additional Evidence," *Review of Economics and Statistics* 38 (Aug. 1956): 286–93.

the chances of finding larger firms being more capital intensive than smaller firms in the same industry are less in the middle ranges of concentration than they are in the competitive and highly concentrated industries.

Intraindustry regressions by concentration ratio: capital intensity and profitability. It was expected that rates of return and capital intensity would be positively related (Hypothesis VII). This, however, is strongly refuted by the findings of a negative relationship between asset/output ratios and rates of return in earlier interindustry analysis. This hypothesis is tested again by the analysis within industries.

In regressing implicit operating returns before taxes (IORB) against the ratio of total assets to sales, a negative relation is found in 53 of the 79 industries; thus, in only 26 industries is the expected positive relation found (see Table 12). When analysis is by concentration categories, a rather clear pattern emerges. As concentration increases, the chances of finding a positive association between capital intensity and profitability increases. This is particularly clear when the percentages of positive relations are compared for successive groups of two categories each. The distinction is most evident in the highest concentration category, where the chances of finding a positive relation are better than 50 percent, which is better than double those for all other five categories combined. The tentative conclusion must be that in the most concentrated industries the capital-intensive firms are able to increase profit margins more than enough to compensate for the decreases in asset turnover. For the more competitive industries, this is clearly not the case.

Intraindustry analysis across industries. As in the intraindustry analysis for size, it is determined whether the more capital intensive firms in each industry generally earn the highest rates of return in those industries. To do this, the deviation of each firm's rate of return from its industry average, expressed as a ratio to the industry average, is regressed against the firm's similarly computed deviation in terms of the two measures of capital intensity. The findings of this analysis, which are presented in Table 13, reject this hypothesis and indicate that a negative relationship exists between profitability and asset/output ratios.[9] The analysis by concentration categories presented in Table 13 indicates that the relationship is not affected by concentration. Instead, a rather uniform negative association between relative profitability and relative capital intensity is found throughout all concentration categories. However, for

9. The results for fixed-capital/output ratios are similar and are, therefore, not given.

TABLE 12

INTRAINDUSTRY ANALYSIS OF CAPITAL INTENSITY AND PROFITABILITY FOR 736 FIRMS IN 79 INDUSTRIES BY SIX CONCENTRATION CATEGORIES, 1960–68

ITEM	CONCENTRATION CATEGORIES*						TOTALS
	I (0–29)	II (30–39)	III (40–49)	IV (50–59)	V (60–69)	VI (70–100)	
Census ratios							
Number of industries	11	17	18	16	8	9	79
Number of positive relations	3	3	6	6	2	6	26
Positive as percentage of total	27	18	33	38	25	67	33
Grouped percentages	I–II 21		III–IV 32		V–VI 47		
Shepherd ratios							
Number of industries	44	6	16	13	18	22	79
Number of positive relations	1	1	6	3	3	12	26
Positive as percentage of total	25	17	38	23	17	55	33
Grouped percentages	I–II 20		III–IV 31		V–VI 38		

* The concentration ratio range for each category is in parentheses, below the category designation.

ANALYSIS OF RELATIVE PROFITABILITY AND RELATIVE CAPITAL
INTENSITY FOR 736 FIRMS IN 79 INDUSTRIES BY SIX
CONCENTRATION CATEGORIES, 1960–68

CONCENTRATION		NUMBER OF FIRMS	DEPENDENT VARIABLE (REL: IORB)	CONSTANT	COEFFICIENT OF INDEPENDENT VARIABLE (REL:A/Q) *	$\bar{R}^2$†
CATEGORY	RATIO					
All firms		736	...	2.2×10^{-6}	−.4857 (6.96)	.061
Census ratios						
I	0– 29	71	...	4.7×10^{-7}	−.4529 (1.62)	.036
II	30– 39	175	...	2.3×10^{-6}	−.5155 (3.54)	.063
III	40– 49	166	...	1.8×10^{-6}	−.3469 (2.39)	.028
IV	50– 59	201	...	$3.8\times10.^{-6}$	−.6698 (5.87)	.143
V	60– 69	71	...	1.9×10^{-6}	−.8326 (3.08)	.108
VI	70–100	52	...	3.2×10^{-7}	−.3281 (1.15)	.007
Shepherd ratios						
I	0– 29	23	...	5.6×10^{-7}	−.2946 (0.57)	.000
II	30– 39	49	...	9.5×10^{-7}	−.6721 (2.59)	.106
III	40– 49	149	...	1.2×10^{-6}	−.0085 (0.52)	.000
IV	50– 59	128	...	2.8×10^{-6}	−.5168 (2.78)	.053
V	60– 69	191	...	3.3×10^{-6}	−.6704 (5.23)	.121
VI	70–100	196	...	2.0×10^{-6}	−.4902 (3.74)	.062

* Absolute value of t ratios in parentheses.
† Coefficient of determination adjusted for degrees of freedom.

Census categories, a positive (though weak) association is found in the 70–100 concentration range. The rather tenuous inference would be that only in the highly concentrated industries (using Census ratios) does capital intensity seem to confer an advantage to the larger firms in each particular industry.

Business Risk and Profitability

The hypothesis that the greater the temporal risk, the higher are the rates of return (Hypothesis X) is not supported by the results which are presented in Table 14. Instead of rates of return being positively associated with the temporal standard deviation and negatively associated with temporal skewness, they are negatively associated with the temporal standard deviation and positively associated with temporal skewness. In other words, these results would support a hypothesis that these firms were risk-takers rather than risk-averters during the 1960–68 period.

Two similar yet different approaches are taken to measure temporal risk. First, risk is attributed to the variability and the skewness of the rate-of-return distribution over the entire time period, i.e., the standard deviation and skewness are computed around the period-average rate of return—the proxy for the expected return. Fisher and Hall criticize this measure of risk on the grounds that risk would be indicated even though a firm could predict with certainty each year's rate of return.[10] By emphasizing the year-to-year predictability of returns as meaning risk, Fisher and Hall's computation of the standard deviation and skewness around predicted rates of return (from simple time-series regression) is readily understandable. However, I contend that there is no reason to expect an upward or downward trend in any firm's profitability except that which may result from general business conditions or temporary disequilibrium in demand and supply conditions. Yet these factors should be considered an integral part of the risk of doing business. Specifically, the 1960–68 time period generally represents a movement out of a recession (though mild) through a prolonged expansionary period to a peak in general business. Should one firm have experienced an upward trend in profit rates and another no trend, then I argue that this may indicate the comparative risks associated with the effects of general business conditions on each firm's overall performance. The findings (in Table 14), however, are "not heartening," to borrow Stigler's description of similar findings.[11]

10. I. N. Fisher and G. R. Hall, "Risk and Corporate Rates of Return," *Quarterly Journal of Economics* 83 (Feb. 1969): 79–92.
11. George J. Stigler, *Capital and Rates of Return in Manufacturing Industries* (Princeton, N.J.: Princeton University Press, 1963), p. 63.

TABLE 14

ANALYSIS OF TEMPORAL RISK AND PROFITABILITY FOR 768 FIRMS, 1960–68

EQUATION	DEPENDENT VARIABLE RATE OF RETURN*	CONSTANT	INDEPENDENT VARIABLES†				R^2
			COEFFICIENT‡	VARIABLE	COEFFICIENT‡	VARIABLE	
1	IORB	.1456	−.0204 (0.26)	TSD	.0100 (2.38)	TS	.001
2	IORB	.1473	−.0661 (0.74)	TSDP	.0199 (4.25)	TSP	.025
3	IORA	.0835	−.0917 (1.72)	TSD	.0072 (3.64)	TS	.222
4	IORA	.0835	−.1230 (2.04)	TSDP	.0119 (5.51)	TSP	.048
5	SRB	.2172	.0648 (1.34)	TSD	.0372 (5.59)	TS	.040
6	SRB	.2249	−.0008 (0.15)	TSDP	.0414 (5.22)	TSP	.035
7	SRA	.1237	−.1385 (4.24)	TSD	.0172 (5.01)	TS	.065
8	SRA	.1256	−.2075 (5.79)	TSDP	.0160 (4.10)	TSP	.068

* IORB stands for implicit operating return on assets before taxes; IORA, for implicit operating return on assets after taxes; SRB, for stockholders' returns before taxes; and SRA, for stockholders' returns after taxes.

† TSD stands for the temporal standard deviation of a firm's annual rates of return around the period average; TS for the temporal skewness (third moment) of a firm's annual rates of return around the period average; TSDP for the temporal standard deviation of a firm's annual rates of return around predicted returns; TSP for the temporal skewness of a firm's annual rates of return around predicted returns.

‡ Absolute value of *t* ratios in parentheses.

As a consequence, Fisher and Hall's approach to the measurement of risk is taken by computing these risk variables around the predicted values from a simple linear time-series regression for each firm. However, these results (the risk variables are denoted TSDP and TSP to indicate their being computed around predicted values) are very similar and likewise are not heartening (see Table 14). The degree of explanatory power, though remaining very low, is improved slightly for the two measures for return on total assets, while not changing for stockholders' returns.

Before we explore risk further, one important observation needs to be made. In the original panel of 787 (instead of 768), the findings were astounding. The original model measuring risk around the period-average return explained 81 percent of the variation ($R^2 = .81$) in before-tax stockholders' returns.[12] It was later discovered that a good number of firms in the panel had *negative* stockholders' equity in one or more years. When computing rates of return, a negative equity strongly suggests the likelihood of finding denominators very close to zero (positive or negative). As a result, some of these firms have average-annual rates of return up to 1300 percent. What I am suggesting is that the inclusion of these types of firm in any sample can distort the results profoundly.

Business risk and the structural variables

Commonly cited as the fundamental reason for the findings that large firms have lower variances in rates of return than smaller firms is the diversification of larger firms. To the extent that greater diversification lessens the variance among large firms' rates of return, it would seem that diversification would also lessen the temporal variance (standard deviation) of rates of return for large firms. In other words, an advantage

---

12. It is important to note that Fisher and Hall (see footnote 10) computed risk for stockholders' returns. The fitted model for these 787 firms is:

$$SRB = .182 + .328TSD + .0830TS; \quad R^2 = .809$$
$$(55.50) \qquad (8.14)$$

This same regression was run again after eliminating from the panel those nine firms with period-average rates of return less than −50 percent and greater than 100 percent. This panel produced the following fitted regression:

$$SRB = .225 - .0291TSD + .0445TS; \quad R^2 = .057$$
$$(0.94) \qquad (6.68)$$

In the final panel, all firms with negative stockholders' equity in any one year are eliminated. These results are found in Table 14.
(Notations: SRB for stockholders' returns before taxes; TSD, for temporal standard deviation; TS, for temporal skewness.)

of size is the ability to lessen temporal business risk. I contend that, in fact, one reason that firms become large is to minimize business risk.[13]

Indeed, one could hypothesize that the other two fundamental structural variables—capital intensity and concentration—are similarly related to risk. Capital intensity might be a proxy for the ratio of fixed to total costs and, therefore, one might expect capital-intensive firms, *ceteris paribus,* to evidence greater temporal variability (Hypothesis VIII). On the other hand, capital intensity might simply indicate the degree of vertical integration.[14] Certainly one of the advantages of both forward and backward integration would be the lessening of business uncertainty and risk. Thus, it is ambiguous, on an a priori basis, whether the temporal variability of rates of return is positively or negatively associated with the capital intensity.

It is hypothesized that the higher the concentration ratio (hence the greater the market power), the less the business risk (the temporal variability of rates of return) (Hypothesis XI). Therefore, all three structural variables are seen to influence the temporal variability of rates of return. To determine the influence of each on profit variability, the two measures of temporal variability (over the entire time period, and year-to-year) are regressed against size, concentration, and capital intensity.[15] The results presented in Table 15 are not those that are expected. Size of firm and capital intensity are negatively related to both measures of temporal variability. However, firms in concentrated industries are shown to be subject to greater temporal variability in rates of return. In terms of the relative importance of each structural variable's impact on variability, size is clearly the most important, followed distantly by concentration and capital intensity.[16]

13. The expected return on a portfolio of two different assets (two product lines) is just the weighted average of the expected returns on each. As long as the correlation between the returns of each is less than one, the standard deviation of the return on the portfolio is less than the weighted average of the standard deviations of the returns of each asset. See, for example, Eugene F. Fama and Merton H. Miller, *The Theory of Finance* (New York: Holt, Rinehart & Winston, 1972), chap. 7.

14. It is noted in the Introduction that two elements of market structure are the ratio of fixed to total costs and the degree of vertical integration. Both of these are captured by a measure of capital intensity.

15. The logarithm of firm assets is taken as the size variable, because one would not expect that equal absolute increases in size would result in equal decreases in variability. Relative increases in size, however, might have such a result.

16. The relative importance can be indicated from the beta coefficients. It is noted earlier that capital intensity might be either negatively related or positively related to variability (depending on the relative advantages of vertical integration compared to high ratios of fixed to total costs). Thus, what is measured is the net influence for these two offsetting influences.

Table 15

ANALYSIS OF THE VARIABILITY OF RETURNS AND STRUCTURE FOR 768 FIRMS, 1960–68

Equation	Standard Deviation*		Regression Coefficients—Independent Variables†				R^2
		Constant	Concentration (CCR)	Size (LogA)	Capital Intensity (A/Q)	
1	TSD:IORB	.0880	.0296 (3.89) *.127*	−.0285 (16.17) *−.536*	−.0051 (1.40) *−.045*	.276
2	TSD:SRB	.1919	.0445 (1.96) *.069*	−.0563 (10.74) *−.385*	−.0206 (1.91) *−.067*	.154
3	TSDP:IORB	.0726	.0219 (3.33) *.109*	−.0240 (15.83) *−.527*	−.0046 (1.48) *−.048*	.270
4	TSDP:SRB	.1575	.0376 (1.93) *.068*	−.0477 (10.59) *−.380*	−.0195 (2.11) *−.074*	.152

* TSD:IORB and TSD:SRB stand for the temporal standard deviation of a firm's annual rates of return around their period average for rate of return defined as implicit operating return on assets before taxes (IORB) and stockholders' returns before taxes (SRB), respectively. TSDP:IORB and TSDP:SRB stand for the temporal standard deviation of a firm's annual rates of return around their predicted returns for IORB and SRB, respectively.

† Absolute value of t ratios in parentheses, beta coefficients in italics.

Three conclusions are tentatively drawn. The first is that size of firm not only increases the amount of profits but also the quality of profits. That is, if managers are generally averse to risk and require a premium for high temporal variability in returns, the previously observed difference between large-firm rates of return and small-firm rates of return would be even greater for risk-adjusted or risk-comparable returns.[17] The second tentative conclusion might be that the advantage of vertical integration in lessening temporal profit variability more than offsets the attendant disadvantages of an increase in the ratio of fixed to total costs.[18] Here, it is assumed that capital intensity is a proxy for each of these two opposite influences on temporal variability—the ratio of fixed to total costs and the degree of vertical integration.

The third tentative conclusion is quite unexpected. Concentrated industries apparently do not have the capability to stabilize earnings. At this point suffice it to say that there must be some common element among concentrated industries which leads to instability in returns.[19] As a consequence, it is important to observe that rates of return in concentrated industries might be overstated compared to those in unconcentrated industries because of a disproportionately large risk premium included in their observed profitability measures.

The importance of these findings, however, goes beyond these immediate results. If there is a true behavioral model upon which managers act, which is similar to the one here and which describes the trade-offs between expected rates of return (averages) and the variance and skewness of the distribution, it would not be observed in a panel of large and capital-intensive firms. That is, these structural conditions or variables,

17. This raises an interesting question, which cannot be answered in this study. Might the frequently observed greater profitability of large firms be principally due to risk because large firms with diversified portfolios make investment decisions based on expected values of returns rather than expected utilities? That is, are their utility functions linear, or at least closer to linear than those for smaller firms?

18. The relation between rates of return and capital intensity indicates a rather strong negative association. Thus, capital intensity reduces both the average return and the variability of that return stream. Capital intensity may not, in itself, reduce risk because the reduced variability is traded for a reduced expected return. That is, if risk-adjusted of return were regressed against capital intensity, one might not find this strong negative association.

19. The two-variable fitted models result in consistent negative associations between temporal profit variability and concentration. Obviously, these results are heavily influenced by the positive collinearity of concentration with firm size and capital intensity. Caves and Yamey, of course, offer another explanation centered around the collusive breakdowns in concentrated industries. (R. E. Caves and B. S. Yamey, "Risk and Corporate Rates of Return: Comment," *Quarterly Journal of Economics* 85 [Aug. 1971]: 513–17.)

in part, are ways in which the manager can change the business risks associated with particular employments of assets. On the other hand, this suggests that, while in this panel of firms, which are, generally, large and capital intensive, one cannot observe the model upon which managers act, the true relation might be observed among small, non–vertically integrated firms in competitive industries.[20]

Business risk and profitability by concentration categories

Within each of the six concentration categories, the relations between average rates of return and the two risk variables are determined. It is expected that, because large, capital-intensive firms in concentrated industries could lessen the temporal variability in rates of return, the true relation between risk and expected returns could be observed only in small, non–vertically integrated firms in competitive industries. Because capital intensity and size increase with concentration, the firms which for our purposes would be termed pure firms might be found in the lowest concentration category (see Table 17, page 90). Thus, an alternative methodology to determine risk is to take this panel of firms. The results given in Table 16 are, to harken back to Stigler, quite heartening.[21]

In Concentration Category I for both sets of concentration ratios and for both measures of profitability (implicit operating return on assets befores taxes [IORB] and stockholders' returns before taxes [SRB]) the higher the temporal standard deviation, the higher the average rate of return. For both sets of concentration ratios and for rates of return defined as IORB (the principal measure of profitability) the skewness of returns is, as expected, negatively associated with average profitability.[22] However, skewness is positively associated with profitability for SRB.[23]

For Categories I through III it is clear that, as concentration increases (and firm size and capital intensity), the regression coefficients for the

20. The variety of results of previous research on risk might be attributed simply to the nature of the samples. In this study, this hypothesis is not tested directly. However, some evidence is gathered which strongly indicates its validity. See the next section on the analysis of temporal risk within concentration categories. The reader is also referred to Chapter 1 for the discussion of the concept of business risk.

21. The measurement of the risk variables (around the period-average returns as opposed to around the predicted returns) does not materially alter the results. Therefore, only those results where the risk variables are computed about the period-average returns are given.

22. In fact, for Category II for Shepherd ratios (which must be considered to include small, non-capital-intensive and competitive firms), the expected signs are also found.

23. The use of return to stockholders' equity to measure risk, as noted earlier, confounds business risk with financial risk because of the managerial prerogatives with regard to the debt-equity ratios. Therefore, these results are not presented.

TABLE 16

ANALYSIS OF TEMPORAL RISK AND PROFITABILITY FOR 736 FIRMS IN 79 INDUSTRIES BY SIX CONCENTRATION CATEGORIES, 1960–68*

| CONCENTRATION | | NUMBER OF | | DEPENDENT VARIABLE (IORB)* | CONSTANT | REGRESSION COEFFICIENTS INDEPENDENT VARIABLE† | | $\bar{R}^2$‡ |
CATEGORY	RATIO	FIRMS	INDUSTRIES			STANDARD DEVIATION (TSD)	SKEWNESS (S)	
All firms		736	79	...	.1478	−.0839 (1.08)	.0110 (2.61)	.008
Census ratios								
I	0– 29	71	11	...	.1077	.4734 (1.70)	−.0176 (1.09)	.026
II	30– 39	175	17	...	.1507	−.1718 (1.57)	.0043 (0.53)	.004
III	40– 49	166	18	...	.1733	−.4422 (1.98)	.0031 (3.26)	.072
IV	50– 59	201	16	...	.1211	.1941 (1.38)	.0056 (0.83)	.002
V	60– 69	71	8	...	.1708	−.2874 (1.03)	−.0063 (0.44)	.000
VI	70–100	52	9	...	.1502	.5843 (1.38)	.0238 (1.45)	.029
Shepherd ratios								
I	0– 29	23	4	...	.0879	1.0809 (2.32)	−.0318 (0.89)	.142
II	30– 39	49	6	...	.1332	.3806 (1.11)	−.0155 (0.85)	.000
III	40– 49	149	16	...	.1357	.0741 (0.47)	.0035 (0.40)	.000
IV	50– 59	128	13	...	.1591	−.4328 (3.24)	.0013 (0.14)	.066
V	60– 69	191	18	...	.1467	−.2205 (1.26)	.0213 (2.67)	.35
VI	70–100	196	22	...	.1536	.1043 (0.56)	.0158 (1.84)	.000

* Profitability is implicit operating return (on assets) before taxes (IORB).
† The standard deviation and skewness are computed around the 1960–68 firm period-average rate of return. (Absolute value of t ratios in parentheses.)
‡ Coefficient of determination adjusted for degrees of freedom.

standard deviation decrease and the regression coefficients for skewness increase, even after the signs are the reverse of those expected. For the higher concentration categories, no discernible pattern is found, except that for the highest concentration class (for both sets of concentration ratios) temporal variability is once again positively associated with higher average returns.

If one argues that the risk/return relation can only be observed among the small, non–vertically integrated firms in competitive industries, then one might argue that, as concentration increases, risk does in fact increase.[24] Therefore, for concentrated industries, the observed rates of return are overstated due to the proportionately higher risk premiums included in them. It does not seem likely that concentration leads to riskier situations. Rather what appears more likely is that riskier industries become concentrated, and that this is most evident for the most highly concentrated industries.

Many explanations might be given for the phenomena observed in Table 16. However, it is not within the scope of this study to examine risk in detail. Rather, all that is intended is to determine if a systematic relation between risk and return, and concentration exists. The conclusion here must be that, however latent, one does indeed exist. The nature of the explanation must be the subject of later study, but several very general explanations can be offered here. First, it appears that there is a very complex relationship between size of firm (a proxy for geographic and product-line diversification), capital intensity (a proxy for vertical integration), concentration, and risk. The larger and the more capital-intensive the firm, the less the risk. The greater returns associated with size along with the attendant reduction in risk from increased diversification and integration results in the appearance of these firms' being risk takers. That is, the same attributes which lead to higher returns also lead to less variability and greater market power with which the firm can successfully prevent large losses (negative skewness).

Much along this same line of reasoning, one might argue that something on the order of the Friedman-Savage hypothesis concerning individuals and their willingness rationally to become risk-takers may be offered.[25] That is, small firms may opt for risky investments on the outside chance that they might become eminently successful and break into the big-business elite or at least into a dominant position within certain

---

24. Recall that temporal variability is positively correlated with concentration and negatively correlated with both capital intensity and size.

25. Milton Friedman and L. J. Savage, "The Utility Analysis of Choices Involving Risk," *Journal of Political Economy* 56 (Aug. 1948): 279–304.

industries. This risk-taker behavior continues until the firm, in fact, attains that goal. At that point (highest concentration categories), they return to being averse to risk in attempts to maintain acquired positions.

Interindustry Analysis within Concentration Categories

The central thrust of this study is that the relation between concentration and profitability is confounded by perhaps indeterminable interrelations among several other structural variables. After beginning with simple interindustry analysis of differences in firm profitability, the potential effects of intraindustry relations among these same variables is explored. This section again returns to the simple interindustry analysis; however, here the influence of concentration is isolated by studying the relationships between profitability, firm size, capital intensity and growth within each of the six concentration categories.

Analysis of basic firm variables by concentration categories

Before presenting and discussing the results of these regressions, a brief pause to examine the basic-variable descriptive measures by these six concentration categories seems warranted. Table 17 summarizes the basic variables by their means and standard deviations for each of the six concentration categories according to Census and Shepherd ratios.

Rate of return. The increases in rates of return as concentration increases are not as clear as one might expect. When successive categories are taken two at a time, the resulting group averages display a clearer pattern. These group averages are given below:

Concentration Category	Implicit Operating Return Before Taxes (IORB)	Stockholders' Return Before Taxes (SRB)
Census		
I–II	.1387	.2098
III–IV	.1387	.2197
V–VI	.1642	.2498
Shepherd		
I–II	.1509	.2300
III–IV	.1361	.2067
V–VI	.1464	.2288

For the Census ratios the upward trend with concentration is quite clear for both measures of profitability. The returns for the highest two concentration categories are about 3 percentage points higher than the lower categories. For Shepherd ratios, the returns are highest for the

TABLE 17

KEY VARIABLE SUMMARY DATA BY SIX CONCENTRATION CATEGORIES FOR 736 FIRMS, 1960–68 AVERAGES

Concentration (1)	Category Ratio (2)	No. of Firms (3)	IORB		SRB		A		A/Q		K/Q		AG		SG	
			X̄ (4)	σ (5)	X̄ (6)	σ (7)	X̄ (8)	σ (9)	X̄ (10)	σ (11)	X̄ (12)	σ (13)	X̄ (14)	σ (15)	X̄ (16)	σ (17)
All firms		736	.1429	.0779	.2214	.1365	279.7	858.1	.7608	.3316	.2819	.2437	2.040	4.032	1.942	4.924
							Census Ratios									
I	0– 29	71	.1322	.0771	.2088	.1507	71.7	112.6	.5554	.1746	.1576	.0885	2.307	3.171	2.041	2.687
II	30– 39	175	.1413	.0729	.2102	.1246	99.2	164.6	.7049	.2067	.2359	.1619	2.480	5.807	2.245	5.347
III	40– 49	166	.1505	.0952	.2430	.1729	138.9	335.0	.7107	.3435	.2235	.1733	2.318	4.554	2.226	7.671
IV	50– 59	201	.1289	.0612	.2004	.1135	500.3	1,246.5	.9177	.3892	.3990	.3247	1.684	2.785	1.552	2.651
V	60– 69	71	.1589	.0751	.2390	.1147	254.6	544.3	.7236	.2655	.2931	.2106	1.603	1.809	2.057	3.961
VI	70–100	52	.1715	.0850	.2645	.1136	802.2	1,712.5	.8343	.3769	.3252	.2965	1.274	1.026	1.203	0.894
							Shepherd Ratios									
I	0– 29	23	.1555	.1010	.2516	.2007	53.4	59.7	.5660	.1344	.1564	.0970	3.402	4.389	2.675	2.665
II	30– 39	49	.1488	.0745	.2199	.1267	79.0	120.8	.5879	.2417	.1787	.1410	1.600	1.904	1.211	1.021
III	40– 49	149	.1383	.0711	.2105	.1209	117.2	178.9	.6761	.2023	.2465	.1654	1.882	3.516	1.755	3.332
IV	50– 59	128	.1335	.0727	.2072	.1398	91.2	150.3	.7493	.3414	.1945	.1245	2.881	6.365	2.532	5.648
V	60– 69	191	.1354	.0768	.2138	.1402	431.6	1,241.3	.8059	.3689	.3256	.2604	1.851	2.973	1.703	2.634
VI	70–100	196	.1571	.0837	.2432	.1339	454.9	1,057.5	.8550	.3604	.3640	.3190	1.744	3.845	2.027	7.339

Note: Key variables are represented by the following notations: IORB, implicit operating returns on assets before taxes; SRB, stockholders' returns before taxes; A, total assets; A/Q, total assets/output ratio; K/Q, fixed capital/output ratio; AG, asset growth; SG, sales growth.

competitive industries. Returns for the highly concentrated categories are a close second. Perhaps the most substantive conclusion to be drawn from these data is simply that it would be hazardous to make inferences about concentration and profitability here because of the apparent sensitivity of the results to the assignment of concentration ratios and designation of categories.

The standard deviation of returns among firms in each category (columns 5 and 7, Table 17) show no obvious tendency either to rise or to fall with increases in concentration. Variances within Category I are, however, generally higher than the variances in other categories.

Absolute size. Average size of firm increases monotonically with increases in concentration with but two exceptions—Census and Shepherd Categories IV (see column 8 of Table 17). The average size of firm in the most highly concentrated industries is roughly ten times the size of the firm in the lowest category. Standard deviations of firm sizes within categories increase considerably faster. The collinearity between firm size and concentration is clear.

Capital intensity. For both measures of capital intensity, there is a nearly monotonic increase with increases in concentration (columns 10 and 12). Again, as with size, the exceptions to the monotonic increase are found in Category IV. It should be noted that, because asset/turnover ratios (the reciprocal of asset/output ratios) decline markedly with increases in concentration, one would expect profit margins to increase with concentration even if rates of return do not.[26] The relevant question is whether the increases in profit margins are less than or greater than those necessary to maintain rates of return, given the increases in the ratios of capital to output. Obviously, profit margins must increase faster than necessary to maintain rates of return; otherwise one would not find the positive association between rates of return and concentration. Therefore the question is, How much faster do they increase than is needed to maintain rates of return? The question which cannot be answered here, however, is whether this premium is more than enough consideration for the greater capital commitment required to generate a dollar of sales.

Multiplying the implicit operating rates of return before taxes (IORBs) by the asset/output ratios gives an estimate of the implied or actual

26. Norman R. Collins and Lee E. Preston use profit margins as the performance variable in their profitability concentration study. See *Concentration and Price-Cost Margins in Manufacturing Industries* (Berkeley, Calif.: University of California Press, 1970), pp. 60–69.

(average) profit margins by the six concentration categories. These data are shown below (ACTUAL columns). Also shown are those margins needed to obtain the all-firm-average return of .1429, given the various asset/output ratios (CONSTANT RETURN columns).

CONCENTRATION CATEGORY	CENSUS RATIOS		SHEPHERD RATIOS	
	ACTUAL	CONSTANT RETURN	ACTUAL	CONSTANT RETURN
I	.0734	.0793	.0880	.0809
II	.0996	.1007	.0875	.0840
III	.1070	.1016	.0935	.0966
IV	.1183	.1312	.1000	.1070
V	.1150	.1035	.1091	.1152
VI	.1430	.1192	.1343	.1222

Actual margins do increase substantially with increases in concentration. This increase, however, is very much in line with those expected in order to maintain constant rates of return. For the highest concentration category, the "excess" margins are from one to two-and-a-half cents per dollar of sales.[27]

Growth. Asset-growth rates for Census ratios show a marked decrease with increases in concentration. This negative association is not as apparent for Shepherd ratios. Sales-growth rates appear to decrease for Census ratios; however, no apparent trend is evident for Shepherd ratios.[28]

Profitability regressed against firm size, capital intensity, and growth—by concentration categories

In this section rates of return are again regressed against firm size, capital intensity, and firm growth (the basic interindustry firm variables, exluding concentration), except that here the effects of concentration are isolated by repeating the regressions within each of the six concentration

27. Collins and Preston have used the profit margin as the performance measure. It is clear that a strong positive relation would be found. However, what is not clear is that profit margins increase faster than would be expected from the increases in the asset/output ratios. In their article, "Price-Cost Margins and Industry Structure," *Review of Economics and Statistics* 51 (Aug. 1969); 271–86, Collins and Preston present a table of price-cost margins and capital/output ratios for the 417 four-digit manufacturing industries classified by 1963 Census concentration ratio deciles. (See Table 1, page 272.) Based on the data in this table, a similar computation of actual margins versus constant-return margins indicates very clearly that the actual margins do *not* increase by concentration deciles as fast as would be necessary to maintain rates of return. That is, these data imply a *negative* relation between concentration and average rates of return.

28. *See* Chapter 4 for an extensive discussion of growth and concentration.

categories. Table 18 presents the regression results for each of the primary rates of return (IORB and SRB) for each concentration category determined according to the two sets of concentration ratios (Census and Shepherd ratios). Because of the differences in the number of observations in each category, the adjusted coefficients of determination, denoted $\overline{R}^2$, are given to obtain comparability. Comparability among the regression coefficients is again obtained by computing the beta coefficients. These beta coefficients are presented in Table 19. The following brief analysis is based on these beta coefficients.

Generally, these results reaffirm several earlier tentative conclusions. The relative importance of each independent variable depends heavily on the rate of return measure and the concentration category. Asset growth rates are generally the most important determinants of firm rates of return in the lower concentration categories, while capital intensity is indicated to be the most important in the highest concentration categories. Taking all twenty-four regressions together, size is the most important determinant in only four cases, capital intensity in nine cases, and growth in eleven cases. Again, however, the relative importance of each variable seems to vary according to categories and also according to the rate-of-return measure used. Several tentative conclusions can be offered on the relative effects of each variable as one moves from concentration category to category.

Absolute size. No clear pattern emerges for the importance of absolute size to profitability as concentration changes. The absolute-size profitability hypothesis is consistently affirmed in the lowest concentration category by both measures of profitability (IORB and SRB). In the slightly concentrated industries (Census Category II and Shepherd Categories II and III) size is either not important or has a negative association with profitability. Absolute size is then seen to have an important influence on profitability for the moderate to high concentration categories (Census Categories III–V and Shepherd Categories IV and V). Finally, absolute size seems to evidence very little positive advantage to those firms in the highest concentration category. Generally, the effect of size on rates of return does not seem too sensitive to which measure of profitability is used.

Capital intensity. The importance of capital intensity to profitability generally increases as concentration increases. That is, the negative influence of capital intensity on rates of return becomes stronger in the higher concentration categories. This finding would support the hypothesis that firms in concentrated industries do not maintain the high profit margins necessary to compensate for the decreases in asset-turnover.

TABLE 18

ANALYSIS OF PROFITABILITY AND STRUCTURE FOR 736 FIRMS IN 79 INDUSTRIES BY SIX CONCENTRATION CATEGORIES, 1960–68

Concentration		Number of Firms	Dependent Variable*	Constant	Regression Coefficients— Independent Variables†			$\overline{R}^2$‡
Category	Ratio				Size (RLogA)	Capital Intensity (A/Q)	Growth (AG)	
All firms		736	IORB	.2014	−.0319 (4.78)	−.0581 (6.96)	.0035 (5.19)	.110
		736	SRB	.3267	−.0682 (6.08)	−.1052 (7.51)	.0100 (8.83)	.183
Census ratios								
I	0– 29	71	IORB	.1311	−.0275 (1.27)	−.0218 (0.51)	.0144 (6.11)	.344
II	30– 39	175	IORB	.2056	−.0021 (0.20)	−.0949 (3.67)	−.0017 (1.83)	.079
III	40– 49	166	IORB	.2218	−.0620 (4.11)	−.0514 (2.57)	.0041 (2.71)	.144
IV	50– 59	201	IORB	.1803	−.0214 (1.65)	−.0492 (4.51)	.0038 (2.56)	.124
V	60– 69	71	IORB	.2541	−.0861 (3.06)	−.0798 (2.58)	.0095 (2.11)	.217
VI	70–100	52	IORB	.2375	.0330 (0.45)	−.0748 (2.21)	−.0151 (1.09)	0.77
I	0– 29	71	SRB	.2064	−.0635 (1.63)	−.0432 (0.56)	.0315 (7.40)	.442
II	30– 39	175	SRB	.3278	−.0127 (0.77)	−.1773 (4.28)	.0070 (4.75)	.192
III	40– 49	166	SRB	.3866	−.1222 (4.60)	−.1089 (3.09)	.0091 (3.43)	.193

IV	50– 59	201	SRB	.3003	−.0720 (3.17)	−.0871 (4.54)	.0133 (5.11)	.213
V	60– 69	71	SRB	.3816	−.1058 (2.48)	−.1429 (3.04)	.0159 (2.33)	.229
VI	70–100	52	SRB	.3363	−.0100 (0.10)	−.1013 (2.25)	.0063 (0.34)	.079
Shepherd ratios								
I	0– 29	23	IORB	.2162	−.0466 (0.83)	−.1308 (0.87)	.0142 (3.20)	.491
II	30– 39	49	IORB	.0762	.0368 (2.45)	.0380 (0.96)	.0140 (2.77)	.217
III	40– 49	149	IORB	.1912	−.0195 (1.14)	−.0706 (2.47)	.0044 (2.40)	.059
IV	50– 59	128	IORB	.1933	−.0433 (3.18)	−.0413 (2.29)	.0019 (1.96)	.110
V	60– 69	191	IORB	.2271	−.0488 (4.57)	−.0843 (6.27)	.0050 (3.06)	.248
VI	70–100	196	IORB	.2324	−.0416 (1.96)	.0681 (4.22)	.0030 (2.02)	.099
I	0– 29	23	SRB	.3581	−.1270 (1.37)	−.2134 (0.86)	.0322 (4.37)	.646
II	30– 39	49	SRB	.1062	.0459 (1.73)	.0716 (1.03)	.0229 (2.58)	.158
III	40– 49	149	SRB	.3135	−.0277 (1.01)	−.1575 (3.41)	.0117 (4.08)	.150
IV	50– 59	128	SRB	.3070	−.0901 (3.62)	−.0666 (2.02)	.0074 (4.20)	.201
V	60– 69	191	SRB	.3593	−.1081 (6.14)	−.1334 (6.01)	.0189 (7.02)	.386
VI	70–100	196	SRB	.3836	−.0554 (1.67)	−.1383 (5.51)	.0044 (1.89)	.145

* IORB = implicit operating return (on assets) before taxes; SRB = stockholders' returns before taxes.
† Absolute value of *t* ratios in parentheses.
‡ Coefficient of determination adjusted for degrees of freedom.

TABLE 19

BETA COEFFICIENTS FOR ANALYSIS OF PROFITABILITY AND STRUCTURE FOR 736 FIRMS IN 79 INDUSTRIES BY SIX CONCENTRATION CATEGORIES, 1960–68

CONCENTRATION		NUMBER OF FIRMS	RATE OF RETURN*	BETA COEFFICIENTS		
CATEGORY	RATIO			SIZE	CAPITAL INTENSITY	GROWTH
Census ratios						
I–VI		736	IORB	—.169	—.247	.182
I	0– 29	71	IORB	—.123	—.049	.594
II	30– 39	175	IORB	—.015	—.269	.134
III	40– 49	166	IORB	—.331	—.185	.195
IV	50– 59	201	IORB	—.114	—.313	.172
V	60– 69	71	IORB	—.328	—.282	.229
VI	70–100	52	IORB	.080	—.332	—.182
I–VI		736	SRB	—.206	—.256	.297
I	0– 29	71	SRB	—.146	—.050	.664
II	30– 39	175	SRB	—.053	—.294	.325
III	40– 49	166	SRB	—.322	—.216	.240
IV	50– 59	201	SRB	—.207	—.299	.327
V	60– 69	71	SRB	—.264	—.331	.251
VI	70–100	52	SRB	.019	—.336	.057
Shepherd ratios						
I–VI		736	IORB	—.169	—.247	.182
I	0– 29	23	IORB	—.146	—.174	.618
II	30– 39	49	IORB	.313	.123	.356
III	40– 49	149	IORB	—.094	—.201	.193
IV	50– 59	128	IORB	—.267	—.194	.166
V	60– 69	191	IORB	—.293	—.405	.194
VI	70–100	196	IORB	—.136	—.293	.139
I–VI		736	SRB	—.206	—.256	.297
I	0– 29	23	SRB	—.201	—.143	.704
II	30– 39	49	SRB	.230	—.136	.345
III	40– 49	149	SRB	—.078	—.263	.312
IV	50– 59	128	SRB	—.289	—.163	.331
V	60– 69	191	SRB	—.356	—.351	.402
VI	70–100	196	SRB	—.113	—.372	.126

* IORB = implicit operating return (on assets) before taxes; SRB = stockholders' returns before taxes.

That is, it appears that as concentration increases, the capital-intensive firms maintain profit margins more nearly comparable to the less capital-intensive firms in industries of comparable concentration.[29]

Asset growth. The beta coefficients for growth show a distinct decline as concentration increases, indicating quite clearly that as concentration increases asset growth becomes a less important determinant of profitability. In fact, for Census concentration ratios, growth rates have practically no influence on returns to stockholders and a negative influence on returns on assets.[30] The importance of asset-growth rates on profitability in the lowest concentration category far outweighs the importance in the other categories and the other variables within these competitive industries. The hypothesis that the relationship between growth and profitability is affected by concentration (Hypothesis XIV) is strongly supported by these results.[31]

Empirical Results for 79 Industries

Early in this study the use of industry variables to study performance and structure is criticized. Basically, the criticism centers around the use of averages to determine the influences of structure on performance. Averages of firm variables are likely to distort relationships, especially intraindustry relations. In this section, however, industries are analyzed. Essentially a special set of hypotheses is tested by the use of only industry variables, and consequently these results are not comparable to earlier results.

The panel and computation of industry variables. Industry averages are the simple averages of those 736 firms classified in each of the 79 industries. In only one case is a weighted average of firm variables used.[32] Thus, all other industry variables are unweighted means of member-firm variables for the 1960–68 time period.[33] Table 20 summarizes the basic industry variables by presenting their descriptive measures.

29. This conclusion, however, conflicts with the preceding analysis of capital intensity by concentration ratios.

30. This could result from the use of borrowed equity (increased leverage) to finance asset expansion.

31. Table 17 gives the means and standard deviations of growth rates by these concentration categories.

32. In order to further test the interrelation between the size-profitability relation within industries and concentration, a weighted-average (weighted by assets) return is computed.

33. For the details of these computations see Appendix C.

TABLE 20

DESCRIPTIVE MEASURES OF BASIC INDUSTRY VARIABLES, 79 INDUSTRIES (736 FIRMS), 1960–68 AVERAGES

VARIABLE	NOTATION	MEAN	STANDARD DEVIATION	RANGE	
				MINIMUM	MAXIMUM
Rates of return					
Implicit operating return before taxes	IORB	.1459	.0470	.0682	.3047
Implicit operating return after taxes	IORA	.0810	.0223	.0478	.1577
Stockholders' return before taxes	SRB	.2255	.0786	.0768	.4878
Stockholders' return after taxes	SRA	.1156	.0391	.0397	.2383
Concentration ratios					
Census concentration ratio	CCR	.4680	.1766	.1000	.9900
Shepherd concentration ratio	SCR	.5996	.1871	.1600	.9500
Average firm size					
Average total assets (millions of dollars)	AA	253.9	519.7	21.47	3,991.
Average capital intensity					
Average asset/output ratio	AA/Q	.7491	.2734	.1849	1.680
Average fixed capital/output ratio	AK/Q	.2696	.2067	.0785	1.147
Average growth					
Average asset growth	AAG	1.871	1.301	.4202	7.770
Average sales growth	ASG	1.780	1.376	.3100	9.862

Note: All industry variables are simple (unweighted) averages of each industry's member firms' period averages used in firm analysis. See Appendix C for the definitions and calculations of variables.

Analysis of Profitability and Structure

The results of regressing industry-average rates of return against the industry averages of firm size, asset/output ratios, asset-growth rates, and the industries' concentration ratios are presented in Table 21. As would be expected, the various industry models explain a much higher percentage of the variance in rates of return than do the firm models. (Roughly twice as much is explained.) Accordingly, the beta coefficients are also larger.

For the firm-variable models, only results for Census concentration ratios were given, because results using Shepherd ratios were very similar. For the industry models, however, results are different enough to warrant disclosure of both. When Census ratios are used the coefficients of determination are slightly higher than when Shepherd ratios are used. The other differences are that the regression and beta coefficients for concentration and size are substantially larger for the models using Census ratios. There are no obvious explanations for these findings except that Shepherd ratios are subjective and take international competition into account, whereas Census ratios do not.

A very startling finding is that the industry size variable has a strong negative influence on average rates of return.[34] Since the interpretation of this result might be quite lengthy, a brief discussion of only one possible explanation for this finding will be given. The negative relation may result from taking the means of two variables when these variables are not linearly related. Take a simple, extreme case. Assume the following, where two firms in each of two industries earn the rates of return which would be predicted from the absolute-size profitability relation found in the full-firm model (Equation 1 of Table 4, Chapter 2):

	INDUSTRY A		INDUSTRY B	
	Assets	Rate of Return (Percentage)	Assets	Rate of Return (Percentage)
Firm 1	$2 billion	15.35	$500 million	15.17
Firm 2	2 million	7.35	50 million	14.59
Average	1.001 billion	11.35	275 million	14.88

Clearly, when industry-average firm size is regressed against the industry-average returns, a very strong negative association results. The

---

34. For the industry size variable, a logarithmic form of the function does not explain as much of the variation in rates of return as the simple linear form does. Because there is no compelling reason to argue for any one form for the industry average, the linear form is used. Industry size cannot be taken to be a proxy for capturing true influence of either absolute size or relative size. Rather, it confounds them.

TABLE 21

ANALYSIS OF PROFITABILITY AND STRUCTURE FOR 79 INDUSTRIES (736 FIRMS), 1960–68

EQUATION	INDUSTRY AVERAGE RETURN*	CONSTANT	REGRESSION COEFFICIENTS—INDEPENDENT VARIABLES†						R^2
			CONCENTRATION		SIZE (AA)‡	CAPITAL INTENSITY (AA/Q)‡	GROWTH (AAG)‡		
			(CCR)‡	(SCR)‡					
1	IORB	.1155	.0935 (2.99) *.352*	⋯ ⋯	−.0202 (1.99) *−.222*	−.0439 (2.42) *−.256*	.0132 (3.42) *.366*		.276
2	IORB	.1249	⋯ ⋯	.0586 (2.05) *.233*	−.0138 (1.38) *−.153*	−.0432 (2.29) *−.251*	.0116 (2.97) *.322*		.232
3	SRB	.1529	16.32 (3.26) *.367*	⋯ ⋯	−.0268 (1.65) *−.177*	−.0667 (2.29) *−.232*	.0283 (4.58) *.468*		.338
4	SRB	.1638	⋯ ⋯	.1134 (2.49) *.270*	−.0171 (1.07) *−.113*	−.0668 (2.22) *−.232*	.0257 (4.11) *.425*		.301

* IORB = implicit operating return before taxes; SRB = stockholders' return before taxes.

† Absolute value of t ratios in parentheses, beta coefficients in italics.

‡ Notations are as follows: CCR, Census concentration ratios; SCR, Shepherd concentration ratios; AA, average total assets; AA/Q, average asset/output ratio; AAG, average asset growth.

conclusion is that the use of industry averages to capture the structure-performance relation between size and profitability, at least, is wholly inappropriate.[35] If the firms in each of the 79 industries were of comparable size, this problem would not arise.

For the other three structural influences on profitability, the problem is not as critical, because simple linear relations are likely. Indeed, the regression coefficients for concentration, capital intensity, and growth are all of the same order as those found for the similar firm regressions. Generally the size of the marginal effects of each structural variable is increased. The marginal effect of concentration in this model suggests that a highly concentrated industry with a concentration ratio of .90 would earn an implicit operating return before taxes (IORB) of 18.63 percent as opposed to an 11.15 percent return for a competitive industry with a ratio of .10—a 67 percent higher return.[36]

Spatial business risk and industry profitability

It is hypothesized that the greater the risk associated with a firm's ability to predict its average rate of return upon entering an industry because firms in that industry earn different rates of return, the higher are average (industry) rates of return (Hypothesis IX). To test this hypothesis, industry-average rates of return are regressed against the standard deviation and skewness of member-firm rates of return computed around industry averages. If firms are, as assumed, averse to risk, then the standard deviation and skewness ought to be positively and negatively related to industry-average returns. In other words, a firm contemplating investment in one of two industries would enter that industry which has the smallest dispersion of existing-firm rates of return and the highest positive skewness, *ceteris paribus*—e.g., identical expected average rates of return. As a result, the rate of return in the more risky industry would remain high while the returns in the less risky industry would fall with the new entrant.

The empirical results presented in Table 22 lend support to this hypothesis. For the principal measure of profitability, implicit operating return before taxes (IORB), the signs of the regression coefficients for

35. The arguments here are against unweighted averages. This problem may be avoided with the use of weighted averages. However, another problem is introduced—confounding intraindustry relations with interindustry relations. Later, weighted-average returns are used.

36. The marginal effect from the firm model suggests a 44 percent larger return for the highly concentrated industry.

TABLE 22

ANALYSIS OF SPATIAL RISK AND PROFITABILITY FOR
79 INDUSTRIES (736 FIRMS), 1960–68

EQUATION	INDUSTRY AVERAGE RETURN*	CONSTANT	REGRESSION COEFFICIENTS— INDEPENDENT VARIABLES†		R^2
			STANDARD DEVIATION (ISD) ‡	SKEWNESS (IS) ‡	
1	IORB	.1165	.5399 (2.80) *.313*	−.0106 (1.25) *−.140*	.098
2	IORA	.0749	.0202 (1.18) *.135*	.0017 (0.44) *.051*	.022
3	SRB	.1875	.3671 (1.99) *.226*	.0079 (0.60) *.068*	.062
4	SRA	.1078	.1315 (0.78) *.088*	.0119 (1.93) *.217*	.050

* IORB and IORA = implicit operating return before and after taxes, respectively; SRB and SRA = stockholders' return before and after taxes, respectively.

† Absolute value of t ratios in parentheses, beta coefficients in italics.

‡ The spatial risk variables ISD and IS respectively stand for the industry standard deviation and industry skewness computed from the distribution of member-firm period-average returns around their respective industries' period-average returns.

the standard deviation and skewness are, as expected, positive and negative, respectively. However, for the other measures of profitability both risk variables are positively associated with average rates of return.[37] These results, especially for profitability defined as IORB, support the hypothesis that the uncertainties attached to entering an industry are an effective barrier to entry reflected in industry-average rate-of-return patterns. Taking the two extreme industries in this panel (highest and lowest risk) the fitted model for IORB suggests that the rate of return

37. Again, however, only the implicit operating rates of return should be free of confounded relations because of managerial discretions in adjusting debt-equity ratios. Because of the differences in a firm's handling of taxes on financial statements (e.g., with regard to investment credits and tax allocation) and because of the very nature of income tax in smoothing rates of return and reducing the difference between firms' rates of return, it is difficult to make any meaningful statement about after-tax returns and business risk.

for the riskiest industry of 20.4 percent is comparable to the 10.6 percent rate of return in the so-called safest industry.[38]

Risk-comparable rates of return. Because observed industry-average rates of return reflect different exposure to spatial risk, the use of these observed measures in regressions with the structural variables may bias the results because of a salient collinearity between some or all of the structural variables with spatial risk. One solution is to rerun the basic model with this modification: use risk-comparable rates of return (actual rates of return adjusted for risk). If the model for risk is $R_j = a + bISD_j + cIS_j$, then risk-comparable rates of return for each industry can be estimated by the following computation:

$$RAR_j = R_j - bISD_j - cIS_j$$

where:

RAR_j is the risk-adjusted or risk-comparable rate of return for industry j.

Regressing these risk-adjusted industry rates of return (RAR_js) against the structural variables may result in a more accurate assessment of the influence of each structural variable on performance.

These results for the risk-adjusted IORB profitability measure are:

$RAR_j (IORB) =$

	$.08104 + .09289CCR_j -$	$.00002120AA_j -$	$.03585AA/Q_j +$	$.01294AAG_j$
t ratios	(3.12)	(2.19)	(2.07)	(3.53)
beta coefficient	.368	−.247	−.220	.377

$$R^2 = .273$$
$$N = 79 .$$

These results are very similar to those for the unadjusted rates of return. The importance of the structural variables (judged by the size of the beta coefficients) is only slightly increased for all variables except capital

---

38. For this computation, it is assumed that the industries with the highest and lowest dispersions are also the industries with the lowest and highest measures of skewness respectively. This, however, is not necessarily the case. Actually, this model suggests that the "risk free" rate of return is 11.65 percent (the constant). This is the rate of return for no dispersion in firm rates of return, and for a zero value for skewness. However, skewness is both negative and positive. A "riskless" industry with zero skewness is less attractive than one with a positive skewness. This industry has a positive skewness and hence is better off than the "riskless" industry, *ceteris paribus*.

intensity when risk-adjusted rates of return are employed.[39] This suggests that none of the structural variables is highly correlated with spatial risk. Therefore, to ignore spatial risk in regressing industry-average rates of return against these structural variables does not seem to create bias.

Although it has been argued that the dispersion of firm rates of return (around the industry average) is risk, this study has explored several reasons for differences in firm rates of return within the same industry which should not be considered indicators of risk. Spatial risk as a barrier to entry is predicated on the assumption that the potential entrant cannot identify which firm it would be similar to. However, if, for example, the larger firms in an industry earn higher rates of return than the smaller firms, the potential entrant might be able to predict with certainty its rate of return given the size of its commitment.[40] Thus, differences in returns among an industry's member firms may not be indicative of risk of entry so much as they are indicative of an absolute-capital-requirement barrier to entry.

Analysis of industry variables by concentration categories

Let us continue the presentation of the empirical results with a short discussion of the basic industry variables and their descriptive measures. Table 23 gives the variables' means and standard deviations by the six categories for both Census and Shepherd concentration ratios.

Rates of return. The industry pattern of average returns by concentration categories (see Table 12)—as with the firm data for average rates of return by concentration categories shown in Table 17—does not manifest an abundantly clear association between profitability and concentration. Grouping industries by Census concentration ratios does show, however, that industries in the two highest concentration categories (ratios from 60–100) earn the highest rates of return before taxes on assets and on stockholders' equity. However, when these same industries are classified by their Shepherd concentration ratios, the highest returns are found in the lowest concentration category, and the highest concentration category shows the second highest returns. Category V shows the lowest and second lowest average returns for returns on assets and returns to

---

39. As would be expected, the percentage of the variance explained (R^2) has fallen, though ever so slightly. Compare these results to those given for Equation 1 of Table 21.

40. For a fuller discussion see: Daryl Winn, "Profitability and Industry Concentration," Working Paper No. 7, Bureau of Business Research, Graduate School of Business Administration, The University of Michigan, 1970, pp. 80–85. (Multilith.)

TABLE 23

KEY VARIABLES SUMMARY DATA BY SIX CONCENTRATION CATEGORIES
FOR 79 INDUSTRIES (736 FIRMS), 1960–68 AVERAGES

| Concentration | | No. of Firms | No. of Indus- tries | Variable* | | | | | | | | | | | | | | | |
Category (1)	Ratio (2)	(3)	(4)	IORB X (5)	IORB σ (6)	IORBω X (7)	IORBω σ (8)	SRB X (9)	SRB σ (10)	SRBω X (11)	SRBω σ (12)	AA X (13)	AA σ (14)	AA/Q X (15)	AA/Q σ (16)	AAG X (17)	AAG σ (18)	ASG X (19)	ASG σ (20)
All industries		736	79	.1459	.0470	.1511	.0564	.2255	.0786	.2350	.0896	253.9	519.7	.7491	.2734	1.67	1.30	1.78	1.38
								Census Ratios											
I	0– 29	71	11	.1366	.0612	.1366	.0681	.2115	.1081	.2096	.1154	65.0	45.2	.5605	.1401	2.44	2.00	2.23	1.69
II	30– 39	175	17	.1561	.0506	.1570	.0488	.2299	.0733	.2341	.0690	90.8	85.7	.7305	.1551	2.08	1.21	1.86	1.11
III	40– 49	166	18	.1392	.0484	.1447	.0659	.2286	.0950	.2383	.1137	110.0	83.7	.7099	.2326	2.11	1.47	1.98	2.07
IV	50– 59	201	16	.1335	.0305	.1358	.0426	.2024	.0486	.2145	.0551	380.9	526.4	.8962	.3394	1.47	0.73	1.32	0.68
V	60– 69	71	8	.1615	.0243	.1793	.0517	.2403	.0510	.2638	.0823	324.0	208.4	.8014	.3330	1.49	0.72	1.57	0.54
VI	70–100	52	9	.1597	.0571	.1725	.0571	.2558	.0800	.2724	.0944	792.3	1,236.3	.7855	.3570	1.64	0.35	1.69	1.18
								Shepherd Ratios											
I	0– 29	23	4	.1659	.0995	.1650	.1042	.2602	.1741	.2628	.1770	46.2	20.6	.5725	.0959	3.68	3.05	2.77	1.71
II	30– 39	49	6	.1378	.0418	.1283	.0399	.1986	.0730	.1949	.0732	76.0	49.9	.6024	.2256	1.47	0.66	1.11	0.55
III	40– 49	149	16	.1438	.0465	.1509	.0510	.2192	.0685	.2263	.0719	101.6	89.1	.6713	.1191	1.92	1.21	1.88	1.28
IV	50– 59	128	13	.1492	.0396	.1554	.0488	.2246	.0526	.2313	.0570	105.3	106.1	.7422	.3298	2.16	1.40	1.86	1.18
V	60– 69	191	18	.1338	.0370	.1361	.0549	.2146	.0765	.2276	.0995	261.4	495.0	.8283	.2280	1.61	0.71	1.51	0.58
VI	70–100	196	22	.1540	.0501	.1646	.0604	.2403	.0830	.2556	.0967	532.6	813.7	.8214	.3505	1.66	1.21	1.88	1.97

* Notations are as follows: IORB, implicit operating return on assets before taxes; SRB, stockholders' return before taxes; AA, average total assets; AA/Q, average asset/output ratio; AAG, average asset growth; ASG, average sales growth. Subscript ω indicates category average of industry weighted average.

stockholders respectively. These conclusions, however, are limited by the nature of the methodology. The six categories are arbitrarily preselected and the number of industries (firms) included in each varies considerably. For example, the first two categories for Shepherd ratios combined include only 10 of the 79 industries and only 72 of 736 firms. Different results might obtain from arbitrarily grouping the 79 industries into concentration categories by taking 13 industries at a time proceeding from the lowest to the highest concentration ratios.

Also presented in Table 23 and denoted with the subscript ω (see columns 7 and 11) are category averages of industry weighted averages. (Firm-average returns are weighted by their period-average assets to obtain the industry weighted average.) Comparing the weighted-average returns with the unweighted averages by concentration categories allows an interesting observation to be made. For the lowest concentration categories, the weighed-average returns are generally lower than the unweighted averages suggesting that *within* these industries large firms earn lower rates of return than the smaller firms. However, as concentration increases the weighted-average returns become larger and the discrepancy between weighted and unweighted returns is generally the greatest in the highest concentration category. This shift suggests that the discrepancy between the rates of return of large and small firms in the same industry increases with concentration. In order to verify this finding, the differences between weighted- and unweighted-industry average returns are regressed against concentration, size, and capital intensity. This model and the results for the two before-tax rates of return and Census ratios are given below:

$$IORB_{\omega j} - IORB_j = .00876 + .00975CCR_j + .0000193AA_j - .0174AA/Q_j \quad R^2 = .152$$
$$\qquad\qquad\qquad\quad (0.49) \qquad\quad (2.88) \qquad\qquad (1.51)$$
$$\text{beta coefficient} \quad .060 \qquad\qquad .348 \qquad\qquad -.166 \qquad N = 79$$

$$SRB_{\omega j} - SRB_j = .02029 + .0211CCR_j + .0000273AA_j - .0367AA/Q_j \quad R^2 = .140$$
$$\qquad\qquad\qquad\quad (0.64) \qquad\quad (2.49) \qquad\qquad (1.94)$$
$$\text{beta coefficient} \quad .079 \qquad\qquad .302 \qquad\qquad -.214 \qquad N = 79$$

Again (reaffirming earlier conclusions), as concentration increases an industry's larger firms have only a moderately increased advantage over the smaller firms (see the beta coefficients). In other words, firm scale economies are either not clearly present in the concentrated industries or "X-inefficiency" conceals their presence. The most important determinant of the difference between weighted returns and unweighted returns is the average size of firm. It is difficult to interpret this result without ambiguity, principally because of the difficulty in attaching any unambiguous meaning to averages of firm sizes and their relationship to average returns. (See the earlier discussion in this chapter of the results from regressing average returns against average size, pages 99–101). The result that the greater the average capital intensity, the less profitable are the large firms is likewise difficult to interpret. This is primarily because there are several reasons for differences in capital intensity (e.g., degree of vertical integration, the nature of the production function), and also simply because of the dynamics of demand and the firm's investment responses.

The standard deviations of category-average returns generally decrease as concentration increases. In all cases the largest variance in rates of return among industries is in the lowest concentration category. This would be expected because this category is composed of the smallest firms.[41] While the variance falls throughout the middle ranges of concentration, it increases sharply in the highest concentration category. Several reasons may be given for the rise. First, the variance of industry sizes increases sharply for the last category. To the extent that absolute size does influence industry-average rates of return within the highly concentrated categories, then the variance of those returns would be high. Because regressions on industry data are not run within the concentration categories, there exists no empirical evidence from which to draw an answer. However, it is recalled that, as cited earlier, the evidence that absolute size affects profitability within the highest concentration category is inconclusive. Another explanation might be that, as Stigler observed, "concentration, itself . . . is associated with characteristics . . . which make for dispersion of profits."[42]

Support for this possibility is given in the section on risk where temporal variances of firm rates of return are found to be positively associated with concentration.[43] One last explanation is offered, which is suggested in a review of Bain's first study.[44] Some industries may be concentrated because they face a declining or stable market demand and, consequently,

---

41. See earlier discussion on the problems of unequal variances and weighted regressions. Note also that the standard deviation of firm size increases rather consistently with concentration as would the coefficient of variation. This is especially clear for Shepherd concentration ratios.

42. George J. Stigler, *Capital and Rates of Return,* p. 70.

43. Recall, however, that temporal variance is also found to be negatively associated with firm size and capital intensity. In the highest concentration category, both these factors are highest.

44. Joe S. Bain, "Relation of Profit Rate to Industry Concentration: American Manufacturing, 1936–40," *Quarterly Journal of Economics* 65 (Aug. 1951): 293–324.

the few remaining firms are the more successful. The marginal firms may have diversified into other markets and are no longer appropriately classified in the original industry.

Average size. It is quite clear that average size of firm is strongly and positively associated with concentration. It is likewise clear that the variance of average size increases much faster as concentration increases. Because of this, there is a marked upward trend in the coefficient of variation—implying that, to the extent that absolute and relative size become a factor influencing firm rates of return, it might be quite difficult to sort out the independent influences of concentration by solely relying on industry data.

Capital intensity. Again as observed for firm variables, capital intensity increases rather consistently and strongly with concentration. A comparison of the implied or actual (average) profit margins against those necessary to maintain the all-industry average rate of return of .1492 (as was done for firm data) reveals that profit margins do rise substantially. However, this rise is closely in line with those expected for the maintenance of rates of return. These data are presented below:

CONCENTRATION CATEGORY	CENSUS RATIOS		SHEPHERD RATIOS	
	ACTUAL	CONSTANT RETURN	ACTUAL	CONSTANT RETURN
I	.0766	.0818	.0950	.0835
II	.1140	.1066	.0830	.0879
III	.0990	.1036	.0965	.0979
IV	.1196	.1308	.1107	.1083
V	.1294	.1169	.1101	.1201
VI	.1255	.1147	.1265	.1198
All	.1039	.1093	.1093	.1093

For the Census ratios, the actual margins are moderately higher for the highest concentration categories. These so-called excess margins, however, amount to only about one cent on a dollar of sales.

Growth. For Census ratios, average growth rates of both sales and assets show a marked decrease with increases in concentration. Asset growth evinces the stronger decrease. The variances of growth rates within each category generally decrease also along with increases in concentration. The variance of sales growth rates, however, increases very substantially in the highest concentration category. For Shepherd ratios, no clear pattern emerges for the relation between average growth rates, their variances, and concentration. An interesting observation comes from comparing asset growth with sales growth for each of the categories. In the lower concentration categories (for both Census and Shepherd ratios) asset growth is higher than sales growth. This difference diminishes until sales growth becomes actually greater than asset growth in the highest concentration categories. Reasons for this phenomenon could range all the way from (1) concentrated industries' being less responsive to increases in demand, to (2) concentrated industries' building excess capacity in anticipation of future demand.[45]

45. See Chapter 4, pages 127 ff. for an extensive discussion of these points.

4

SUMMARY AND CONCLUSIONS

Chapters 2 and 3 directly or indirectly test many hypotheses (some implicit) by a variety of approaches. This chapter summarizes the evidence and states conclusions. The order in which the evidence is discussed follows the order of the hypotheses given in Chapter 1. At the outset, it should be recalled that the integrative purpose of all hypotheses is the eventual culmination of evidence on a single hypothesis: **After accounting for the independent influences of size, capital intensity, growth, business risk, and distortions arising from historical-cost accounting, firms in concentrated industries are found to earn above-average long-run rates of return.**

To accomplish the test of this hypothesis, this study seeks to determine the nature of the interrelation between profitability, concentration, and each of the other influencing factors.

Profitability and Concentration

The initial hypothesis that **firms in concentrated industries earn above-average long-run rates of return** (Hypothesis I) is first tested in the usual manner by interindustry analysis, using both firms and industries as units of observation. A tabular presentation (Table 17, Chapter 3) of firm-average rates of return by six concentration categories indicates no clear linear relation between levels of concentration and profitability. Generally, the return pattern by concentration categories is found to be U-shaped, with above-average returns in both unconcentrated and highly concentrated industries. The lowest returns in all cases are found in the 50/59 concentration ratio category (Category IV). The U-shaped distribution is also found in a similar tabular presentation of industry variables (Table 23, Chapter 3).

The firm regression results (Table 4, Chapter 2) indicate that a firm

110

in an industry with a concentration ratio (CCR) of .10 would earn a return (IORB) of 12.0 percent in contrast to a return of 17.2 percent for a firm with a ratio of .90—a 44 percent increase in profitability. Though this is a large difference, comparing the beta coefficients for concentration, firm size, capital intensity, and growth indicates that concentration has the least influence, regardless of the profitability measure. When industries are the unit of observation, the marginal effect of concentration on rates of return increases (Table 21, Chapter 3). A highly concentrated industry with a concentration ratio of .90 would earn an 18.6 percent rate of return (IORB), as opposed to an 11.2 percent rate of return for a competitive industry with a ratio of .10—a 67 percent higher return. The remaining part of this study determines whether and how this association between concentration and profitability might be influenced by other factors affecting profitability. To do this, a set of interrelated hypotheses is tested.

Firm Size

Because previous research finds firm size to be positively associated with both profitability and concentration, an attempt is made to study the interplay of these two structural variables and to determine their separate influences.

Absolute size and profitability

The hypothesis that **large firms earn higher rates of return than small firms** (Hypothesis II) is tested by again using both firms and industries as units of observation. For firms as the unit of observation and expressing size as the reciprocal of the logarithm (base 10) of assets, the absolute-size hypothesis is confirmed (Table 4, Chapter 2). However, absolute size is found to have very little influence on profitability for firms beyond the $10-million—$20-million asset range. This finding confirms earlier conclusions where, using IRS data, this plateau is also observed.

According to the beta coefficients, absolute-size of firm is only slightly more important than concentration and considerably less important than either capital intensity or growth in influencing rates of return.

When an industry average of firm size is regressed against industry-average profitability, a negative association is consistently found (Table 21, Chapter 3). This result may in part be due to the impropriety of taking the means of two variables in obtaining industry averages when the two variables (profitability and size) are not linearly related, and in part, it may also arise from confounding the absolute-size–profitability relationship with the relative-size–profitability relationship.

Relative size, concentration, and profitability

A relative-size–profitability hypothesis that **the positive effect of firm size on firm rates of return is greater within concentrated industries than within unconcentrated industries** (Hypothesis III) is tested. A positive association between size and profitability is found in only 48 of the 79 industries. This hypothesis is tested by three different approaches.[1] First, the number of positive and negative intraindustry relations is analyzed by concentration categories. No clear pattern emerges (Table 9, Chapter 3). In other words, economies of scale and/or greater market power of each industry's larger firms do not appear to confer a greater advantage to the larger firms in concentrated industries.

Second, relative-size and relative-profitability variables—i.e., relative to the industry average—are computed for each firm. The regressions between these two variables by the six concentration categories yield a weak indication that relative size is more important in the higher concentration categories (Table 10).

The third approach to the test of the influence of concentration on the relation between size and profitability within industries is made through the use of industry weighted- and unweighted-average returns. Where an industry's average return weighed by firm size is found to be higher than its unweighted-average return, one can conclude that there is a positive association between profitability and firm size in that industry. In Table 23 (Chapter 3), it is shown that for the lowest concentration categories the weighted-average returns are generally lower than the unweighted averages, suggesting that within these industries large firms earn lower returns than small firms. However, as concentration increases, the weighted-average returns become larger than the unweighted returns and the discrepancies between weighted and unweighted returns are generally greatest in the highest concentration category (Table 23). This suggests that as concentration increases, larger firms have an increased advantage over the smaller firms in the same industry. However, in the regression of the difference between weighted and unweighted averages against concentration ratios, average firm size, and average capital intensity, concentration is found to have a very small, though positive, influence on these differences. Average firm size particularly and average capital intensity to a lesser extent are found to have far greater influences.[2]

---

1. The differences in the numbers of firms in various industries rendered direct comparisons of the size of the regression coefficients an inappropriate methodology.

2. See Chapter 3, page 106.

Absolute size, concentration, and profitability

Finally, the possibility that the absolute-size profitability relationship confounds the relationship between profitability and concentration is explicitly considered. The importance of this consideration lies in the possibility that concentrated industries earn above-average rates of return simply because they are typically composed of larger firms. The test of the hypothesis that **concentrated industries are composed of larger firms than unconcentrated industries** (Hypothesis IV) establishes whether this collinearity may be a problem. The collinearity between absolute size and concentration is quite clear when firms are grouped by the six concentration categories.[3] The mean size of firm increases monotonically with but one exception—Category IV (Table 17, Chapter 3). The average size of firm in the most highly concentrated industries is roughly ten times the average size of firm in the lowest category. This same result is found when industry averages are analyzed by the six concentration categories.

After it is established that absolute size and concentration are correlated, the use of industry dummy variables in a bivariate regression between firm rates of return and the firm-size variable results in an industry-average rate of return which is adjusted for absolute size. These dummy variables are interpreted as each industry's average rate of return after the rate of return of each member firm has been adjusted for the overall relationship between firm size and profitability. Regressing the size-adjusted rates of return against concentration ratios suggests that the collinearity between size and profitability is such that it affects the concentration-profitability findings and causes more importance to be attributed to concentration than ought to be. The marginal effect of concentration on size-adjusted rates of return (IORB) from this model indicates that an industry with a size-adjusted rate of return would earn a 15.9 percent return if it had a concentration ratio of .10 as opposed to a 16.7 percent return for an industry with a concentration ratio of .90— a rather small difference.

Absolute size and profitability within concentration categories. When firm rates of return are regressed against firm size, capital intensity, and growth within each of the six concentration categories, another aspect of the interplay between the influences of absolute size and concentration on profitability is captured. These results (Tables 18 and 19, Chapter 3)

---

3. The simple coefficients of correlation between the logarithm of firm assets and Census concentration ratios are .302 for firms as units of observation and .593 for industries as units of observation.

suggest that absolute size is less important in the lower concentration categories (Census Categories I–III) and in the highest category (Category VI) than in the middle ranges of concentration. The conclusion might be that large (absolute) firms have a marked advantage over smaller firms when market power is emerging. However, this finding is difficult to interpret unambiguously. Recall that in these ranges of concentration the average size of firm is quite large (around $200–300 million in assets). Absolute size is found to have little influence on profitability when firm size rises above the $10-million–$20-million plateau. Again, the closely woven interplay between size and concentration is clear.

Capital Intensity

Capital intensity and firm size

The hypothesis that **large firms have higher capital/output ratios than do small firms** (Hypothesis V) is affirmed for interindustry analysis. When capital intensity is regressed against the three different functional expressions of firm size—total assets (A), the logarithm (base 10) of total assets (Log$A$), and the reciprocal of the logarithm of assets (RLog$A$)—the greatest percentage of the variance in capital intensity is explained by the logarithm of total assets (Log$A$). The bivariate regression results for the two measures of capital intensity—the ratios of fixed assets to sales (K/Q) and total assets to sales (A/Q)—are (t ratios in parentheses):[4]

$$K/Q_i = .0510 + .1273 \; \mathrm{Log} A_i \qquad R^2 = .134$$
$$(10.87) \qquad\qquad N = 768$$

$$A/Q_i = .5255 + .1303 \; \mathrm{Log} A_i \qquad R^2 = .076$$
$$(7.92) \qquad\qquad N = 768$$

Capital intensity and firm size within industries. Another test of Hypothesis V explores the association between firm size and capital intensity within each of the 79 industries. Davis had concluded that in the industries where large firms have higher capital/output ratios, any "market advantages possessed by the large firms . . . [enable] them to undertake activities requiring more capital than those commonly undertaken by the small operators."[5] Of the 79 industries in this study, a posi-

---

4. These results indicate that the capital/output ratios for a $10 million firm and a $1 billion firm respectively would be: K/Q of .1783 and A/Q of .6558 for the $10 million firm and K/Q of .4329 and A/Q of .9164 for the $1 billion firm.

5. Hiram S. Davis, "Relation of Capital/Output Ratios to Firm Size in American Manufacturing: Some Additional Evidence," *Review of Economics and Statistics* 38 (Aug. 1956): 287.

tive relation between size and capital intensity (A/Q) is found within 50 (Table 11, Chapter 3). Analysis of the effects of different levels of concentration on the intraindustry relation between capital intensity and size reveals no clear pattern, except that the chances of finding larger firms being more capital intensive are less in the middle ranges of concentration than they are in both the competitive and highly concentrated industries (Table 11).

Capital intensity and concentration

The hypothesis that **concentrated industries have higher capital/output ratios than do unconcentrated industries** (Hypothesis VI) is affirmed. The first order coefficients of correlation between the two measures of concentration and the two measures of capital intensity using firms (768) as units of observation are:

	TOTAL ASSETS/SALES	FIXED ASSETS/SALES
Census concentration ratio	.2030	.2087
Shepherd concentration ratio	.2531	.2769

Taking firm averages by the six concentration categories reveals a very clear and strong positive association between average capital intensity and levels of concentration. For both measures of capital intensity, there is an almost monotonic increase with increases in concentration (Table 17, Chapter 3). Again, as with size, the exceptions to the monotonic increase are found in Category IV.[6] The importance of this finding lies in the use of capital intensity as a barrier-to-entry variable. It is argued earlier that larger firms may be in a position to undertake more capital-intensive operations. Large firms and firms in concentrated industries may be more capital intensive, however, not only because of particular production function characteristics but also because of a higher degree of vertical integration. Both conditions may serve as a barrier to entry.

Capital intensity and profitability

Because capital intensity is positively associated with both size and concentration, which are, in turn, positively associated with profitability, it is hypothesized that **firms with high capital/output ratios earn above-average rates of return** (Hypothesis VII). Obviously, the intent of establishing this relationship is to determine whether the frequently observed

6. These results are also found when industries are the unit of observation (Table 23, Chapter 3).

association between concentration and profitability is explained to any degree by a latent relationship between capital intensity and concentration. However, both measures of capital intensity (A/Q and K/Q) are consistently found to be negatively associated with profitability across firms (Table 4, Chapter 2). The general strength of this negative association is attested to by the findings that the beta coefficients for capital intensity are roughly twice the size of the beta coefficients for size of firm and concentration.[7] These findings lend support to Schor's hypothesis that large firms are under less competitive pressure to use capital efficiently than are smaller firms, particularly in an oligopolistic industry.[8] On the one hand, this hypothesis is consistent with the determined relation between capital intensity and size, and, on the other, it would explain the negative association between capital intensity and profitability.

A more direct test of Schor's hypothesis is made by analyzing the intraindustry relation of capital intensity and profitability.

Capital intensity and profitability within industries. Within 53 of the 79 industries, the more capital-intensive firms earn lower rates of return (Table 12, Chapter 3). Thus the interindustry results are generally confirmed to hold within industries as well. When these results are analyzed by the six concentration categories a rather clear pattern emerges, which refutes Schor's hypothesis that inefficient use of capital obtains in oligopolistic industries. The chances of finding a positive intraindustry relation in the category of the most concentrated industries (Category VI) are better than 50 percent—more than double the chances of finding a positive relation in the other concentration categories. Analysis of the percentage of positive intraindustry relations by concentration categories, taking successive categories two at a time, shows a rather marked increase in the chances of a positive intraindustry relation as concentration increases (Table 12).

Capital intensity, profit margins, and concentration

A negative association between profitability and capital intensity indicates that as capital intensity increases (or as asset/turnover ratios decrease) firms are not able to increase profit margins enough to maintain rates of return. However, as concentration increases there is an increased

---

7. These results are similar to those obtained using industries as units of observation.

8. Stanley S. Schor, "The Capital-Product Ratio and Size of Establishment for Manufacturing Industries" (unpublished Ph.D. dissertation, University of Pennsylvania, 1952).

capability of firms to offset the effects of decreases in asset/turnover on rates of return through higher profit margin. This apparent capability is verified by a tabular presentation of the implied or actual (average) profit margins arranged by concentration categories. Against these actual profit margins, a so-called constant-return profit margin is compared. The constant-return margins are computed by multiplying each concentration category's actual (average) asset/outset ratio by the all-firm average rate of return of .1429. The actual profit margins are smaller than the constant-return margins in the less concentrated industries and higher than the constant-return margins in the highly concentrated industries. The conclusion is that, as concentration increases, the more capital-intensive firms can and do increase profit margins more than enough to offset the effects of lower asset turnover. In other words, capital intensity—a proxy for vertical integration and absolute capital requirements—is an advantage only in the more concentrated industries. Or—to view any inferred causation from another angle—when capital intensity is, in fact, an advantage, it can be said to lead to industrial concentration.[9]

Capital intensity and profitability within concentration categories. In order to capture another aspect of the interplay of capital intensity, concentration, and profitability, rates of return are regressed against firm size, capital intensity, and asset growth within each of the six concentration categories without regard to any intraindustry relations. The behavior of the beta coefficients clearly indicates that the importance of capital intensity increases as concentration increases. That is, the negative influence of capital intensity on rates of return becomes stronger in the higher concentration categories. This finding supports the hypothesis that firms in concentrated industries do not maintain the high profit margins necessary to compensate for the decreases in asset turnover.

9. This line of causation is implied by Victor R. Fuchs in his analysis, "Integration, Concentration, and Profits in Manufacturing Industries," *Quarterly Journal of Economics* 75 (May 1961): 278–91. Fuchs shows that in the typical manufacturing industry the plants owned by firms with more than one establishment operating in more than one industry are on the average larger and have more value added per employee than do either firms with only one establishment or firms with more than one establishment but all of them in the same industry (nondiversified firms). Among the reasons for this phenomenon, Fuch suggests, are greater efficiency and/or more intensive use of capital by multiunit and multiindustry firms. He argues that "the percentage of an indusry's value added accounted for by multi-unit . . . [firms] is a useful measure of the ease or difficulty of entry into that industry" (pp. 284–85). Fuchs finds that 70 percent of the variance of concentration ratios is explained by this entry-barrier variable and another related variable defined as the value added per firm, concluding as follows: "The percent[age] of an industry's value added accounted for by multi-unit plants provides a better basis for predicting rates of return than does concentration . . ." (p. 291).

On first glance, this finding contradicts the results of earlier analysis and suggests that concentrated industries do not use capital efficiently. Thus Schor's hypothesis seems to be supported by interindustry analysis. It remains unsupported by intraindustry analysis, however. Perhaps what the interindustry analysis within the concentrated industries shows is that, for firms of roughly comparable market power, the inverse relation between profitability and capital intensity is tautological rather than structural. Unfavorable demand conditions produce both a low profit profile *and* low sales volume reflected in a high asset/output ratio. That is, in this case asset/output ratios become a performance variable rather than a structural variable. Reasons for the increased strength of this influence as concentration increases could be the generally greater degree of capital intensity among concentrated industries, on the one hand and the inability of firms in concentrated industries to shift (perhaps more highly specialized) resources to more favorable markets, on the other. In other words, this interindustry phenomenon may indicate a longer-run risk associated with the employment of assets in certain industries, i.e., concentrated industries.

Capital intensity and variability of profitability

It is hypothesized that **the higher the firm's capital/output ratio, the greater the variability in rates of return over time** (Hypothesis VIII). Two measures of temporal variability (variance of firm annual returns around their period average and a variance around predicted returns) are regressed against capital intensity, firm size, and concentration (Table 15, Chapter 3). Capital intensity is found to have an influence on temporal variability, which, though small, judged by the size of the beta coefficients, is negative. Because capital intensity could be a proxy for either the ratio of fixed costs to total costs *or* the degree of vertical integration (two opposite influences on variability over time), it is tentatively concluded that the advantage of vertical integration in lessening temporal variability more than offsets the attendant disadvantage of an increase in the ratio of fixed to total costs.

Business Risk

Profitability and temporal risk

Concern for the variability of returns leads to the hypothesis that **the greater the risk associated with a firm's ability to predict its rate of return over time, the higher are its average rates of return** (Hypothesis IX). Labeled temporal business risk, this type of risk is quantified by determining the association between a firm's period-average rate of return and the standard deviation and skewness of its annual rates of return around an expected return. Both the firm's period-average return and the predicted returns (from time-series regression) are used as proxies for the expected return. Generally, the proxy for expected returns does not materially alter the results (Table 14, Chapter 3).

When average returns are regressed against the standard deviation and skewness across all 768 firms, the results consistently find the relation of standard deviation and of skewness to average returns to be, respectively, negative and positive—just the opposite of that hypothesized (Table 14). In other words, the greater the risk the *lower* the rates of return. Being of the strong belief that managers do have an aversion to risk, as defined here, I will briefly explore a rather complex hypothesis—that, although managers are averse to risk, the resultant observed relationship between average returns and risk is distorted. Essentially, I believe that, when faced with a risky situation, firms have alternatives other than requiring a higher return. Two very likely alternatives are diversification and vertical integration. Usually the accomplishment of both accompanies growth in the size of the firm. In other words, the result is a reemphasis or an extension of Baumol's argument that larger firms, with easier access to financial markets, have an advantage over smaller firms in their increased opportunity to diversify geographically, to offset cyclical products, etc., and to control through integration.[10]

Temporal risk and structure

Insight into this possibility is obtained by regressing firm temporal standard deviations against the three structural variables—concentration, firm size, and capital intensity. The results are rewarding. About 27 percent of the variance in firm standard deviations (computed on returns defined as IORB) is explained by these structural variables. Increases in firm size and capital intensity are indicated as reducing the temporal variability of returns (Table 15, Chapter 3). While size has a considerable influence (judging from the size of the beta coefficients), the influence of capital intensity is found to be negligible.[11] Concentration, on the other hand, is positively associated with temporal variability, an association we shall discuss shortly.

10. Or, to weaken Baumol's argument, large firms may earn higher rates of return simply because they may, more easily, base their individual investment decisions on expected monetary values (as opposed to expected utility). Assuming managers are averse to risk, firm-wide average returns would be highest for these large firms.

11. Recall that when capital intensity is hypothesized to be positively associated with variability, capital/output ratios are argued to serve as a proxy for two opposing influences—ratio of fixed to total costs and the degree of vertical integration.

If, as is argued, increased firm size decreases risk *and* increases rates of return, the model used here on a panel of large firms would not capture a true risk-return relationship. A solution to this dilemma is found by regressing returns against the measures of variation and skewness within each of the six concentration categories. In the lower categories, firm size, asset/output ratios, and concentration ratios are small. The relation of the standard deviation and skewness to average returns is, as hypothesized, positive and negative respectively (Table 16, Chapter 3). Thus evidence of risk aversity is found for the small, nonintegrated firms in competitive industries. It cannot be concluded, however, that risk aversity is nonexistent among the larger and capital-intensive firms in concentrated industries. Too many influences confound the relation and, in this study at least, further attempts to disentangle these problems are unwarranted.

Profitability and spatial risk

The second type of business risk explored is that of spatial risk, or risk as barrier to entry. It is hypothesized that **the greater the risk associated with a firm's ability to predict its average rate of return upon entering an industry (because firms in the industry earn different rates of return), the higher are the industry's average rates of return** (Hypothesis X). Spatial risk is measured by regressing industry-average rates of return against the standard deviation and skewness of member-firm rates of return around these industry averages. The results find variability and skewness to be, respectively, positively and negatively related to industry-average returns, thus supporting the hypothesis (Table 22, Chapter 3).

Business risk and concentration

The study of risk *per se,* however, is not the purpose of this undertaking. Rather, the ultimate design is to determine whether there is any systematic, albeit latent, relationship between risk and concentration. Accordingly, it is hypothesized that **both temporal risk and spatial risk are less in concentrated industries than in unconcentrated industries** (Hypothesis XI).

Temporal risk and concentration. Although the relationship between risk and returns cannot be captured directly among the concentrated industries (where larger and more capital-intensive firms are found), it is possible to determine how concentration is associated with temporal variability and skewness. In Table 24 temporal deviations and skewness

TABLE 24

ANALYSIS OF TEMPORAL RISK AND STRUCTURE FOR 736 FIRMS, 1960–68

| | | | REGRESSION COEFFICIENTS—INDEPENDENT VARIABLES‡ | | | | |
| | | | CONCENTRATION† | | SIZE | CAPITAL INTENSITY | |
EQUATION	DEPENDENT VARIABLE*	CONSTANT	(CCR)	(SCR)	(LOGA)	(A/Q)	R^2
1	TSD:IORB	.0880	.0296 (3.89)	···	−.0285 (16.17)	−.0051 (1.40)	.276
2	TSD:IORB	.0808	···	.0400 (5.70)	−.0293 (16.81)	−.0070 (1.94)	.292
3	TSDP:IORB	.0726	.0219 (3.33)	···	−.0240 (15.83)	−.0046 (1.48)	.270
4	TSDP:IORB	.0682	···	.0275 (4.52)	−.0245 (16.23)	−.0058 (1.87)	.278
5	TS:IORB	−.1258	−.0179 (0.11)	···	.0250 (0.66)	−.0014 (0.02)	.006
6	TS:IORB	−.1521	···	.0507 (0.33)	.0207 (0.55)	−.0073 (0.09)	.007
7	TSP:IORB	−.3882	.0913 (0.63)	···	.1434 (4.29)	.0317 (0.46)	.032
8	TSP:IORB	−.4317	···	.1759 (1.31)	.1376 (4.12)	.0208 (0.30)	.034

* Notation: TS: IORB and TSD: IORB = temporal skewness and temporal standard deviation computed around firm period-average returns; TSP:IORB and TSDP:IORB = the same variables computed around firm yearly predicted returns.
† Measures of concentration are Census ratios and Shepherd ratios.
‡ Absolute value of t ratios in parentheses.

for IORB are regressed against concentration, firm size, and capital intensity. The standard deviation and skewness are computed around firm period-average returns (denoted TSD:IORB and TS:IORB respectively) and around firm yearly predicted returns (denoted TSDP:IORB and TSP:IORB respectively). Both Census and Shepherd concentration ratios are used.[12] The results indicate that concentration increases both the temporal variability and the skewness. In other words, while concentration is associated with increased risk from profit variability, it is also associated with lessened risk from unfavorable skewness—i.e., a lesser chance of large losses. It is difficult to conclude at this point whether or not concentrated industries are less risky—as temporal risk is defined here. However, if one takes the risk-return relationship determined for the 23 firms in the lowest Shepherd concentration category and treats this as the true managerial preference for tradeoffs,[13] one can estimate a risk-adjusted rate of return for each of the six concentration categories.[14]

12. Table 15 (Chapter 3) gives the results for only TSD:IORB and TSDP:IORB and only for Census concentration ratios.

13. One may be skeptical of the use of parameters estimated from a regression on 23 firms to estimate risk-adjusted rates of return for the entire panel of firms. However, in a similar risk-return regression conducted by Fisher and Hall on a sample of 88 firms, comparable regression coefficients are obtained. Their regression coefficients for the temporal standard deviation and skewness are +1.181 and −.0193 respectively. For the 23-firm panel, these are +1.0809 and −.03175 respectively. (Fisher and Hall, "Risk and Corporate Rates of Return," *Quarterly Journal of Economics* 83 [Feb. 1969], Table 1, p. 85).

14. One might initially be tempted to take the category means of temporal standard deviations (TSD:IORB) and of temporal skewness (TS:IORB) and, using the relationship between risk and rates of return (given below), compute risk premiums for each of the six categories. Unfortunately, such straightforward methodology ignores the previously determined collinearity between size, capital intensity, and concentration ratios and the findings that both size and capital intensity (especially size) influence risk. Because of this collinearity, each category's mean risk variables are estimated from the determined relations between each risk variable and firm size, capital intensity, and concentration. (The fitted models are given in Table 24.) By holding firm size and capital intensity at their mean values, predicted risk variable values are obtained for each category, given the fitted relation between concentration ratios and the risk variables. The predicted risk variables are obtained by using the mean concentration ratios in each class, rather than the category midpoint. Having obtained these estimated risk variables for each category, the next step is to estimate a risk premium based on the risk-return relationship established in Shepherd Category I. This is found to be (Table 16, Chap. 3):

$$IORB_i = .08788 + 1.0809 TSD_i - .03175 TS_i.$$

Multiplying the predicted TSD and TS category means by +1.0809 and −.03175 respectively and summing gives an estimated category risk premium. This risk premium, however, cannot be interpreted as the average risk premium associated with firms in each category. Rather, it is the risk premium which is due solely to

Table 25 gives the observed category means (IORB), the estimated risk premiums, and the adjusted returns. It is noted, however, that these risk-adjusted rates of return are adjusted only for the collinearity between risk and concentration. Based as they are on what must be regarded as a somewhat tenuous methodology, the risk-adjusted category means, because of the positive collinearity between risk and concentration, clearly weaken any pattern of increased profitability as concentration increases.

TABLE 25

RISK-ADJUSTED RETURNS (IORB) FOR 736 FIRMS BY SIX
CONCENTRATION CATEGORIES, 1960–68 AVERAGES

CONCENTRATION		NUMBER OF FIRMS	OBSERVED MEAN	ESTIMATED* PREMIUM	ADJUSTED RETURNS
CATEGORY	RATIO				
Census ratios					
I	0– 29	71	.1322	.0382	.0940
II	30– 39	175	.1413	.0408	.1005
III	40– 49	166	.1505	.0477	.1028
IV	50– 59	201	.1289	.0510	.0779
V	60– 69	71	.1589	.0535	.1054
VI	70–100	52	.1715	.0582	.1133
Shepherd ratios					
I	0– 29	23	.1555	.0303	.1252
II	30– 39	49	.1488	.0355	.1133
III	40– 49	149	.1383	.0403	.0980
IV	50– 59	128	.1335	.0451	.0884
V	60– 69	191	.1354	.0488	.0866
VI	70–100	196	.1571	.0568	.1003

* Adjusted only for collinearity between risk and concentration. See text for explanation.

For Census ratio categories any positive association between observed returns and concentration has become more obscure. For example, the difference of four percentage points between average returns in Category I and in Category VI has been reduced to two percentage points for the adjusted returns. For Shepherd concentration ratio categories, the

the changes in risk associated with changes in concentration. When these concentration-risk premiums are subtracted from observed category mean rates of return, risk comparable rates of return result—returns adjusted for the collinearity between concentration and risk. Admittedly, this procedure is somewhat tenuous. However, it does indicate the potential magnitude of this problem and the need to consider it in the study of concentration and profitability.

adjusted returns indicate a rather strong and consistent *negative* concentration-profitability relation. Adjusted returns decrease monotonically until Category VI is reached, when adjusted returns increase, although they remain lower than those estimated for the two most competitive categories.

While these conclusions are tentative because of the indirect nature of these procedures, this analysis does indicate the potential impropriety of ignoring differences in temporal risk exposure in concentration-profitability studies.

Spatial risk and concentration. When the spatial-risk–return relation within the 79 industries has been determined, the relation between spatial risk and concentration is directly determinable. From the fitted relation between rates of return and spatial risk (standard deviations and skewness), industry risk-adjusted returns are calculated. These are then regressed against industry concentration ratios, average firm size, capital intensity, and growth rates.[15] The results are substantially unchanged from those where observed industry-average rates of return are used. The conclusion is, therefore, that it does not bias the observed relation to ignore spatial risk in regressing industry-average rates of return against these structural variables. Specifically, industry concentration does not appear to be associated with spatial risk—i.e., risk as a barrier to entry.

Rates of Growth

Growth and concentration

The findings between concentration and each of the several other independent variables—size, capital intensity, and risk—having been summarized, the findings between concentration and growth are summarized. It is hypothesized that **firms in concentrated industries grow more slowly than do firms in unconcentrated industries** (Hypothesis XII). Several approaches are taken to the test of this hypothesis.

First, as a means of summarizing the general relation between concentration and the several structural variables, Census and Shepherd concentration ratios are regressed against firm and industry measures of size, capital intensity, and growth rates. With firms used as units of observation the results are (*t* ratios in parentheses, beta coefficients in italics):[16]

---

15. See Chapter 3, p. 103, for the regression results.

16. When industry variables are used the results are similar, except that better than one-third of the variance in concentration ratios is explained.

$$CCR_i = .3146 + .05990 \text{Log} A_i + .5962 A/Q_i - .004008 AG_i + .002908 SG_i$$

$$(7.38) \qquad\qquad (3.48) \qquad\quad (1.59) \qquad\quad (1.41)$$
$$.242 \qquad\qquad\quad .124 \qquad\quad -.102 \qquad\quad .090$$

$$R^2 = .109$$
$$N = 768$$

$$SCR_i = .4072 + .06482 \text{Log} A_i + .09234 A/Q_i - .003388 AG_i + .003888 SG_i$$

$$(7.44) \qquad\qquad (5.02) \qquad\quad (1.25) \qquad\quad (1.76)$$
$$.263 \qquad\qquad\quad .177 \qquad\quad -.080 \qquad\quad .111$$

$$R^2 = .130$$
$$N = 768.$$

All of the previously established relations between concentration and the structural variables are upheld. Here, however, the test is of the relation between growth and concentration. These results indicate concentration to be negatively related to asset growth and positively related to sales growth. The analysis of mean growth rates by the six concentration categories (Table 17, Chapter 3) does not produce the conclusion that concentration is positively associated with sales growth. While category means clearly show average asset growth falling as concentration increases, sales growth shows no clear pattern.[17]

Growth and profitability

This analysis necessarily leads to explicitly considering, first, the relation between growth and profitability, and then the more complex relations between growth, profitability, and concentration. It is hypothesized that **above-average growth (industries) earn above-average rates of return** (Hypothesis XIII). The direct test of this hypothesis is made by regressing the four principal rate-of-return measures against the structural variables including both sales and asset growth.[18] In all cases, asset growth is positively related to profitability. Of the eight firm-variable regressions (four measures of the rate of return for each of the two sets of concentration ratios), sales growth is negatively related to profitability in seven. However, the beta coefficients indicate that sales growth is a relatively unimportant factor in determining firm rates of return.[19]

17. Average asset growth in the highest concentration category is roughly one-half that of the lowest concentration category.
18. The sales growth variable was eliminated from previous analysis. Therefore the results of sales growth are not given earlier.
19. The absolute size of the beta coefficients for sales growth ranges from .03 to .10 and for asset growth ranges from .19 to .38.

When industry variables are employed in a full model explaining rates of return, asset growth and sales growth are, respectively, positively and negatively related to industry-average returns in all regressions. Here, however, sales growth is a relatively important factor in the determination of rates of return. In fact, it is second to asset growth in importance (again judging from the size of the beta coefficients).[20]

Growth, concentration, and profitability

Having now determined that asset growth is negatively associated with concentration and positively associated with profitability, and that sales growth is positively associated with concentration and negatively associated with profitability, we now explicitly consider the nature of the interrelation of growth, concentration, and profitability. First it is observed that the relation between growth, profitability, and concentration is such that the observed relation between concentration and profitability cannot be a direct result of collinearity between growth (either sales or asset) and concentration.

It is hypothesized that **the relation between growth and profitability is affected by concentration** (Hypothesis XIV). The direct test of this hypothesis is accomplished by regressing profitability against size, capital intensity, and (asset) growth[21] within each of the six concentration categories (Tables 18, 19, and Chapter 3). The results of comparing the size of the beta coefficients in the concentration categories reveals that as concentration increases asset growth becomes less important as a determinant of profitability.[22] The importance of asset growth rates to profitability in the lowest concentration category far outweighs their importance in the other categories and the importance of other variables within these competitive industries. In contrast, for Category VI asset growth is indicated to have little or no effect on profitability and, in fact, for profitability defined as IORB in Census Category VI, asset growth accompanies lower profits. The accumulation of this evidence and previous analysis must culminate in the conclusion that the degree of concentration does affect the relation *between* profitability and growth.

20. The ranges of the beta coefficients are: asset growth from +.622 to +.755; sales growth from −.324 to −.362; concentration from +.259 to +.400; asset/output ratios from −.124 to −.230; and size from −.107 to −.242.

21. Because sales growth is found not to be an important factor in determining firm rates of return and its inclusion would add little, it is left out of this analysis.

22. Wenders argues that because oligopoly prices are less sensitive to changes in demand, oligopoly profits ought to be less sensitive to changes in growth. (John T. Wenders, "Profits and Antitrust Policy: The Question of Disequilibrium," *Antitrust Bulletin* 16 [1971]: 255.)

Growth, Concentration, and Profitability—Extended

The question as to the precise nature of the relation and the reasons for its existence remains, however. This section presents four lines of thought as to the explanation.

Cyclical variability in concentrated industries

When concentration ratios are regressed against the asset- and sales-growth variables (and the other structural variables), concentration is associated with lower asset growth and higher sales growth. This result would be consistent with the earlier findings that concentration is positively associated with the temporal variability of profits.

First, the finding that firms in concentrated industries grow more slowly than other firms could indicate that excess capacity was more prevalent among concentrated industries at the beginning of the period. Should concentrated industries be hit with disproportionate severity of fallen demand, not only would excess capacity result but a disproportionate rise in sales would then obtain in the recovery years. The period which this study covers begins with a recession and continues through a protracted general expansionary period, ending with a peak in economic activity.[23] This line of reasoning is advanced by Stigler for his findings that concentration is, in and of itself, associated with larger cyclical variations in demand.[24] In other words, concentrated industries may, in fact, be slow-growth industries as evidenced clearly by the asset-growth means for concentration categories. Therefore, there may be failure to observe a decline in sales growth in these concentration categories only because of the construction of the sales-growth measure and the depressed level of sales in the 1960 base period.[25]

Expansion in anticipation of future demand

Another explanation for these phenomena could be that concentrated industries expand capacity in anticipation of future demand. Should this be the case and had concentrated industries expanded physical

23. The findings given earlier that concentration is positively associated with sales growth and capital intensity and negatively associated with asset growth are consistent with this reasoning. In this analysis, capital intensity becomes a performance as well as a structural variable.

24. George J. Stigler, *Capital and Rates of Return in Manufacturing Industries* (Princeton, N.J.: Princeton University Press, 1963), p. 70.

25. The growth variables are computed by taking the absolute growth in sales (or assets) from 1960 to 1968 and dividing this by the 1960 values.

capacity in the late 1950s in anticipation of demand in the 1960s, one would then find not only "excess" capacity in 1960 but a slower-than-average asset-growth rate in the 1960s.[26]

Disequilibrium

A potentially important theory relating growth and profitability to concentration rests with the "disequilibrium hypothesis" advanced by Brozen and extended by Wenders. Very simply, Brozen argues that large firms are large because in certain industries (concentrated) cost or scale advantages accrue to them which have not yet accrued to the smaller firms. To determine an industry's average return from only these large firms produces an artificial correlation between rates of return and concentration. Brozen argues that the opposite influence occurs in the competitive industries, where the larger firms, while not possessing any similar advantage over their rivals (otherwise they too would be concentrated) are, in fact, at a disadvantage because the smaller (newer) firms can more readily adopt new technology. Hence, in disequilibrium, the use of the larger firms overstates an industry's average return for concentrated industries and understates the returns for unconcentrated industries. While this hypothesis may account for a collinearity between profits and concentration in times of disequilibrium, it fails to explain why disequilibrium is "always" observed.[27] In other words, larger firms' becoming large in concentrated industries and smaller in unconcentrated industries (by disinvestment) cannot continue indefinitely. How and when is equilibrium reached?

Growth and disequilibrium. Part of the difficulty with Brozen's argument rests with his almost exclusive reliance on supply-induced disequilibrium. Wenders adds demand-induced disequilibrium to balance the analysis. Unfortunately, however, beyond the recognition that "disequilibrium may occur when investment flows lag behind changes in demand," Wenders fails to extend the disequilibrium hypothesis into a testable theorem. Simple enough, demand-induced disequilibrium occurs when an industry's investment (asset expansion) is less than its growth in market demand, causing prices and profits to rise. On the other hand,

---

26. Wenders did find that for the 1950s concentrated industries grew at an annual rate of 14 percent compared to an 11 percent rate for unconcentrated industries (i.e., four-firm ratios less than 70 percent). ("Profits and Antitrust Policy, . . ." p. 253.)

27. Because the positive collinearity seems to be consistently observed over different time periods, either this hypothesis is only a partial explanation of the correlation or concentrated industries are always in disequilibrium.

when faced with declining demand, an industry's disinvestment would lag. Accordingly Wenders concludes: "The upshot of this kind of disequilibrium should be a positive correlation between profits and growth."[28] The shortcoming in this hypothesis is a failure to define explicitly the variables which are hypothesized to be related, in this instance whether "growth" is asset growth (investment flows) or sales growth (demand changes). Wenders takes asset growth and determines the interrelation between growth, profits, and concentrations.[29] It is my opinion that to use either asset growth or sales growth alone is an inadequate test of the hypothesis. Rather it seems to be the *relation* between asset growth and sales growth that lies at the core of this argument.

The restatement of the growth theorem of the disequilibrium hypothesis might be as follows: If the rate of sales growth is greater than the rate of asset growth, disequilibrium leads to above-normal profitability; if the sales-growth rate is less than the asset-growth rate (demand falls faster than disinvestment), disequilibrium leads to below-normal profitability. Equilibrium is thus achieved when asset- and sales-growth rates are equal.[30] The test of this hypothesis would then entail the use of both sales and asset growth, recognizing that neither alone is adequate. It is also noted that equilibrium is defined in a dynamic sense wherein neither sales nor asset changes must be zero. The test of the disequilibrium hypothesis comes from an analysis of these growth rates and concentration.

According to this definition of equilibrium, 1960–68 may be a time of slight disequilibrium, in general, for the 736 firms studied. Average sales growth is 1.94 and average asset growth is 2.04.[31]

Before we proceed any further, it must be pointed out that this hypothesis greatly simplifies a rather complex supply-demand analysis. For example, to assume that increases in assets are tantamount to increases in capacity must be tempered by the likelihood that some asset expansion is cost-reducing and not capacity-creating. In other words, the test of this hypothesis in part confounds the two sources of disequilibrium—cost, or technological, disequilibrium and demand-induced disequilibrium. One might therefore simply observe that during the 1960s much of the investment boom cannot be explained as capacity expansion

28. Wenders, "Profits and Antitrust Policy, . . ." p. 252.
29. This is accomplished by a set of three bivariate regressions, relating profits to growth, growth to concentration, and finally profits to concentration.
30. Sales-growth and asset-growth variables are calculated such that should they be equal there would be no tendency for a change in the asset-to-sales ratio (the measure of capital intensity) for the firm.
31. Growth is measured as the ratio of the difference between 1968 and 1960 sales (assets) to 1960 sales (assets).

alone. Indeed, it is argued that much investment was labor saving (because of rapidly rising wage rates and labor shortages) and not adding to capacity. This would explain why assets grew more rapidly than sales. In fact, the amount of cost-reducing investment is probably greatly understated by the overall comparison of asset growth to sales growth. As argued earlier, 1960 was a year of general recession and, with much unutilized capacity in that year, asset growth would not need to match sales growth for the upturn.[32]

In view of these and other rather significant difficulties with using asset growth and sales growth as proxies for changes in capacity and demand, one might conclude that the 736 firms were in equilibrium (as defined here) for the 1960–68 time period. Equilibrium, in general, however, does not preclude conditions of disequilibrium among certain industry groups. Specifically, Brozen's disequilibrium hypothesis assumes a systematic association between disequilibrium and concentration.

Disequilibrium and concentration. Any association between disequilibrium and concentration can be directly observed by comparing asset- and sales-growth rate means by the six concentration categories (Table 17, Chapter 3). Generally, asset growth rates fall rapidly with increases in concentration, leaving the mean growth rate in the highest concentration category roughly one-half of the mean rate in the lowest concentration category. However, sales-growth rates are not observed to decrease with increases in concentration. In the lower concentration categories, asset-growth rates are greater than sales-growth rates. With the fall in asset-growth rates by concentration categories, the difference between asset- and sales-growth rates decreases until asset-growth rates become less than sales-growth rates in the highest concentration categories. Thus disequilibrium may be, indeed, systematically associated with concentration during this time period. Furthermore, the association is such that disequilibrium would lead to above-their-normal[33] returns in concentrated industries and below-norm returns in unconcentrated industries.

Market-share optimism and concentration. Generally, when concentration reaches the 60–100 range, asset growth is either more nearly in line with sales growth or it is less than sales growth. What may be

---

32. For example, manufacturing capacity utilization was 80.1 percent in 1960 and increased to 87.7 percent in 1968.

33. It is only proper to state that, for example, if investment lags behind demand increases, then rates of return for those firms or industries are higher than they might otherwise be for these same firms (above-their-norm). One cannot judge directly whether it is for this reason, and for this reason alone, that these above-their-norm rates of return result in above-all-firm-average rates of return.

occurring is a behavioral phenomenon often attributed to oligopolistic market structures. When rivals are few, interdependence of action is easily recognizable. This interdependence is most frequently cited as influencing price-output decisions. Interdependence may, however, influence investment and long-run supply decisions also. For example, if there were four firms which supplied the major portion of an industry's output, and each firm forecast a one-million unit increase in *industry* demand, no one firm would be so naive (or optimistic) as to increase its capacity by the one million units. Collusion or no collusion in concentrated industries, it would be as unlikely as it would be inefficient to find the combined capacity expansion to be considerably greater than the one million units. Such would probably not be the case, however, were there 30 or 40 firms.

The less the recognition of the interdependence of action (the more "competitive" the structure), the greater the likelihood of combined capacity expansion far in excess of that needed.[34] To be sure, lower prices, greater output (with less profit) would obtain along with firm failures. Whether this is an *undue* misallocation of society's scarce resources would probably be subject to debate.[35]

The operation of this very simple phenomenon is consistent with the general findings here. The point is that while rates of return in concentrated industries are, perhaps, as they should be, those in the competitive industries are lower than they should be, because of the inefficient nature of the investment decision process. If one were to cast these arguments into a simple hypothesis it might be: *As the number of firms in an industry increases, the "market-share optimism" of each firm increases—* where optimism is measured as the ratio of hoped-for market share to realized market share.

It should be noted that this rather systematic change in the relation

---

34. ". . . . in progressive industries, vigorous competitors will be basing their judgement on what they think (or what they are afraid) other leading firms are (or may be) going to do—not simply on what they have already done except insofar as a vigorous, progressive past is properly extrapolated to the future. One or a few firms 'hell-bent for progress' can so stack the cards in the competitive game that others must follow suit or lose out. . . ." (J. Lintner, "Effect of Corporate Taxation on Real Investment," *American Economic Review* 44 [May 1954]: 520–34.)

35. The debate should benefit, however, from a point made by Joseph Schumpeter that is as profound as it is simple. "A system—any system, economic or other— that at *every* given point in time fully utilizes its possibilities to the best advantage may yet in the long run be inferior to a system that does so at *no* given point of time, because the latter's failure to do so may be a condition for the level or speed of long run performance." (*Capitalism, Socialism, and Democracy* [3d ed.; New York: Harper & Brothers, 1950], p. 83.)

between sales-growth and asset-growth rates by concentration categories is not a simple tautological result of the previously observed association between increases in capital intensity (ratios of assets to sales) and increases in concentration. For a given percentage increase in demand (sales), an identical percentage increase in assets is required to maintain a constant asset-output ratio (A/Q).

In summary, the disequilibrium hypothesis states that rates of return are above normal when sales-growth rates exceed asset-growth rates and below normal when asset-growth rates exceed sales-growth rates. Based on this hypothesis, the general conclusion is that disequilibrium, found in both concentrated and unconcentrated industries, is such that the observed rates of return in concentrated industries are above their norm and the returns in competitive industries are below their norm. However, such a simple formulation of the hypothesis seems inadequate in and of itself. Rather it seems necessary to consider explicitly some theorems on the behavioral aspects of the causes of disequilibrium, e.g., with regard to the efficiency of the investment decision process.

Revenue maximization

Three possible explanations for the observed relations between profitability, concentration, and rates of growth have been presented. This section offers but one more—revenue maximization in oligopolistic industries. Baumol advances the hypothesis that "sales volume ranks ahead of profits as the main object of the oligopolist's concern . . .";[36] more specifically, that "the typical oligopolist's objectives can be usefully characterized . . . as sales maximization subject to a minimum profit constraint."[37]

Oligopolistic industries, in general, are thought to earn above-average rates of return. If one assumes that, generally, these profitability levels are above this "minimum profit constraint,"[38] then the cost of greater sales growth[39] in oligopolistic industries ought to be reduced profitability. It is argued in this section that the patterns of profitability, growth, and concentration discussed in the preceding sections may, in part, be caused by this type of effect.

36. William J. Baumol, *Business Behavior, Value and Growth,* (rev. ed.; New York: Harcourt, Brace and World, 1967), p. 47.
37. *Ibid.,* p. 49.
38. A condition more likely to be found over a long expansionary period (1960–68) than during a recession.
39. Baumol formulated a static model for the levels of sales as well as a dynamic model for the growth of sales.

Two rather straightforward approaches are taken in the test of the revenue maximization hypothesis in oligopolistic industries. First, it is observed (Table 19, Chapter 3), that as concentration increases, the importance of asset growth to profitability decreases. In fact, the beta coefficients for asset growth in the highest concentration categories are either very small or negative. The negative coefficient for Census Category VI would result if these firms in highly concentrated industries, on the average, grew at a rate greater than the profit-maximizing rate[40] to achieve greater sales growth. Was "above-normal" sales growth achieved? The use of only asset growth merely indicates that assets grew too rapidly (on the average). To determine whether sales grew too rapidly, both sales and asset growth are studied.

The second piece of evidence supporting Baumol's revenue maximization hypothesis is obtained by combining the results of several sets of regressions on concentration, growth rates, and profitability. First, recall that, when profitability is regressed against concentration, capital intensity, and both growth rates, asset growth is positively associated with profitability while sales growth is negatively associated with profitability. That sales growth is achieved with losses in profitability is consistent with sales-maximizing behavior. These results are for all firms, however—competitive as well as oligopolistic.[41] Yet when concentration is regressed against sales growth, asset growth, and the other basic variables, it is found (results are given on pages 124 and 125 of this chapter) that for firms of similar size and capital intensity, the higher their concentration, the higher their sales growth (and the lower the asset growth). Although disequilibrium could be the cause, so could sales-maximizing behavior. To the extent that oligopolists are revenue maximizers—a hypothesis consistent with the findings in this study—this behavior would, in part, explain why some have observed the correlation between concentration and profitability to be stronger in recessions than in expansion. In upturns, the oligopolist's main objective is sales (having most likely met its minimum-profit constraint) while in the downturn profits become the main concern with profits approaching or falling below the constraint).

---

40. Baumol argues that there is "an optimal (profit-maximizing) rate of growth for the firm. . . ." Baumol, *Business Behavior, Value and Growth*, p. 89. See pages 86–89 for Baumol's development of this argument.

41. Because it is not a purpose of this study to test the sales maximization hypothesis, it should not be inferred that the methodology used here is designed for such purposes. For example, the methodology suggested here would be to regress profitability against both growth measures within each of the six concentration categories with the use of dummy variables.

Summary

Any or all of these lines of reasoning may be valid. The methodological tools used in this analysis are intended for other purposes and are, therefore, not sufficiently refined for these purposes. This study of the relations between growth, concentration, and profitability has as its *primary* object, however, the distortions in observed measures of profitability arising from the universal use of historical-cost accounting techniques.

Current-Cost Rates of Return

Because the distortions from using historical-cost accounting techniques are in large part a function of the age of a firm's assets, and because growth is hypothesized to be related to concentration, the following is hypothesized: **The adjustment to current-cost rates of return affects concentrated industries' rates of return more than it affects unconcentrated industries' rates of return** (Hypothesis XV). Though this hypothesis is supported by the evidence (Tables 7 and 8, Chapter 2), it is concluded that the systematic relation between concentration and the discrepancies between current-cost and historical-cost rates of return would not, by itself, account for the commonly determined relationship between concentration and observed profitability.

Independent Influence of Concentration on Profitability

While each of the previous hypotheses is significant in and of itself, the ultimate purpose of this study is to determine whether the profitability measures, concentration, and the basic variables are interrelated in such a fashion that the commonly observed relation between concentration and profitability may be one of multicollinearity rather than one of direct cause and effect. Through the test of these individual hypotheses, evidence is brought to bear on one final hypothesis.

Thus this study culminates with the fundamental hypothesis that **after the independent influences of size, capital intensity, growth, risk, and the distortions arising from historical-cost accounting are accounted for, firms in concentrated industries are found to earn above-average long-run rates of return** (Hypothesis XVI).

Weighing the accumulated evidence from the many tests of the several hypotheses in this study, I must conclude that there is considerable doubt as to the validity of the fundamental hypothesis.

First, a latent collinearity between (absolute) size, concentration, and profitability alone may account for much of the frequently observed relation between concentration and profitability.

Second, although capital intensity is positively correlated with concentration and negatively correlated with profitability, there is some evidence that capital intensity—a proxy for vertical integration and absolute capital requirements—is an advantage, leading to greater profitability, in the more concentrated industries.

Third, although (generally) asset growth is negatively correlated with concentration and positively correlated with profitability, and although sales growth is positively correlated with concentration and negatively correlated with profitability, there is evidence that there is yet a latent relationship between asset- and sales-growth rates, concentration, and profitability, which may result in the observed correlation between concentration and profitability. This latent relationship is obtained through the analysis of the disequilibrium hypothesis.

Fourth, temporal variability of returns are greater in concentrated industries. Therefore, to the extent that business managers are averse to risk, observed rates of return in concentrated industries are greater than the risk-comparable rates of return. On the other hand, that there is greater variability of returns in certain asset employments may be a reason for the existence of only a few firms in some industries—industrial concentration.

Finally, there is evidence that some correlation between concentration and observed measures of profitability may be attributed to a systematic relation between concentration and discrepancies between historical- and current-cost rates of returns.

Conclusion

The purpose of this study, as stated in its first pages, has been to seek an answer to one fundamental question: "Is the common empirical finding (supported by theoretical expectations) that monopoly power is associated with above-average rates of return, the result of direct cause and effect or can it be explained by the multicollinearity among several phenomena?" To attempt an answer, the study seeks to determine whether and how the multicollinearity among the several phenomena might affect the relation between concentration and profitability. It seems to me at least that this attempt has raised more questions than it has answered and opened more doors than it has closed. Specifically, the evidence of this study does not support the judgment stated by President Johnson's Task Force on Antitrust:

> It is the persistence of high profits over extended time periods . . . that suggests artificial restraints on output and the absence of fully effective competition. The correlation of evidence of this kind with the existence of very high levels of concentration appears to be significant.[42]

Ironically, it is indeed "the correlation of evidence," or rather correlation between various elements of market structure and performance, which precludes such judgment here.

42. U.S., Congress, Senate, White House Task Force on Antitrust Policy, Phil C. Neal, Chairman, "Task Force Report on Antitrust Policy," *Congressional Record,* 27 May 1969, p. S5644.

5

RECOMMENDATIONS FOR PUBLIC POLICY

Though it has been found that, generally, firms in concentrated industries earn above-average returns, as a basis for formulating antitrust policy this conclusion must be regarded as somewhat sterile. Public policy must be predicated in causes and their effects. Although it was the objective of this study to determine the independent effect of concentration on rates of return, statistical analysis is seriously deficient for this purpose. Multicollinearity among the phenomena, misspecification, imperfect data, and inadequate theory limit the ability to form conclusive recommendations. Nevertheless, analysis does provide some illumination on a few key issues in public policy.

Allocative Efficiency—Product Markets vs. Capital Markets

The relations between firm size, concentration, and profitability raise a most important question in public policy: Is it bigness *and/or* monopoly power that is associated with (leads to) high rates of returns? Although the most concentrated industries (those with ratios of 70 percent and more) earn the highest returns, they are also composed of the largest firms—about 10 times the average size of firms in the lowest concentration categories. After finding that size has a "greater apparent effect . . . on profit rates than does concentration," Hall and Weiss recommend action more "toward an attack on capital market imperfections than to anti-trust programs oriented toward divestiture, dissolution, and merger."[1] That conclusion and recommendation are strongly corroborated in this study. Probably the most damaging piece of evidence that absolute size is the more important structural determinant of high returns is obtained from

1. Marshall Hall and Leonard Weiss, "Firm Size and Profitability," *Review of Economics and Statistics* 49 (Aug. 1967): 330.

regressing concentration against size-adjusted rates of return and un-adjusted industry rates of return.

Clearly, if our concern is with "excess" returns (a subject to be discussed shortly), then the *cause* of that concern appears to rest largely with imperfect capital markets[2] and not imperfect production-selling markets. Therefore the evidence in this study strongly suggests that the recommendations of the Neal Report and the evidential basis of Senator Hart's "Deconcentration Act" are improper. Though monopoly power *may* lead to restricted output and artificially high prices, as indicated by above-average rate-of-return measures, the misallocative effects are probably not nearly so critical as those which result from imperfect competition in the money capital markets.

Conduct and the Structure-Performance Relationship

No doubt some above-average returns are earned both because firms are large and because they possess market power. The foregoing paragraphs contain seeds of a line of analysis which, although empirically unmanageable, is perhaps far more relevant than the approach followed here. It has been argued that large firms, with ease of entry to money and to production-selling markets, would earn above-average returns. Is it necessarily the case that these "efficiencies" would or could *not* be passed along to the consumer at lower prices, thereby eliminating any "excess" profits?

When the consumer's welfare is pitted against the stockholders' welfare few Americans have difficulty in assessing the ultimate determination. However, let us suppose that managers with some unorthodox sense of morality are indeed rewarded (not by direct remuneration, and indeed probably not by any remuneration) by maximizing consumer welfare, once suppliers of money capital are adequately paid for their risks. Would we then expect "average" or nearer average returns? Probably

---

2. There are, it seems, two quite separate and extremely important issues within the "imperfect capital market" hypothesis. First, there are the imperfections in the allocations of money capital, and second there are imperfections in the factor market. The first occurs when large firms can more easily obtain larger sums of money capital at lower costs. The second occurs when larger firms (having easier access to the money capital markets) can choose among the same production alternatives as the small firms, plus those unobtainable by the small firms. Because large firms have all the options of small firms in addition to others, it follows that larger firms earn higher returns on the assets employed, irrespective of the costs of capital. Hall and Weiss confound both sources of capital market inefficiencies by using returns on stockholders' equity without considering the effects of differences in the costs of borrowed capital on those rates of return.

not. Were larger firms to reduce their prices or increase their quality while maintaining prices, marginal (smaller) producers would be eliminated eventually. Lower returns among the larger firms would accompany increases in concentration in one, some, or all the product markets the larger firms operate in, and the likelihood (risk) of antitrust action would increase. Historically, divestiture and dissolution result more frequently from a concern for product market power or imperfections in product markets than from a concern for sheer size and "bigness" or imperfections in money capital markets. It is unlikely, therefore, that management of large firms would want to jeopardize their relatively safe position and pass on substantially lower prices obtainable from capital-market scale advantages.

On the other hand, leading firms in concentrated industries which are the largest and the most profitable (assuming production scale economies) might likewise find it disadvantageous to reduce prices and returns to a level which is lower yet satisfactory from the stockholders' point of view. For them, increases in already high market shares would bring them that much closer to unfavorable antitrust action. Any attempt to eliminate or reduce excess profits may be, in the longer run, detrimental to stockholders' interest, because it increases the likelihood of subsequent antitrust action.

There are, however, other alternatives open to the large and/or concentrated firm besides earning excess returns (such as maintaining the numbers of competitors) and reducing prices (such as reducing the number, or health, of competitors). Consciously or unconsciously, the profitable, large firms in concentrated industries may incur nonproductive costs—"X-inefficiency"[3]—or engage in suboptimal decisions, thereby reducing rates of return. Phenomena with these effects may take the form of revenue maximization, managerial emoluments, unnecessary expenditures for advertising, research, and development, for political contributions, antitrust lawyers, or lobbying, or the devotion of resources to the exercise of socially responsive activities not in the firm's narrowly defined interest. Suboptimal decisions might take the form of the company's hiring and maintaining additional work force and/or paying its work force more,[4] trading less risk for lower returns,[5] failing to expand and/or

3. H. Leibenstein, "Allocative Efficiency vs. 'X-Efficiency'," *American Economic Review* 56 (June 1966).

4. Leonard Weiss, "Concentration and Labor Earnings," *American Economic Review* 56 (Mar. 1966): 96–117.

5. Hall and Weiss in "Firm Size and Profitability" and Samuel H. Baker in "Risk, Leverage and Profitability: An Industry Analysis," *Review of Economics and*

innovate with new processes, technology, or improved product quality, and generally failing to employ the combination of input factors which costs least.

In addition to the matrix of more traditional goals of, or values and motives for, business behavior, policy makers ought to study companies' avoidance of potentially detrimental antitrust action by maintaining the number of competitors and clothing so-called excess profits in managerial emoluments or "X-inefficiency." It is hard to imagine that business executives charged with protecting the wealth of an enterprise would ignore the potential effects of future antitrust action in the development of their overall business strategy. Surely they do not. More weight should be given to Lanzillotti's conclusion that oligopolies establish target rates of return, acting more like public utilities than unfettered profit-maximizing monopolists.[6] In short, rather than stating the industrial organization's descriptive paradigm as structure-conduct-performance, the foregoing proposition in essence suggests that it is the simplified structure-performance view embodied in antitrust policy that may determine the conduct in some markets. In weighing antitrust legislation Congress must seek a balance between potential benefits to consumers and potential encouragement of inefficiency.[7]

Deconcentration and the Consumer

It must not be forgotten that the primary goal of antitrust policy must be consumer welfare, though concern for labor and business managers and owners should not be ignored. If, as indicated in this study and others before it, concentrated industries do earn above-average returns, does it necessarily follow that consumers benefit from dissolution? Assume that there are economies of firm size (as opposed to production or plant-

---

Statistics 55 (Nov. 1973): 503–7, argue this point. In addition, it is observed that large firms (in concentrated industries) have more risk-reducing options to choose from than do smaller firms. The major ones would be product and geographic diversification and vertical integration.

6. Robert F. Lanzillotti, "Pricing Objectives in Large Companies," *American Economic Review* 48 (Dec. 1958): 921–40. Rather than describing oligopoly pricing behavior as administered prices, Lanzillotti argues for an "administered profit" thesis.

7. In March 1973, Senator Hart introduced the "Industrial Reorganization Act." One of its provisions reads: "There shall be a rebuttable presumption that monopoly power is possessed . . . by any corporation if the average rate of return . . . is in excess of 15 per centum. . . ." (*Congressional Record—Senate*, S-4362, 12 Mar. 1973.) Obviously, should this provision be passed, firms would be encouraged either to reduce prices *or* to increase costs. Large firms and/or firms in concentrated industries would be especially encouraged to increase costs.

scale economies) which intraindustry analysis does not necessarily reveal.[8]
If the goal is to eliminate so-called excess returns, dissolution of large
firms in concentrated industries may accomplish that end. On the other
hand, if, in the consumer's interest, the goal is to reduce prices and
increase output, the result of dissolution is far more difficult to assess.
The elimination of excess returns through dissolution does not necessarily
mean lower prices if the resulting size of firms is too small to operate
efficiently, even though the resulting numbers of firms is large enough to
ensure competitive behavior—i.e., driving prices close to average costs.[9]

In determining the "dead-weight" monopoly loss it seems it is often
tacitly assumed that the "loss" is a measure of the aggregate net benefits
to be obtained by eliminating monopoly power. This is simply not the
case.

Figure 3 shows the typical simplified diagram of dead-weight monopoly

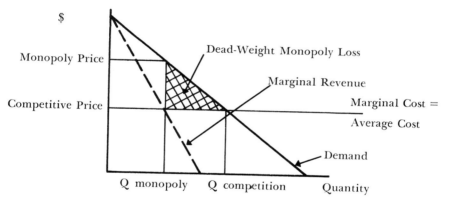

Fig. 3. Typical diagram of dead-weight monopoly loss.

8. Because only the larger firms in each industry are studied here, the failure to find
a positive intraindustry size-profitability relation in some industries should not be
taken as final evidence that no relation exists.
9. The following quotation illustrates a common trap concealed in this point:
Markets with more than rather than fewer firms, particularly if parallel reduc-
tions in market shares are implied, will tend to reduce the exercise of market
power, i.e., the extent to which prices can be advantageously elevated relative to
costs. For example, if a dozen automobile firms of similar size were to supercede
the present structure, there is good reason to believe that the average ratio of
price to cost would be substantially reduced.
(U.S., Congress, Senate, Select Committee on Small Business, *Planning, Regulation,
and Competition: Automobile Industry—1968*, Hearings, before Subcommittee of
the Select Committee on Small Business, 90th Cong., 2d sess., 1968 [Washington,
D.C.: Government Printing Office, 1968], p. 915.)

loss. Obviously, the critical assumption in the diagram is that the monopoly (or oligopoly) has no scale advantage and that, therefore, the average cost for the monopoly is the same that would obtain for enough firms to drive price to their average cost.

In summary, much more research needs to be conducted if the concern to be implemented is with lowering prices, increasing output, quality, innovation, and with other factors determining consumer welfare, rather than with reducing above-average or excessive returns.

Excess Profits

Throughout this study and in similar studies there seems to be a presumption that above-average returns are excessive rather than that below-average returns are deficient. This study has established no basis upon which to determine whether any or all returns are deficient or excessive. In theory, it is easy to establish the concept of normal profits as those just sufficient to compensate the suppliers of capital. This necessarily involves the adjustment for differences in risk as well as in opportunity costs of alternative investments, which in a dynamic economy continually change. Accordingly, while stockholders, especially stockholders of large and publicly held firms, can and do frequently alter their portfolios of financial investments, firms cannot and do not easily alter their commitments in real investments to reflect changing opportunity costs. With government bills yielding 9 percent one would otherwise expect many of the very largest firms with lower returns to alter their portfolios. Indeed it is true that nominal yields in bonds reflect the changing real cost of capital plus changing expectations of inflation. In the assessment of excess or deficient returns the relative ability or inability of firms to alter their returns in similar fashion must be considered. It cannot be presumed that observed nominal rates of return for competitive manufacturing industries during a given time period reflect the movement in normal profits. Disequilibrium or departures from longer-run firm or industry return levels lower or raise a given panel's average returns. For example, above-average returns may be indicated for firms in concentrated industries because returns in unconcentrated industries

---

the Select Committee on Small Business, 90th Cong., 2d sess., 1968 [Washington, D.C.: Government Printing Office, 1968], p. 915.)

On the basis of the hypothetical situation depicted here, this statement and its prediction are valid. However, that prices would be lower to consumers does not follow from the proposition that the "average ratio of prices to costs would be substantially reduced." Antitrust policy should be concerned with prices to consumers rather than with profits to producers.

reflect the inefficiencies of uncoordinated responses to changes in demand and supply conditions. Should returns in concentrated industries be judged excessive if, after careful analysis, returns in unconcentrated industries are judged to be deficient—i.e., below that rate necessary to maintain the capital in those industries?

The assessment of so-called normal profits (and the subsequent determination of excess and deficient returns) is of critical importance in the development and execution of antitrust policy. This study has conspicuously avoided all such considerations, and any inference that above-average profits are excessive, or any public policy based on such inferences, must be regarded as without sufficient foundation within the context of the study. Moreover, the lesser question of whether concentrated industries earn above-average returns remains largely unanswered by the accumulated research.

A Final Admonition

Capitalism and the workings of its many markets constitute a complex process, in Schumpeter's words, a "process of Creative Destruction."

> Since we are dealing with a process whose every element takes considerable time in revealing its true features and ultimate effects, there is no point in appraising the performance of that process *ex visu* of a given point of time; we must judge its performance over time, as it unfolds through decades or centuries.[10]

A period of nine years, from 1960 to 1968, is but a small slice of time. Its eventual individual relevance must derive from its place in history.

---

10. Joseph A. Schumpeter, *Capitalism, Socialism, and Democracy* (3d ed; New York: Harper and Brothers, 1950), p. 83.

APPENDIXES

APPENDIX A

CONCENTRATION RATIOS

This study uses two alternative sets of four-firm concentration ratios to measure market power. Both sets of ratios and the procedures used to compute them are presented in this appendix.

The first set of ratios adjusts the 1963 Bureau of Census ratios to reflect economically meaningful products selling in comparable geographic markets.[1] The procedures used in these adjustments follow those of Hall and Weiss.[2] The other set of ratios is constructed from William G. Shepherd's subjective estimates of concentration ratios for 1966 four-digit industries.[3] Both sets of concentration data are used to construct concentration ratios for those industries included in this study.

Initially, 768 firms are classified into 132 three-, and four- and five-digit SIC industries. These 132 industry definitions are not necessarily mutually exclusive. The purpose of this procedure is to approximate the concentration ratio for each firm for use in regressions, with firms as units of observation. These 768 firms are placed into the narrowest reasonable industry definition consistent with their product mix.[4] For example, Gerber Products can be reasonably placed in the five-digit industry of 20321 Baby Foods. Other firms operating in the three-digit industry 203 Canned and Frozen Foods, however, generally spread their sales among many of the four- and five-digit products within 203, and, therefore, the

---

1. U.S., Congress, Senate, Committee on the Judiciary, Subcommittee on Antitrust and Monopoly, *Concentration Ratios in Manufacturing Industry, 1963,* Parts I and II (Washington, D.C.: Government Printing Office, 1966 and 1967).

2. Marshall Hall and Leonard Weiss, "Firm Size and Profitability," *Review of Economics and Statistics* 49 (1967). Their procedures are discussed in detail in an appendix supplied upon request to the *Review,* "Appendix to Firm Size and Profitability," n.d. (Mimeographed.)

3. William G. Shepherd, *Market Power and Economic Welfare* (New York: Random House, 1970), Appendix Table 8, pp. 263–67.

4. For a full explanation of the procedures for classifying firms into industries see Appendix B.

narrowest reasonable classification is 203. In 28 cases, the concentration ratio in Table A.1 at the end of this appendix is used for a "one-firm industry" and in many cases a two- or three-firm "industry."

When industries are used as the unit of observation, 53 of the 132 concentration ratios are no longer appropriate. Some firms (industries) are dropped from the analysis because they belong to a one- or two-firm "industry" which cannot be pooled with other firms to make a reasonably homogeneous, more broadly defined industry of three or more firms. In industry analysis, industries with fewer than three firms are dropped. For this reason the number of firms falls from 768 in firm analysis to 736 in industry analysis. Table A.2 at the end of this appendix lists the 79 industries and the concentration ratios used in industry regression analysis along with the "industries" from Table A.1 which have been pooled to make these industries.

Index of Concentration—Bureau of Census Ratios

In many cases, the Census concentration ratios for firms classified in four- or five-digit industries need not be adjusted because they reasonably reflect economically meaningful products selling in a national market. In such cases, the four-firm concentration ratio is taken directly from Table 4 of *Concentration Ratios in Manufacturing Industry 1963*, Part I. Where firms could not be reasonably classified into a narrow four- or five-digit industry, the concentration ratio for the more broadly defined industry is a weighted average of four-digit product concentration ratios. If, however, the Census concentration ratio is not economically meaningful, these four-digit ratios are adjusted first, before these procedures are followed.

(*NA*) No adjustment case

Where there are no adjustments in the Census four-digit concentration ratios, the three-digit ratios are computed as:

$$(NA) \ \ CR_3 = \frac{\Sigma \ (PS_4 CR_4)}{\Sigma \ PS_4}$$

where:

CR_3 = three-digit concentration ratio
PS_4 = product shipments (in a few cases, another measure of firm activity) for the indicated four-digit product groups
CR_4 = concentration ratio for the indicated four-digit product groups.

(*N*) Over-aggregation of noncompeting products

Where Hall and Weiss indicate that the five-digit products within the Census four-digit product group are not strongly competing or where producers cannot, in the short run, shift production among these products (or if it is the writer's judgment that this is the case), a weighted average of five-digit concentration ratios is substituted into expression NA (No Adjustment Case). These adjusted four-digit ratios (denoted ACR_4) are computed in a fashion comparable to the three-digit ratio above.

$$ACR_4 = \frac{\sum (PS_5 CR_5)}{\sum PS_5}$$

and therefore:

$$ACR_3 = \frac{\sum (PS_4 ACR_4)}{\sum PS_4}.$$

(*U*) Under-aggregation of competing products

Where five-digit product classes in two different four-digit product groups are competing products and where the concentration ratio is combined in Table 4A of *Concentration Ratios in Manufacturing Industry 1963*, Part I, the four-digit concentration ratios are adjusted. Because Table 4A combines only five-digit ratios, the adjusted four-digit ratio is computed by averaging these five-digit ratios with the other five-digit ratios within the four-digit product group.

(*R*) Regional markets

Where firms sell primarily in regional markets according to Hall and Weiss or according to Table 25 of the *Concentration Ratios in Manufacturing Industries 1963*, Part II, a weighted average of the regional concentration ratios is substituted in expression NA.

$$ACR_4 = \frac{\sum (RPS_4 RCR_4)}{\sum RPS_4}$$

where:

RPS_4 = regional product shipments for the four-digit product group

RCR_4 = regional concentration ratios for the four-digit product group.

If data are not available for a region, it is excluded; or if data are combined for a group of regions, the combined data are treated as a single region.

(L) Local markets

Where firms sell primarily in local markets according to Hall and Weiss or to Table 26 of the above source, a weighted average of state concentration ratios is substituted in expression NA.

$$ACR_4 = \frac{\Sigma\,(SPS_4 SCR_4)}{\Sigma\,SPS_4}$$

where:

SPS_4 = state product shipments for the four-digit product group

SCR_4 = state concentration ratios for the four-digit product group.

If data are not available for a state, it is excluded from the calculation.

(P) Pooling

For several three-digit industry groups, one or more of the constituent four-digit product groups are excluded in the calculation of the three-digit concentration ratio in NA. Generally, it is my intention to develop concentration ratios that will be the most appropriate, given the products manufactured by firms in any particular industry. Therefore, when the firms classified in a three-digit industry group do not manufacture (among their major product lines) a particular four-digit product group, and if the inclusion of the product group in the calculation of the three-digit ratio would change the three-digit ratio substantially, the four-digit group is excluded. In Table A.1, listing the concentration ratios (with the appropriate adjustments indicated), a simple three-digit code—e.g., 201, 202, etc.—means that *all* the constituent four-digit product groups are used in the concentration ratio calculation. On the other hand, when a three-digit code ends in a zero (0), not to be confused with a SIC four-digit industry,[5] this industry excludes one or more four-digit product groups in the calculation of the ratio. In this case, only those four-digit product groups which are included are listed. In addition, the three-digit code ending in zero (0) is also used to indicate the pooling of three-digit

_____
5. The SIC system does not use ending zeros for four-digit product groups.

industries. As with the treatment of the four-digit industries, those industries which are pooled are listed in Table A.1.

In summary, many of the industries could be thought of as being somewhere between a three- and four-digit Census industry.

(S) Special treatment industries

Two industries receive special treatment—Sugar (206) and Floor Covering Mills (227). Again, the special treatment outlined below follows the treatment of Hall and Weiss for these two industries. In these two instances it is judged that there is close competition between the four-digit product groups. Therefore, the problem of under-aggregation existing at the four-digit level needs to be corrected in a manner similar to the problem at the five-digit level. Unfortunately, combined concentration ratios (as in Table 4A) are not available for this purpose. The following method is used to estimate a combined concentration ratio: Both a minimum and a maximum ratio are computed; the estimate is made by interpolation between these.

Minimum ratio. The calculation of the minimum ratio assumes that the four largest firms in the largest industry (subscript L) are all different from the four largest firms in the smallest industry (subscript S).

$$CCR(\text{Min}) = \frac{(CR_L)(PS_L)}{PS_L + PS_L} \quad \text{or} \quad \frac{(CR_S)(PS_S)}{PS_L + PS_S},$$

whichever is larger.

Maximum ratio. The calculation of the maximum ratio assumes that the four largest firms are the same in both industries.

$$CCR(\text{Max}) = \frac{(CR_L)(PS_L) + (CR_S)(PS_S)}{PS_L + PS_S}.$$

Estimate of adjusted concentration ratio. Interpollation between these two ratios is then made on the basis of outside knowledge of the number of leading firms the industries have in common.

Index of Concentration—Shepherd Ratios

The second set of concentration ratios used in this study are developed from William G. Shepherd's subjective estimates of 1966 four-firm, four-digit industries.[6] In commenting on these estimates Shepherd states:

6. Shepherd, *Market Power and Economic Welfare*, Appendix Table 8, pp. 263–67.

. . . The 1966 U.S. ratios were adjusted by the author where necessary to represent the "average" degree of concentration in relevant markets, allowing for spatial submarkets and divisions among noncompeting products as well as import competition. Some 225 of the 417 Census industries needed adjusting; in each case care was taken to be on the low side. Although other researchers might differ on details, they would probably reach the same general results.[7]

Tables A.1 and A.2 give the concentration ratios calculated from Shepherd estimates[8] as well as those from Census ratios. Many of Shepherd's ratios differ from those contained here because many of Shepherd's industries (four-digit SIC industries) are combined to be consistent with the industry definitions in this study. Because Shepherd's ratios are for only four-digit industries, whenever a five-digit ratio is needed, adjusted Census ratios are used.

7. *Ibid.,* pp. 107–8.

8. Shepherd's adjusted ratios are given as a range. The midpoint of each range is used here as the adjusted four-digit ratio.

TABLE A.1

CONCENTRATION RATIOS FOR 768 FIRMS IN 132 INDUSTRIES
(FOR FIRM REGRESSION ANALYSIS)

INDUSTRY	ADJUSTED CONCENTRATION RATIOS		CENSUS ADJUSTMENTS AND COMMENTS*
	CENSUS	SHEPHERD	
201 Meat products	27	37	2011 U and 2012U
202 Dairy products	42	59	2024L, 2026L
203 Canned and frozen foods	32	46	2032N, 2035N
20321 Baby foods	95	95	
204 Grain mill products	43	46	2041U and 2045U, 2042R
2041 Flour	45	45	U
2042 Prepared feeds	33	35	R
2044 Rice	46	45	
2046 Wet corn	65	67	
2051 Bread and other bakery products	41	50	L
2052 Biscuits, crackers, and pretzels	60	70	N
206 Sugar	42	42	S
207 Confectionary	50	59	2071R, 2072U
2071 Candy	38	45	R
2072 Chocolate and cocoa products	66	85	U
2073 Chewing gum	86	88	
2082 Beer	67	65	R
2085 Liquor	56	55	
2086 Soft drink bottlers	38	35	R
20873 Soft drink flavoring	89	89	
2092 Soybean mills	48	57	
2111 Cigarettes	80	81	
2121 Cigars	59	58	
2210 Broad woven fabric mills, except wool	33	43	P, 2211, 2221 (using Table 2)
2231 Broad woven fabric mills, wool	46	60	
2241 Narrow fabrics	15	23	
225 Knitting mills	19	30	
227 Floor covering mills	34	39	S2271 and 2272
228 Yarn and thread mills	26	33	
2298 Cordage and twine	30	38	
2310 Men's and boys' clothing	21	30	P, 2311, 232
2330 Women's, children's and infants' clothing	10	16	P, 233, 234, 236
251 Household furniture	11	28	
2610 Pulp, paper and board	39	46	P, 2611, 2621N, 2631N, 2661N
2640 Converted paper and paperboard products	39	50	P, 2641N, 2642, 2649N
265 Paperboard containers and boxes	28	39	
2711 Newspapers	57	90	L

Continued

* Adjustments and comments apply only to the adjusted Census ratios. For the adjustments for Shepherd's ratios, see William G. Shepherd, *Market Power and Economic Welfare* (New York: Random House, 1970), Appendix Table 8.

TABLE A.1—Continued

INDUSTRY	ADJUSTED CONCENTRATION RATIOS		CENSUS ADJUSTMENTS AND COMMENTS*
	CENSUS	SHEPHERD	
2721 Periodicals	40	60	N
2731 Books	39	35	N
2750 Printing	35	31	P, 2751L, 2752L, 2761R, 2771
2761 Manifold business forms	56	47	R
2771 Greeting cards	53	85	
281 Basic chemicals	50	67	2812N, 2818N, 2819N
2821 Plastics	45	60	U
2823 Cellulosic man-made fibers	79	90	
283 Drugs	43	86	2831N, 2833N, 2834N
2840 Soap and specialty cleaners	60	90	P, 2841, 2842N
2844 Perfumes, cosmetics, and other toilet preparations	48	60	N
2851 Paint	24	45	
28991 Salt	77	77	
2911 Petroleum refining	52	65	2911R
295 Paving mixtures, blocks, asphalt felts and coatings	34	50	2951R
3011 Tires	72	71	
3031 Reclaimed rubber	73	93	
3069 Fabricated rubber products	33	45	N
3141 Footwear	30	45	N
3211 Flat glass	87	96	3211U and 32313U
322 Glass products	65	82	3229N
3241 Cement	54	80	R
3250 Structural clay products	42	67	P, 3251R, 3253
3270 Concrete	35	56	P, 3271L, 3272L, 3273L, 3274
3275 Gypsum products	82	80	
329 Non-metallic mineral products	55	62	3291N, 3292N
3291 Abrasives	64	70	N
3293 Gaskets	26	33	
3296 Mineral wool	68	71	
331 Steel	52	78	3312U, 3313U, 3315U, 3316U, 3317 (involves averaging of 5-digit products)
332 Iron and steel foundries	39	43	3321R
3331 Primary copper	69	80	3331U and 33412U
3334 Primary aluminum	77	95	3334U and 3341U and 3352U
335 Nonferrous rolling and drawing	56	68	Many of the 5-digit products in the 4-digit product groups are competing; therefore, 5-digit product classes are averaged to obtain the 3-digit ratio.
3411 Metal cans	73	90	
34212 Razor blades and razors, except electric	95	95	

Continued

* Adjustments and comments apply only to the adjusted Census ratios. For the adjustments for Shepherd's ratios, see William G. Shepherd, *Market Power and Economic Welfare* (New York: Random House, 1970), Appendix Table 8.

TABLE A.1—Continued

INDUSTRY	ADJUSTED CONCENTRATION RATIOS		CENSUS ADJUSTMENTS AND COMMENTS*
	CENSUS	SHEPHERD	
3429 Hardware	48	65	N
343 Heating and plumbing fixtures	32	52	3433N
344 Fabricated structural metal products	20	48	3443N
345 Screw machine products	16	28	3451R
3461 Metal stamping	27	55	N
349 Miscellaneous fabricated metal products	28	46	3494N
3492 Safes and vaults	87	95	
351 Engines and turbines	69	79	3519N
3522 Farm machinery	53	70	N
353 Construction, mining and materials handling machinery	46	61	3531N
3531 Construction machinery	56	70	N
3533 Oil field machinery	27	50	
3534 Elevators	55	63	
3536 Hoists, cranes, and monorail systems	27	44	
3540 Metalworking machinery	35	53	P, 3541N, 3542N, 3545, 3548N
355 Special industrial machinery	32	42	3551N, 3559N
356 General industrial machinery	31	48	3561N
3562 Ball and roller bearings	57	70	
3564 Blowers, exhaust, and fans	20	35	
3567 Industrial process furnaces and ovens	34	35	
357 Office and computing machines	65	85	3571N
3581 Automatic merchandising machines	59	61	
3585 Refrigeration machinery	36	55	
3610 Basic electrical equipment	50	61	P, 361 and 362, 3611N, 3629N
363 Household appliances	60	69	3634N, 3639N
3631 Household cooking equipment	45	60	
3633 Household laundry equipment	71	79	
3634 Electric housewares and fans	47	70	N
3635 Vacuum cleaners	64	78	
3536 Sewing machines	82	80	
364 Electric wiring and lighting equipment	33	46	

Continued

* Adjustments and comments apply only to the adjusted Census ratios. For the adjustments for Shepherd's ratios, see William G. Shepherd, *Market Power and Economic Welfare* (New York: Random House, 1970), Appendix Table 8.

TABLE A.1—Continued

Industry	Adjusted Concentration Ratios		Census Adjustments and Comments*
	Census	Shepherd	
3651 Radio and television receiving sets	47	60	N
3652 Phonograph records and tapes	68	71	
366 Communication equipment	51	59	3662N
367 Electronic components and accessories	35	53	3679N
3690 Batteries	66	68	P, 3691, 3692
3694 Electrical equipment for internal combustion engines	76	85	N
3711 Passenger cars	99	94	use 37171
3713 Trucks	81	35	use 37172
3714 Motor vehicle parts and accessories	60	60	use 3714 from Table 5 of *Concentration Ratios in Manufacturing*, Part 1, (1967) Special Report of 1967 Census of Manufacturers
3720 Aircraft engines, parts, and auxiliary equipment	48	75	P, 3722N, 3723, 3729N
3721 Aircraft	58	90	
37212 Complete personal aircraft	85	85	
3731 Ship-building and repairing	48	65	
3732 Boat-building and repairing	21	45	
3742 Railroad and street cars	52	60	
3751 Bicycles, motorcycles	47	50	
3791 Trailer homes	23	21	
3811 Engineering, laboratory, and research equipment	41	45	N
382 Mechanical measuring instruments	48	56	3821N
3831 Optical instruments and lenses	37	56	
384 Medical instruments and supplies	43	59	3842N
3861 Photographic equipment	62	80	
38612 Reproduction equipment	82	82	
3871 Watches	42	45	
3911 Jewelry	17	35	
3931 Musical instruments	51	60	N
3940 Games, toys, and dolls	15	26	P, 3941, 3942
3950 Pencils, pens, and artist's supplies	44	43	P, 3951, 3952N

* Adjustments and comments apply only to the adjusted Census ratios. For the adjustments for Shepherd's ratios, see William G. Shepherd, *Market Power and Economic Welfare* (New York: Random House, 1970), Appendix Table 8.

TABLE A.2

CONCENTRATION RATIOS FOR 736 FIRMS IN 79 INDUSTRIES
(FOR INDUSTRY REGRESSION ANALYSIS)

INDUSTRY		POOLED INDUSTRIES (FROM TABLE A.1)		ADJUSTED CONCENTRATION RATIOS	
INDUSTRY	NUMBER OF FIRMS	INDUSTRY	NUMBER OF FIRMS	CENSUS	SHEPHERD
201	8			27	37
202	6			42	59
203	12	203	11	32	43
		20321	1		
204	14	204	5	43	46
		2041	1		
		2042	4		
		2044	1		
		2046	3		
205	8	2051	5	45	55
		2052	3		
206	9			42	42
207	5	2071	3	50	59
		2072	1		
		2073	1		
2082	10			67	65
2085	9			56	55
20873	4			89	89
2100	7	2111	4	77	77
		2121	3		
2210	13			33	43
2231	5			46	60
228	4			26	33
2310	8			21	30
2330	10			10	16
251	4			11	28
2610	16			39	46
2640	3			39	50
265	9			28	39
2711	3			57	90
2721	5			40	60
2731	7			39	35
2750	13	2750	9	35	31
		2761	2		
		2771	2		
281	26			50	67
282	5	2821	3	53	67

Continued

TABLE A.2—Continued

INDUSTRY		POOLED INDUSTRIES (FROM TABLE A.1)		ADJUSTED CONCENTRATION RATIOS	
INDUSTRY	NUMBER OF FIRMS	INDUSTRY	NUMBER OF FIRMS	CENSUS	SHEPHERD
		2823	2		
283	18			43	86
2840	6			60	90
2844	10			48	60
2851	7			24	45
2911	23			52	65
3011	9			72	71
3069	7			33	45
3141	6			30	45
321	9	3211	2	70	86
		322	7		
3241	12			54	80
3250	6			42	67
3270	4			35	56
329	6	329	3	55	62
		3291	1		
		3293	1		
		3296	1		
331	33			52	78
332	5			39	43
3331	5			69	80
3334	5			77	95
335	10			56	68
3411	4			73	90
3429	6			48	65
344	6			20	48
345	6			16	28
349	6			28	46
351	7			69	79
3522	5			53	70
353	18	353	3	46	61
		3531	7		
		3533	5		
		3534	1		
		3536	2		
3540	12			35	53
355	17			32	42
356	14	356	5	31	48

Continued

TABLE A.2—Continued

INDUSTRY		POOLED INDUSTRIES (FROM TABLE A.1)		ADJUSTED CONCENTRATION RATIOS	
INDUSTRY	NUMBER OF FIRMS	INDUSTRY	NUMBER OF FIRMS	CENSUS	SHEPHERD
		3562	4		
		3564	1		
		3567	4		
357	12			65	85
3585	5			36	55
3610	25			50	61
363	10	363	3	60	69
		3631	1		
		3633	2		
		3634	2		
		3635	1		
		3636	1		
364	6			33	46
3651	14			47	60
366	22			51	59
367	32			35	53
369	6	3690	3	72	77
		3694	3		
3711	5			99	94
3714	17			60	60
3720	13			48	75
3721	9			58	90
37212	3			85	85
3731	4			48	65
3742	5			52	60
3811	7			41	45
382	15			48	56
3831	3			37	56
384	4			43	59
3861	4			62	80
3871	4			42	45
3931	3			51	60
3940	3			15	26

APPENDIX B

FIRM CLASSIFICATION

One of the more important (and more time-consuming) requirements of this study is to classify firms into industries. The importance of this task is underscored by the heavy reliance on the industry's concentration ratio as a measure of industry market structure. The purpose of this appendix is to outline the approach to what is essentially the development of a set of industry definitions.

The primary objective of firm classification follows directly from the primary objective of the study—an analysis of industry performance through the analysis of firms in those industries. As a result, industries must be homogeneous. This objective of homogeneity leads to the operational criteria of classifying firms into narrowly defined industries, i.e., at the four- and five-digit level.[1]

Others' Approaches to Industry Definition and Firm Classification

Because there have been relatively few studies where individual firms are the units of observation, I have had little precedent from which to borrow. In these few studies, the small numbers of firms made it practical to give ample consideration to each firm. Probably the most notable

1. It should be noted that four-digit industries, while generally, are not always, more homogeneous than three-digit industries. The most obvious example is where the three-digit industry is composed of only one or two four-digit industries which are closely related in the methods of production and have high cross-elasticities of demand. An example of a relatively homogeneous three-digit industry and a relatively heterogeneous four-digit industry might be industries 206 and 2834 respectively. Industry 206 includes only the two four-digit industries of 2061 (Cane Sugar Refineries) and 2062 (Beet Sugar Refineries). On the other hand, 2834 (Pharmaceutical Preparations) includes products for the myriad of human ailments (respiratory, cardiovascular, skin, nutritional, etc.), but also includes products for veterinary use. Within the four-digit industry of 2834, the cross-elasticity of demand between many of the products would, no doubt, be zero.

160

example is Weiss's and Hall's study which ends up with about 350 of the largest 500 industrial firms. Through much effort, no doubt, they essentially compute a separate concentration ratio for each firm by using Fortune's *Plant and Product Directory*.[2] Each firm's concentration ratio is a weighted average of its several plants' five-digit product classes. The weights used are each plant's employment figures, the assumption obviously being that the various products are of comparable labor intensity.

Other studies of individual firms generally limit themselves to analysis of each industry's dominant firms (two, three, or four firms) and, in addition, limit the number of industries to thirty or so. One would find that were he to limit himself to, say, thirty industries he could easily pick those particular industries in which the dominant firms are readily identified and data for which are easily obtainable. Any subsequent findings that dominant firms in those concentrated industries earn higher rates of return than dominant firms in unconcentrated industries must be interpreted with caution. To conclude from this that concentrated industries earn higher rates of return or even that, in general, dominant firms in concentrated industries earn higher rates of return than their counterparts in unconcentrated industries is extremely hazardous. The sample may prejudice the results.[3]

While I do not necessarily dispute the dominant firm theory,[4] I contend that the empirical test of the hypothesis is fraught with great difficulties. Specifically, to limit the study to dominant firms might also limit the resulting industry list to "dominant" industries, or might otherwise bias the industry sample. That is, the dominant firms in many small, highly concentrated industries cannot be classified in that industry because the great majority of their sales are in other (large) industries. For example, should one rule out the refrigerator industry because General Motors (a dominant firm) is not principally a refrigerator manufacturer? This writer thinks not. Consequently, in this study industries (hence firms) are not deleted when the industry's dominant firms could not be included.

The approach taken in this study generally resembles Weiss's and Hall's efforts at classifying firms into industries defined at the narrowest level practical. One basic difference should, however, be kept in mind. Hall and Weiss do not analyze industries. They analyze firms. In doing

---

2. Fortune Magazine, *Plant and Product Directory of the 1,000 Largest U.S. Manufacturing Corporations* (New York: Time, Inc.).

3. For a brief discussion of this, see Yale Brozen, "Bain's Concentration and Rates of Return Revisited," *Journal of Law and Economics* 14 (Oct. 1971): 351–69.

4. Joe S. Bain, *Barriers to New Competition* (Cambridge, Mass.: Harvard University Press, 1956), p. 191.

so, therefore, the criterion for grouping firms into industries is not necessarily homogeneity, but rather whether the "industry's" concentration ratio appropriately represents the market power of the firm. In other words, Hall and Weiss use the concept of the industry only as a tool to derive measures of firm market power.

Published Sources for Firm Classification

Although any one of several sources could have been used to classify all the firms, because of the rigidity inherent in the use of any one classification scheme, I have employed several sources in conjunction with one another.

As even the casual student of industrial organization realizes, many firms are highly diversified. Hence they operate in several perhaps related product markets within the same basic or broad industrial categories. For example, most firms that manufacture products classified in SIC industry 2611 also manufacture in 2621, 2631, and 2661. Rigidity in each source results from the practical problem of needing mutually exclusive industrial categories. To continue with the example, while many (diversified) firms operate in all four three-digit industries, many operate in just two or even one of the four. The system then must either classify all firms into the one broad industry (which includes the four three-digit industries) and essentially misclassify the nondiversified firms, or classify all firms into the narrow four-digit industries and essentially misclassify the diversified firms. Meaningful classification of each firm would result only from a scheme that does not insist on mutually exclusive industrial categories.

When one adopts categories which are not mutually exclusive, he opens up Pandora's box to a geometrically expanding list of industries limited only by the number of firms. Somewhere in between there must be a reasonable compromise, and I have tried to find one. In the resulting list of industrial categories (see Table A.1, Appendix A) the industries are not mutually exclusive. The extent to which they are not is simply a function of the nature of the diversification of the firms in the panel.

Before I explain my approach to firm classification, a brief description of the different sources would seem helpful. Those sources which classify a firm's products into the most narrowly defined industries (four- and five-digit SIC) are discussed first, followed by classification schemes with broader industry definitions.

In Fortune's 1966 *Plant and Product Directory,* the plants of 1,000 firms are classified into five-digit product classes. Because total employment figures are for each plant, it is possible to determine, as Hall and Weiss did,[5] the extent of a firm's involvement in various product classes. This source is used for only a few firms in this study. At times it is consulted to determine whether firms in three-or four-digit industries produce in certain five-digit product classes. This information becomes desirable because it is used in the calculation of concentration ratios. Specifically, it helps answer the question of whether there is overaggregation within a four-digit industry.[6]

At the four-digit level of classification both the Dun and Bradstreet *Million Dollar Directory* and Standard and Poor's *Register* are used extensively. While the Standard and Poor's *Register* is available for each year in the study, the Dun and Bradstreet *Directory* was available for only 1968 and 1971.[7] Although each of the directories usually lists from one to four or five (sometimes more) four-digit product groups which represent the major product groups, only Dun and Bradstreet acknowledge their attempt to list them in descending order of importance. Another limitation on the use of both sources is that these major product groups are those of the corporate parent organization. Therefore, these four-digit sources do not list the major product classes for all consolidated subsidiaries combined. Because this study uses consolidated data, the propriety of using these four-digit sources becomes doubtful should a parent firm be small in relation to its consolidated subsidiaries. The writer found no convenient way to disentangle these considerations.

At the three-digit level of classification the consolidated subsidiaries are not excluded and therefore this problem is avoided. Both the News Front *Directory* and the Securities and Exchange Commission *Directory* are used extensively.[8] For the 1959 classification, News Front seems to follow the Standard Enterprise Classification System, which often pools several SIC three-digit industries. (For example, industry 261 includes the three-digit SIC industries of 261, 262, 263, and 266.) Likewise, the Commission's *Directory* follows the SEC System. Both of these sources are

5. Marshall Hall and Leonard Weiss, "Firm Size and Profitability," *Review of Economics and Statistics* 49 (Mar. 1967): 162–68.

6. See Appendix A.

7. To a subscriber to Dun and Bradstreet's *Million Dollar Directory*, typically only the most recent year will be available. This is because the new volume is issued under the condition that the old volume be returned.

8. News Front, *News Front Directory of 7,500 Leading U.S. Manufacturers* (New York: News Front, 1961), and News Front, *25,000 Leading U.S. Corporations* (New York: News Front, 1970). U.S., Securities and Exchange Commission, *Directory of Companies Filing Annual Reports with the Securities and Exchange Commission* (Washington, D.C.: Government Printing Office, 1961, 1963, 1969).

often found to be too broad in industry definition. Their general use is in checking the propriety of a narrower classification. The 1970 News Front *Directory* (which classifies firms as of 1967 or earlier) is found to be probably the best source because it generally does not pool three-digit industries, and therefore it is frequently used.

The final source of firm classification is the Standard and Poor's *Compustat Information Manual*. Standard and Poor's Corporation pre-classifies all the firms into what appear to be two-, three-, and four-digit SIC categories. At the outset of this study it was hoped that this classification scheme could be used with only minor modifications. Unforunately, their approach is to define industries (classify them) by the end markets rather than by the nature of the product or production process. Often firms are grouped simply because they manufacture jointly demanded products. For example, the Compustat industry 2510 (Home Furnishings) groups into one industry firms which sell such diverse products as furniture, floor coverings, appliances, heating and plumbing fixtures, and air conditioning. Another problem which stems from classifying firms by end markets is that firms which are primarily wholesalers and retailers are often classified with firms which are primarily manufacturers.

Firm Classification Procedures

Given the objectives of classification and the nature of available sources, the following procedure is adopted for classifying firms into industries. First, for each firm Dun and Bradstreet's product groups are listed in descending order of importance. It is likely that by looking at these major four-digit product groups one could "predict" the three-digit industry code for the firm in the Securities and Exchange and News Front directories. When this prediction is verified by these three-digit sources,[9] the writer is confident that the proper three-digit industry has been selected. When there is considerable disagreement among the different sources and within the same source but among years, the firm is dropped from the study. About 150 firms are dropped for this reason.

Once the three-digit industry has been determined, a narrower four-digit (or 5-digit) classification is considered. For many firms a narrower classification seems warranted. In this instance the first Dun and Bradstreet four-digit code has to fall in the determined three-digit classifica-

---

9. Although the SEC *Directory* for 1963 and News Front, *25,000 Leading U.S. Corporations* (1970), receive primary consideration for this purpose, the 1961 and 1969 SEC directories are also used extensively.

tion. Furthermore, no other four-digit code can appear in the same three-digit industry among the first two or three industries listed.

Perhaps three examples will serve to make this point clearer. Take the following three hypothetical cases:

I.

Source	Classification
D & B	2011, 2334, 2818
S.E.C. ('63, '69)	201
N.F. ('67)	201

Result: Can confidently classify firm in the 4-digit industry of 2011.

II.

Source	Classification
D & B	3634, 3631, 3811, 3622, 3639
S.E.C. ('63, '69)	363
N.F. ('67)	363

Result: Cannot confidently classify this firm into a 4-digit industry but can into the 3-digit industry 363.

III.

Source	Classification
D & B	3634, 3648, 2818, 3714
S.E.C. ('63, '69)	364 and 344
N.F. ('67)	344

Result: Cannot confidently classify this firm based on this information; it should be noted, however, that the written product description may clarify the issue.

It is hoped that these short examples make the general procedure for classification clear. In addition, several guides or specific principles of classification essentially qualify application of the general produre.

When other four-digit product groups within the three-digit industry groups are either quite dissimilar in production methods and/or product characteristics, or the concentration ratios are of materially different magnitude, then I opt for the narrower classification at the four-digit level. With regard to product and production characteristics, I rely on my knowledge of the industry in question, the guide set forth by Weiss and Hall, and the product list of other firms in the three-digit industry. When several firms in the same three-digit industry manufacture different combinations of the four-digit products, this is taken as evidence that similar production characteristics exist among these four-digit products. In other words, this occurence is taken to indicate that firms could readily shift production among the four-digit products, and therefore this lessens the significance of differences in concentration ratios among these four-digit products.

If the firm which marginally meets the criteria for a four-digit classification is the only one of all the firms classified in the same three-digit industry that manufactures that four-digit product, then I choose to separate this firm from the other firms so that a more homogeneous three-digit industry results. This principle rests on the assumption that the other four-digit products are produced in various combinations by these other firms.

When I think it advisable to retain a firm despite the fact that the classification changes from an earlier period (1959, '61, or '63, depending on the sources involved) to a later period (1967, '68, '69), I opt for the later classification. There are several reasons for this. First, an important aspect of the classification process is that the firm's management often classifies itself by responding to questionnaires. When this is the case, one might argue that the management will not identify its newly achieved emphasis until it is clearly established as the major product line—that is, that the fact happens before the firm proclaims it has. On the other hand, should the classification be made by the sources from secondary data, a time lag would naturally exist because of the data collection and the decision process. One would think that the source would naturally be reluctant to *change* a classification until it is clear indeed that a new dominant product class is established. Otherwise, the source's classification runs the risk of varying from year to year and hence might be thought of as unreliable by the user. In either case, the change in classification would seem to lag behind the fact.

Second, if a change in classification occurs, then of necessity the old product line is declining or slowing its rate of expansion as compared to the new product line. In this case, I would argue, more emphasis is probably being given to the emerging product line both in terms of committed assets and in terms of research, marketing, and managerial effort. In short, its prospects of profits must be greater.

Certain groups of firms do not conform to SIC industries because they typically produce two or more four-digit products in different three-digit industries. In this case, I simply pool the firms into a single industry, though several could have been classified into the separate four-digit industries. A good example of this is the SIC industries 3433 (Heating Equipment) and 3585 (Air Conditioning). It has been quite common for firms in either industry to diversify into the other In addition, the concentration ratios for these two industries are of the same magnitude. Therefore, I felt justified in pooling most of the firms involved in one industry. In this case, the industry is designated—granted, arbitrarily— as 3585.

To avoid such arbitrary classification of firms, and to be consistent with the objectives of the study, the option of dropping firms from the sample is exercised frequently. However, firms are dropped only because the industry classification would otherwise be arbitrary and of doubtful meaning or because it lacks the necessary financial data.[10] The major reasons for dropping firms because of industry classification are outlined below:

1. The firms are primarily nonmanufacturing.

2. There appears to be no apparent agreement in classification among the sources.

3. The firms are heavily engaged in widely diversified product lines, i.e., among considerably different three-digit industries or among different two-digit industries.

4. The industry in which the firm is classified contains no other firms and its inclusion seems to add little to the study. (Only a couple of firms are affected.)

Some SIC industries are intentionally very heterogeneous—e.g., those "miscellaneous" and "not elsewhere classified" industries. The concentration ratio in these industries is of doubtful meaning, and therefore these industries and their firms are dropped from the analysis. Table B.1 lists the 768 firms classified into the 132 industries.

10. The 1969 *Compustat* tapes list 1,234 manufacturing firms—industry codes 2000 to 3999. Of these, 245 are dropped because of difficulties in industry classification and 221 firms are dropped because of deficiencies in data. The remaining 768 firms become the basic panel.

PANEL OF 768 FIRMS CLASSIFIED INTO 132 INDUSTRIES

INDUSTRY DESIGNA-TION	INDUSTRY NAME AND FIRM NAME	INDUSTRY DESIGNA-TION	INDUSTRY NAME AND FIRM NAME
201	*Meat products*	2042	*Prepared feeds*
	Armour		Allied Mills
	Cudahy		Ralston Purina
	Hormel		Associated Products
	Rath Packing		National Alfalfa
	Swift	2044	*Rice*
	Hygrade Foods		Riviana Foods
	Needham Packing	2046	*Wet corn*
	Tobin Packing		C.P.C. Intl.
202	*Dairy products*		Staley
	Beatrice Foods		National Starch
	Borden	2051	*Bread and other bakery*
	Carnation		American Bakeries
	Fairmont Foods		General Hosts
	Kraftco		Interstate Brands
	Pet		Tasty Baking
203	*Canned and Frozen Foods*		Ward Foods
	Campbell Soup	2052	*Biscuits, crackers and*
	Del Monte		*Pretzels*
	Di Giorgio		Helme Products
	Green Giant		Keebler
	Heinz		National Biscuits
	Libby	206	*Sugar*
	Stokely-Van Camp		American Sugar
	Castle & Cooke		National Sugar Ref.
	Consolidated Foods		Sucrest Corp.
	General Foods		U.S. Sugar
	Smucker		North American Sugar
20321	*Baby foods*		Amalgamated Sugar
	Gerber Products		American Crystal Sugar
204	*Grain mill products*		Holly Sugar
	General Mills		Michigan Sugar
	Kellogg	207	*Confectionary*
	Pillsbury	2071	*Candy*
	Quaker Oats		Tootsie Roll
	Archer-Daniels-Midland		Barton's Candy
2041	*Flour*		Fanny Farmer Candy
	Seaboard Allied Midland	2072	*Chocolate and cocoa prod.*
			Hershey Foods

Continued

TABLE B.1—Continued

INDUSTRY DESIGNATION	INDUSTRY NAME AND FIRM NAME	INDUSTRY DESIGNATION	INDUSTRY NAME AND FIRM NAME
2073	*Chewing gum*	2210	*Broad woven fabric*
	Wrigley		*mills, except wool*
2082	*Beer*		Burlington Indus.
	Anheuser-Busch		Cone Mills
	Associated Brewing		Dan River
	Duquesne Brewing		Graniteville
	Grain Belt Breweries		Indian Head
	Falstaff Brewing		Lowenstein
	Lone Star Brewing		Reeves Bros.
	Olympia Brewing		Riegel Textile
	Pabst Brewing		Stevens (J.P.)
	Pittsburg Brewing		West Point Pepperell
	Schlitz Brewing		Avondale Mills
2085	*Liquor*		Bates Mfg.
	American Distilling		Liberty Fabrics
	Barton Brands	2231	*Broad woven fabric*
	Brown Forman		*mills, wool*
	Distillers Corp.		Collins Aikman
	Heublein		United Merchants
	National Dist.		Mount Vernon Mills
	Schenley		Wyandotte Ind.
	Walker (Hiram)		Huyck
	Glenmore	2241	*Narrow fabrics*
2086	*Soft drink bottlers*		Wyomissing
	Coca-Cola Bottling	225	*Knitting mills*
	Pepcom		Adams Millis
20873	*Soft drink flavorings*		Wayne Gossard
	Coca-Cola	227	*Floor covering mills*
	Dr. Pepper		Roxbury Carpet
	Pepsico		Mohasco Ind.
	Royal Crown Cola	228	*Yarn and thread mills*
2092	*Soybean oil mills*		Belding Heminway
	Central Soya		Bibb Mfg.
2111	*Cigarettes*		Opelike Mfg.
	American Brands		Duplan
	Liggett & Myers	2298	*Cordage and twine*
	Philip Morris		American Mfg.
	Reynolds	2310	*Men's and boy's clothing*
2121	*Cigars*		Blue Bell
	Bayuk Cigars		Cluett, Peabody
	General Cigar		Hart Schaffner Marx
	Universal Cigar		Manhattan Ind.

Continued

TABLE B.1—Continued

INDUSTRY DESIGNATION	INDUSTRY NAME AND FIRM NAME	INDUSTRY DESIGNATION	INDUSTRY NAME AND FIRM NAME
	Phillips Van Heusen		Papercrraft
	Angelica		Nashua
	Chadbourn	265	*Paperboard containers*
	McGregor-Doniger		*and boxes*
2330	*Women's, children's and*		Federal Paper Board
	infants' clothing		Fibreboard
	Bobbie Brooks		Inland Container
	Genesco		Maryland Cup
	Jonathan Logan		Stone Container
	Kayser-Roth		Simkins Ind.
	Munsingwear		Connelly Containers
	L'Aiglon Apparel		Hoerner-Waldorf
	Russ Togs		United Board
	V. F. Corp.	2711	*Newspapers*
	Warnaco		Boston Herald Trav.
	Wentworth Mfg.		N.Y. Times Mirror
251	*Household furniture*	2721	*Periodicals*
	American Seating		Cowles
	Kroehler Mfg.		Time
	Simmons		Esquire
	Weiman		McGraw-Hill
2610	*Pulp, paper and board*		Meredith
	Crown Zellerbach	2731	*Books*
	Hammermill Paper		Crowell-Collier
	International Paper		Grolier
	Kimberly-Clark		Harcourt Brace
	Mead		Prentice-Hall
	Riegel Paper		Scott Foresman
	St. Regis Paper		Allyn & Bacon
	Scott Paper		W. F. Hall Printing
	Union Camp	2750	*Printing*
	Westvaco		American Bank Note
	Brown		Cuneo Press
	Chesapeake		Donnelley (R. R.)
	Standard Packaging		Goodway
	Paterson Parchment		Ennis Business Forms
	Whippany Paperboard		Moore
	Masonite		Reynolds & Reynolds
2640	*Converted paper and*		Wallace Bus. Forms
	paperboard products		Western Publishing
	Avery Products		

Continued

TABLE B.1—Continued

INDUSTRY DESIGNATION	INDUSTRY NAME AND FIRM NAME	INDUSTRY DESIGNATION	INDUSTRY NAME AND FIRM NAME
2761	*Manifold business forms*		
	Standard Register		Baxter Lab.
	Uarco		Bristol-Myers
2771	*Greeting cards*		Carter Wallace
	American Greetings		Cutter Lab.
	Rust Craft Greetings		Eli Lilly
281	*Basic chemicals*		Merck & Co.
	Publicker Ind.		Miles Lab.
	Air Reduction		Parke, Davis
	Allied Chemical		Pfizer
	American Cyanamid		Plough
	Chemetron		Richardson-Merrell
	Commercial Solvents		Schering
	Diamond Shamrock		Searle
	Dow Chemical		Smith Kline/French
	Dupont de Nemours		Sterling
	Filtrol		Syntex
	F.M.C.		Upjohn
	Monsanto	2841	*Soaps and specialty*
	Olin		*cleaners*
	Pennwalt		Colgate Palmolive
	Reichhold Chemical		Economics Lab.
	Rohm/Haas		Procter and Gamble
	Stauffer Chemical		Unilever N.V.
	Union Carbide		West Chemical
	Witco Chemical		Purex
	Emery Ind.	2844	*Perfumes, cosmetics*
	Essex Chemical		*and other toilet*
	Great Lakes Chem.		*preparations*
	Stepan Chemical		Avon Products
	Michigan Chemical		Chemway
	Diversey		Chesebrough Pond's
	Ethyl		Fabergé
2821	*Plastics*		Max Factor
	Rowland Products		Helena Rubinstein
	Pantasote		Helene Curtis Ind.
	NVF		Revlon
2823	*Cellulosic manmade fibers*		Shulton
	American Enka		Nestle-Lemur
	Celanese	2851	*Paint*
283	*Drugs*		National Lead
	American Home Prod.		Cook Paint Varnish

Continued

TABLE B.1—Continued

INDUSTRY DESIGNATION	INDUSTRY NAME AND FIRM NAME	INDUSTRY DESIGNATION	INDUSTRY NAME AND FIRM NAME
	De Soto		Mansfield Tire
	Sherwin Williams		Mohawk Rubber
	Valspar		Uniroyal
	Guardsman Chem.		Carlisle
	Sun Chemical	3031	*Reclaimed rubber*
28991	*Salt*		U.S. Rubber Reclaim.
	International Salt	3069	*Fabricated rubber products*
2911	*Petroleum refining*		Amerace Esna
	Comonwealth Oil Ref.		Dayco
	Ashland Oil		Rubbermaid
	Atlantic-Richfield		Electric Hose
	Cities Service		Acme-Hamilton Mfg.
	Continental Oil		American Biltrite
	Getty Oil		O'Sullivan Rubber
	Kerr McGee	3141	*Footwear*
	Marathon Oil		Brown Shoe
	Murphy Oil		Green Shoe
	Phillips Petroleum		Interco
	Quaker State Oil		U.S. Shoe
	Shell Oil		Weyenberg Shoe Man.
	Skelly Oil		Wolverine Worldwide
	Standard Oil (Ind.)	3211	*Flat glass*
	Standard Oil (Ohio)		PPG Ind.
	Sun Oil		Libby Owens Ford
	Union Oil	322	*Glass products*
	Crown Central		Anchor Hocking
	Gulf Oil		Owens-Illinois
	Mobil Oil		Brockway Glass
	Standard Oil (Calif.)		Dorsey
	Standard Oil (N.J.)		Richford, Ind.
	Texaco		Corning Glass
295	*Paving mixtures, blocks, asphalt felts, and coatings*		Jeannette Glass
		3241	*Cement*
	Certain Teed Prod.		Alpha Portland
	Flintkote		American Cement
3011	*Tires*		General Portland
	Armstrong Rubber		Giant Portland
	Cooper Tire Rubber		Ideal Basic Ind.
	Firestone Tire		Kaiser Cement
	B. F. Goodrich		Lehigh Portland
	Goodyear Tire		Lone Star Cement

Continued

TABLE B.1—Continued

INDUSTRY DESIGNA-TION	INDUSTRY NAME AND FIRM NAME	INDUSTRY DESIGNA-TION	INDUSTRY NAME AND FIRM NAME
	Marquette Cement		Inland Steel
	Medusa Portland		Interlake
	Missouri Portland		Jones & Laughlin
	Penn-Dixie Cement		Kaiser Steel
3250	*Structural clay products*		Lukens Steel
	D.C.A. Development		McLouth Steel
	Texstar		National Steel
	U.S. Ceramic Tile		Republic Steel
	Glengerry		U.S. Steel
	General Refractories		Alan Wood Steel
	Sayre & Fisher		Byers (A.M.)
3270	*Concrete*		Cyclops
	Colonial Sand		Easco
	Maule Ind.		Harsco
	Texas Ind.		Latrobe Steel
	Warner		Northwestern Steel
3275	*Gypsum products*		Phoenix Steel
	National Gypsum		National Standard
	U.S. Gypsum		Hofmann Ind.
329	*Nonmetallic mineral products*		Michigan Seamless
			Welded Tube Co.
	Johns-Manville		Standard Alliance
	Basic	332	*Iron and steel foundries*
	Vulcan Materials		Central Foundry
3291	*Abrasive products*		Shahmoon Ind.
	Carborundum		Amsted Ind.
3293	*Gaskets*		General Steel Ind.
	Garlock		Duraloy
3296	*Mineral wool*	3331	*Primary copper*
	Owens-Corning		Anaconda
331	*Steel*		Copper Range
	Allegheny Ind.		Inspiration Cons.
	Armco Steel		Kennecott Copper
	Bethlehem Steel		Phelps Dodge
	Bliss & Laughlin	3334	*Primary aluminum*
	C.F. & I. Steel		Alcan Aluminium
	Carpenter Tech		Aluminum Co. of America
	Continental Steel		
	Copperweld Steel		Harvey Aluminum
	Detroit Steel		Kaiser
	Florida Steel		Reynolds Metals
	Granite City Steel		

Continued

TABLE B.1—Continued

INDUSTRY DESIGNATION	INDUSTRY NAME AND FIRM NAME	INDUSTRY DESIGNATION	INDUSTRY NAME AND FIRM NAME
335	*Nonferrous rolling and drawing*		V.S.I.
	PA Ind.		Lamson & Sessions
	Ansonia Wire		Screw & Bolt
	Belden		Standard Pressed
	General Cable		Steel
	Revere Copper	3461	*Metal stamping*
	Scovill Mfg.		Mirro Aluminum
	Simplex Wire	349	*Miscellaneous fabricated*
	Triangle Ind.		*metal products*
	Hoskins Mfg.		Walworth
	Kennametal		Crane
3411	*Metal cans*		Universal Container
	American Can		Automtd. Bldg. Compt.
	Continental Can		Parker Hannifin
	Crown Cork & Seal		Associated Spring
	National Can	3492	*Safes and vaults*
34212	*Razor blades and razors,*		Diebold
	except electric	351	*Engines and turbines*
	Gillette		Foster Wheeler
3429	*Hardware*		Outboard Marine
	Avis Ind.		Cummins Engine
	Stanley Works		Briggs/Stratton
	Cole National		Cooper Ind.
	Jervis		Babcock & Wilcox
	S.O.S. Cons.		Combustion Engr.
		3522	*Farm machinery*
343	*Heating and plumbing*		Allis Chalmers Mfg.
	fixtures		Case (J.I.)
	American Standard		Deere & Co.
	Masco		International
344	*Fabricated structural*		Harvester
	metal products		Massey-Ferguson
	Nuclear of America	353	*Construction, mining,*
	Daryl Ind.		*and materials handling*
	Rusco Ind.		*machinery*
	Season-All Ind.		Joy Mfg.
	Ceco		Gardner-Denver
	Keller Ind.		Unarco Ind.
345	*Screw machine products*	3531	*Construction machinery*
	Allied Products		Bucyrus-Erie
	Buell Ind.		Caterpillar Tractor

Continued

TABLE B.1—Continued

INDUSTRY DESIGNATION	INDUSTRY NAME AND FIRM NAME	INDUSTRY DESIGNATION	INDUSTRY NAME AND FIRM NAME
	Clark Equipment		Compo
	Jaeger Machine		Cosmodyne
	Koehring		McNeil
	Rex Chainbelt		Pneumatic Scale
	American Hoist		Wood Ind.
3533	*Oil field machinery*		Lynch
	Baker Oil Tools		Marley
	Dresser Ind.		Dorr-Oliver
	G. W. Murphy Ind.		Hobart Mfg.
	Smith International		U.S.M.
	Dover	356	*General industrial*
3534	*Elevators*		*machinery*
	Otis Elevators		Ingersoll-Rand
3536	*Hoists, cranes, and*		Pall
	monorail systems		Struthers Wells
	Harnischfeger		Dymo Industries
	Whiting		Stewart Warner
3540	*Metal-working*	3562	*Ball and roller bearings*
	machinery		Hoover Ball Bearing
	Brown & Sharpe Mfg.		New Hampshire Ball
	Skil		Bearings
	Warner & Swasey		Federal Mogul
	Black & Decker		Timken
	Lodge & Shipley	3564	*Blowers, exhausts, and*
	Chicago Pneumatic		*fans*
	Mesta Machine		American Air Filter
	Starrett (L.S.)	3567	*Industrial process*
	Cincinnati Milacron		*furnaces and ovens*
	Giddings & Lewis		Buffalo Forge
	Monarch Machine		Selas Corp. of
	Tool		America
	Ex-Cell-O		B.T.P. Engr.
355	*Special industrial*		Ajax Magnethermic
	machinery	357	*Office and computing*
	Van Dorn		*machines*
	Cherry Burrell		Addressograph-Multi.
	Crompton Knowles		Burroughs
	Emhart		Dictophane
	Harris-Intertype		Electronic Asso.
	Leesona		International
	Bethlehem		Business Machines

Continued

TABLE B.1—Continued

Industry Designation	Industry Name and Firm Name	Industry Designation	Industry Name and Firm Name
	National Cash Reg.		Electronics
	Pitney-Bowes		Vocaline
	S.C.M.		Avnet
	Victor Comptometer		International
	Clary		Rectifier
	Veeder Ind.		C.T.S.
	Mangood		John Fluke Mfg.
38612	*Reproduction*		I.M.C. Magnetics
	equipment		High Voltage
	Xerox	363	*Household appliances*
	American Photocopy		Norris Industries
3581	*Automatic merchandising*		Republic
	machines		National Presto Ind.
	U.M.C. Ind.	3631	*Household cooking*
	Vendo		*equipment*
3585	*Refrigeration*		Welbilt
	machinery	3633	*Household laundry*
	Carrier		Maytag
	Copeland Refg.		Whirlpool
	Fedders	3634	*Electric housewares*
	Tecumseh Prod.		*and fans*
	Trane		Sunbeam
3610	*Basic Electrical*		Schick Electric
	equipment	3635	*Vacuum cleaners*
	General Electric		Hoover
	Westinghouse Elec.	3636	*Sewing machines*
	Century Electric		Singer
	Echlin Mfg.	364	*Electric wiring and*
	Emerson Electric		*lighting equipment*
	Federal Pacific Elec.		Continental Conn.
	McGraw-Edison		Thomas & Betts
	Ohio Brass		Duro-Test
	Reliance Electric		AMP
	Sangamo Electric		El-Tronics
	Allied Control		Thomas Ind.
	Pyle National	3651	*Radio and television*
	Bourns		*receiving sets*
	Crouse-Hinds		R.C.A.
	Cutler-Hammer		Admiral
	Leads Northrup		Magnavox
	Square D		Motorola

Continued

TABLE B.1—Continued

Industry Designa- tion	Industry Name and Firm Name	Industry Designa- tion	Industry Name and Firm Name
	National Union Elec.		Airpax Electronics
	Standard Kollsman		Dynalectron
	Zenith Radio		Electron Research
	Andrea Radio		G.T.I.
	Automatic Radio Mfg.		Industrial Electronic
	Esquire Radio & Elec.		Jetronic Ind.
	Pilot Radio & Tele.		Microdot
	Ampex		National Video
	Muter		Oak Electronetics
	Oxford Electric		Pepi
3652	*Phonograph records and tapes*		Silicon Transistor
	Capitol Ind.		Vernitron
366	*Communication equipment*		Lear Siegler
	Hoffman Electronics		Mallory (P.R.)
	Texas Instruments		Sprague Elec.
	Excutone		Telex
	Narco Scientific Instr.		General Instr.
	National Radio		Hewlett Packard
	Collins Radio		Raytheon
	Fairchild Camera		Transitron Elec.
	General Signal		Varian Associates
	Hazeltine		Electronic Assist.
	Sanders Associates		Loral
	Technical Material		Polarad Elec.
	Dynamics Corp. of America		Servo
	Edo		Sparton
	Milgo Electronic		Varo
	Cohu Electronics		Bowmar Instr.
	Cook Electric		Data-Control Sys.
	Elco		Clarostat Mfg.
	Electronic Engr.		G-L Industries
	Harvard Ind.	3690	*Batteries*
	Microwave Associates		Globe Union
	Reeves Ind.		E.S.B.
	Cubic		Gould
367	*Electronic components and accessories*	3694	*Electrical equipment for internal comb. engines*
			Champion Spark Plug
			Clark Cable
			Standard Motor

Continued

TABLE B.1—Continued

INDUSTRY DESIGNATION	INDUSTRY NAME AND FIRM NAME	INDUSTRY DESIGNATION	INDUSTRY NAME AND FIRM NAME
3711	*Passenger cars*	3720	*Aircraft engines, parts, and auxiliary equipment*
	American Motors		
	Chrysler		
	Ford Motors		Bendix
	General Motors		Pneumo Dynamics
	Checker Motors		Menasco Mfg.
3713	*Trucks*		Curtiss-Wright
	White Motors		Talley Ind.
3714	*Motor vehicle parts and accessories*		Rohr
			Altamil
	Arvin Industries		Breeze
	Borg-Warner		Piasecki Aircraft
	Budd		Royal Ind.
	Dana		Sierracin
	Eaton Yale & Towne		Stanley Aviation
	Kelsey Hayes		United Aircraft
	Maremont	3731	*Shipbuilding and repairing*
	Monroe Auto Equip.		
	Napco Industries		American Shipbuild.
	Purolator		New York Shipbuild.
	Hayes Albion		Todd Shipyards
	Kysor Industrial		Campbell Machine
	McCord	3732	*Boat building and repairing*
	Pierce Governor		
	Ryerson & Haynes		Chris Craft Ind.
	Sheller Globe	3742	*Railroad and street cars*
	A. O. Smith		A.C.F. Industries
3721	*Aircraft*		General American
	Boeing		Pullman
	General Dynamics		Stanray
	Grumman		Youngstown Steel
	Lockheed Aircraft	3751	*Bicycles and motorcycles*
	McDonnell-Douglas		
	North American Rockwell		Murray Ohio Mfg.
		3791	*Trailer homes*
	Northrop		Guerdon Ind.
	United Aircraft	3811	*Engineering, laboratory, and research equipment*
	Fairchild Hiller		
37212	*Complete personal aircraft*		Beckman Instr.
			Cenco Instr.
	Beech Aircraft		G.C.A.
	Cessna Aircraft		Tektronix
	Piper Aircraft		Genisco Tech.

Continued

TABLE B.1—Continued

Industry Designation	Industry Name and Firm Name	Industry Designation	Industry Name and Firm Name
	AMBAC Ind.		Kendall
	Conrac		American Sterilizer
382	*Mechanical measuring*	3861	*Photographic equipment*
	instruments		Anken Chemical Film
	Honeywell		Bell/Howell
	Gulton Ind.		Polaroid
	Systron-Donner		Eastman Kodak
	Tenney Engineering	3871	*Watches*
	Ametek		Benrus Watch
	Neptune Meter		Bulova Watch
	Rockwell Mfg.		Hamilton Watch
	Statham Instr.		Longines-Wittnauer
	Simmonds Precision	3911	*Jewelry*
	Fischer & Porter		Swank
	Standard-Thomson	3931	*Musical instruments*
	Foxboro		*and parts*
	Johnson Service		Baldwin (D. H.)
	Ranco		Wurlitzer
	Robertshaw Controls		Hammond
3831	*Optical instruments*	3940	*Games, toys, and dolls*
	and lenses		Aurora Products
	Bausch/Lomb		Milton Bradley
	Perkin Elmer		Mattel
	Kollmargen	3950	*Pencils, pens, and*
384	*Medical instruments*		*artist supplies*
	and supplies		Parker Pen
	American Hospital		Binney & Smith
	Johnson & Johnson		

APPENDIX C

VARIABLE DEFINITIONS AND CALCULATIONS

The definitions and calculations of all basic variables except concentration ratios and the current-cost variables are given in this appendix.[1] For most variables, several distinguishable computational steps are necessary before use in this study. First, a check is made to ensure that necessary data for each firm are available for each year of the study. These data are classified as critical and noncritical. If missing data are critical, that firm is eliminated from the study. For noncritical data, various estimating procedures are used to make the data complete and thereby avoid eliminating the firm from the panel. Second, the raw data as given on the Compustat Tapes are changed to conform with the variable definitions used. The third step is to generate from firm data for all years the 1960–68 period variables used in the study. Finally, industry 1960–68 period variables are generated using the firm period variables. This appendix outlines each of these four steps.

Compustat Data

Table C.1 lists the variables appearing on the Compustat Industrial Tape by their compustat number. Those variables followed by a code letter are used in this study.[2]

The following are Standard and Poor's definitions of the relevant variables. The Standard and Poor's number (see Table C.1) precedes each definition.

---

1. Concentration ratios and current-cost variables are discussed in Appendixes A and D, respectively.

2. These codes denote how the data are treated for missing data. This is explained later in this appendix.

180

[5] *Total current liabilities*

  A. *Total current liabilities* represents liabilities due within one year, including the current portion of long-term debt.

  B. U.S. government securities are not deducted from the tax liability in current liabilities (treated as a current asset).

  C. Customers' deposits on bottles, cases, kegs, etc., are excluded from liaabilities (treated as a long-term liability).

  D. For finance companies, reserves for unearned insurance premiums are are excluded from current liabilities (treated as other noncurrent liabilities).

  E. For retail companies, deferred income taxes due to installment sales are included.

[6] *Total assets liabilities*

  A. *Total assets* represents current assets plus net plant plus other non-current assets (including intangible assets and deferred items).

  B. U.S. government securities that have been netted by the company in its public reports against tax liability on the current liability side of the balance sheet are considered as current assets.

[7–8] *Gross and net plant*

  A. *Gross plant* represents tangible fixed property (generally at cost)—such as land, buildings, and equipment—which is used in the production of revenue. *Net plant* represents gross plant minus accumulated reserves for depreciation, depletion, amortization, etc.

  B. The following items are included in both gross and net plant:

    1. Improvements on leased property (plus depreciation on reserve for gross plant when it is available)
    2. Advances to vendors for plant expansion programs
    3. Construction in progress
    4. For soft drink, beer, and similar companies—bottles, kegs and cases
    5. Funds for construction
    6. Equipment leased to others
    7. For shipping companies, statutory reserve funds and allowances from the Maritime Administration for vessels traded in (to be used for vessels under construction)
    8. For publishing companies, book plates
    9. Patterns
    10. Net prepaid mine development and stripping costs
    11. For forestry and paper companies, timberlands, and timber rights
    12. Tools and dies not charged to operating expense. If charged to operating expense, they are excluded from gross property
    13. Leaseholds

  C. Excluded from gross and net plant are the following items:

    1. Tools and dies amortized over less than two years, less amortization (treated as other noncurrent assets)
    2. Excess carrying value over cost of property (treated as intangibles)

Table C.1

VARIABLES APPEARING ON THE COMPUSTAT INDUSTRIAL
TAPES BY STANDARD AND POOR'S NUMBER

NUMBER	CODE*	NAME OF VARIABLE
		Balance sheet variables
1		Cash and equivalent
2		Receivables
3		Inventories
4		Current assets
5	B	Current liabilities
6	B	Total assets/liabilities
7	A	Gross plant
8	A	Net plant
9		Long-term debt
10		Preferred stock
11	B	Common equity
		Income statement variables
12	B	Net sales
13	B	Operating income
14	A	Depreciation and amortization
15		Fixed charges
16	B	Income taxes
17		Nonrecurring income expense (not net of tax)
18	B	Net income (before nonrecurring)
19		Preferred dividends
20	B	Available for common
21		Common dividends
		Market variables
22		Stock price—high
23		Stock price—low
24		Stock price—close
25		Number of shares outstanding
26		Dividends per share
27		Adjustment factor
28		Number of shares traded
		Miscellaneous variables
29		Number of employees
30	A	Capital expenditures
31	B	Investment and advances to subsidiaries
32		Investment and advances—other
33		Intangibles

Continued

* The code is for missing data treatment. See discussion in the text which follows. Data used in this study are those for which there is a missing data code letter.

TABLE C.1.—Continued

NUMBER	CODE*	NAME OF VARIABLE
34	C	Debt in current liabilities
35		Deferred taxes and investment credit (B.S. [balance sheet])
36		Number of common shares purchased/sold (net)
37		Total invested capital
38		Minority interest and subsidiary preferred stock (B.S.)
39		Amount of convertible debt and preferred stock
40		Number of shares reserved for conversion
41		Cost of goods sold
42		Labor and related expense
43		Pension and retirement expense
44		Incentive compensation expense
45		Selling and advertising expense
46		Research and development expense
47		Rental expense
48		Nonrecurring income/expense (net of taxes)
49		Minority interest (I.A. [income statement])
50		Deferred taxes (I.A.)
51		Investment credit (I.A.)
52		Carry forward tax—loss
53		Unconsolidated subsidiaries—excess equity
54		Unconsolidated subsidiaries—unremitted earnings
55		Unconsolidated subsidiaries—remitted earnings
56		Preferred stock at redemption value
57		Potentially diluted earnings per share
58		Earnings per share as reported
59		Inventory valuation method
60		Inventory cost or market, whichever is lower

* The code is for missing data treatment. See discussion in the text which follows. Data used in this study are those for which there is a missing data code letter.

  3. Property held for sale and property not used in operations (treated as other noncurrent assets)
  4. Goodwill, patents, and other intangibles (treated as intangibles)
  5. Investment tax credit, when shown as a deduction from plant on asset side of balance sheet

[11] *Common equity*
  A. *Common equity* represents common stock plus the following items:
     1. Retained earnings
     2. Capital surplus
     3. Self-insurance reserves
     4. Unamortized debt premium
     5. Capital stock premium

B. Deducted from common equity are the following items:

1. Common treasury stock
2. Intangibles
3. Accumulated unpaid preferred dividends
4. Excess of involuntary liquidating value of outstanding preferred stock over carrying value

C. Deferred taxes and investment credit (balance sheet) are not included in this figure. See the definitions of deferred taxes and investment credit (balance sheet) in the manual.

D. Negative equity figures are shown where applicable.

[12] *Net sales*

A. *Net sales* represents gross sales and other operating revenue less discounts, returns, and allowances.

B. Royalty income is included (extractive industries only.)

C. For retail companies, sales of leased departments are included, when corresponding costs are available and included in expenses.

D. For shipping companies, operating differential subsidies are included.

E. For shipping companies, income on reserve fund securities is included when shown separately.

F. For finance companies, earned insurance premiums are included.

G. For cigar, cigarette, oil, rubber, and liquor companies, net sales are after deducting taxes.

H. For finance companies, sales are after deducting net losses on factored receivables purchased.

I. Income derived from equipment rental is considered part of operating revenue.

[13] *Operating income before depreciation*

A. *Operating income* represents net sales less cost of sales and operating expenses before deducting depreciation, amortization, and depletion.

B. Operating expenses include, but are not limited to:

1. Cost of goods sold (materials, labor, and overhead)
2. Selling, general, and administrative expenses
3. Repairs and maintenance expense
4. Rent and royalty expense
5. Research and development expense
6. General taxes
7. Strike expense
8. Profit-sharing contributions
9. Bad debt expense
10. Pension costs, including past service pension costs (except when written off in one year)
11. Exploration expense
12. Parent company charges for administrative service
13. For motion picture and entertainment companies, amortization of film costs

14. For finance companies, amortization of development costs of new offices, etc.
15. For finance companies, development costs deferred (credit)
16. For finance companies, discount on notes sold
17. Amortization of tools and dies where the usable life is two years or less (i.e., automobile industry, aircraft manufacturing, etc.)

C. The following items, when separately listed, are treated as other income and deductions rather than as operating expenses:
   1. Moving expenses
   2. Foreign exchange adjustments
   3. Idle plant expenses
   4. Profit on sales of properties (except for securities, etc.) for the companies in the oil, coal, airline and other industries where these transactions are considered a normal part of doing business

D. For finance companies, operating income is stated after deducting additions to reserves for losses.

E. For finance companies, operating income is given after depreciation, if the latter is not stated separately, since it is relatively insignificant.

F. Current year's results of discontinued operations are not considered operating expenses and are shown as nonrecurring income or expense (net or not net of tax).

[14] *Depreciation and amortization*

A. *Depreciation and amortization* represents noncash charges for obsolescence and wear and tear on property, allocation of the current portion of capitalized expenditures, and depletion charges.

B. For oil, gas, and mining companies, this variable also includes dry holes, retirements, abandonments, and other intangible drilling costs. Some companies include these items together and some report them separately. To increase the comparability between companies, the items are lumped together in *Compustat*.

C. Amortization of patents, trademarks, and other intangibles is included.

D. Amortization of book plates is included (if amortized for more than two years).

[15] *Fixed charges*

A. *Fixed charges* represents all interest expense, the amortization of debt discount or premium, and the amortization of expense (i.e., underwriting, brokerage fees, advertising costs, etc.).

[16] *Income taxes*

A. *Income taxes* represents federal, state, other, and deferred income taxes, including charges in lieu of income taxes, a charge equivalent to the investment tax credit, and income taxes on dividends from nonconsolidated subsidiaries when separately stated.

B. Prior years' tax adjustments, when stated separately and reported on a recurring basis, are excluded from both taxes and nonrecurring expense and are treated as other income or other deductions.

C. Tax carry-backs and carry-forwards are excluded from income account (treated as nonrecurring income or expense—net of taxes).

D. Income taxes (both debit and credit) are excluded on extraordinary items that have been stated by the company in its public reports as net of taxes.

E. When prior years' income taxes are shown after net income they are excluded from the income account and shown as extraordinary items.

[18] *Net income*

Net income represents income after all operating and nonoperating income and expense and minority interest, but before preferred and common dividends. It is stated after extraordinary items which are not net of applicable taxes, or where there is a question on this point. However, net income is before all extraordinary items that are listed in the company's public reports as being netted of taxes. In addition, net income is stated before appropriation for general contingencies. These items are treated as surplus adjustments.

[20] *Available for common*

A. *Available for common* represents net income less preferred dividend requirements.

B. Normally, the preferred dividend requirements used in this calculation will be the same as the preferred dividends declared.

1. If more or fewer than four quarterly preferred dividends are declared in one year (where dividends are declared quarterly), then preferred dividend requirements will be used in calculating available for common

2. If all convertible preferred stock is converted into common during the year, no preferred dividends are deducted in calculating available for common

3. If common stock is issued by the company in exchange for preferred stock of another company, the dividends on the old preferred stock are disregarded in calculating available for common.

[30] *Capital expenditures*

Capital expenditures represents the amount spent for the construction or acquisition of facilities and equipment. Capital expenditures of merged companies are included. However, fixed assets acquired through merger, acquisition, or pooling of interests are *not* included.

[31] *Investments in and advances to subsidiaries*

Investments in and advances to subsidiaries includes long-term investments in and advances to unconsolidated subsidiaries and affiliated companies as stated in the consolidated financial statements.

[34] *Debt in current liabilities*

Debt in current liabilities includes notes payable, loans payable, contracts payable, current sinking fund payments, and the current maturity of long-term debt.

Missing Data

For some firms, complete data for a few years were not available on the Compustat tape. If they are critical data (e.g., data used to compute a rate of return), the firm is eliminated from the panel. Otherwise, one of the following procedures is used to estimate the missing data. The treatments differ according to the nature of the data.

Missing data treatment—Code A

Generally, for most of the variables the accuracy of the estimate for missing data is not particularly important. For those variables, denoted by the letter A in Table C.1, estimation is by a simple time-series regression of the form:

$$D_t = a + \text{b}t.$$

The parameters, a and b, are estimated using the data that are available for the period 1960–68. Any missing data could then be predicted. When the predicted value is negative, it is given the value of zero.

Missing data treatment—Code B

If data are missing in the initial year or years, the value of the nearest year for which data are available is taken. If data are missing between years for which data are available, interpolation is the method of estimation. This is accomplished as follows:

1. Let t be the earliest year for which data are missing or for which there is no estimate.
2. Let n be the number of consecutive years of missing data.
3. Let D represent the data.
4. Therefore, D_{t+n} is the first year data become available after n years of missing data.

$$D_t = D_{t-1} + \frac{D_{t+n} - D_{t-1}}{n + 1}.$$

5. This procedure is repeated until all missing data are estimated.

Note: $\dfrac{D_{t+n} - D_{t-1}}{n + 1}$ is the interpolated yearly average increment.

Missing data treatment—Code C

These variables are not estimated, because they are too critical to the study—these variables essentially become the numerator in the rate of return calculation. When these data are missing, the firm is eliminated from the study.

Generation of Variables

From those variables followed by a letter code in Table C.1 new variables are defined and calculated for use in this study.

Definitions and calculations of rate of return

Three basic rate-of-return concepts are used in this study, each of which is defined before and after taxes. In the following presentation, it is helpful to view a rate of return as two separate calculations, one for the numerator and the other for the denominator—the income concept and the investment base concept.

Income definitions. The basic income concept, called *operating profit* (OP), is defined broadly to include profits to stockholders (common and preferred) plus interest to creditors. Operating profits are computed both before and after income taxes, and both with and without an implicit interest on trade liabilities. Thus, there are four operating profit variables. The following paragraphs define and label these variables using the Compustat variables as a basis. The Compustat variables are given by Standard and Poor's name with the identifying number immediately below in parentheses. (See Table C.1.)

Operating Profit before Taxes (OPB)

$$OPB = \text{Operating Income} - \text{Depreciation and Amortization}$$
$$(13) \qquad\qquad\qquad (14)$$

Operating Profit after Taxes (OPA)

$$OPA = OPB - \text{Income Taxes}$$
$$(16)$$

Implicit Operating Profit before Taxes (IOPB)

$$IOPB = OPB + II$$

where:

II is the implicit interest on trade liabilities (see calculation below).

Implicit Operating Profit after Taxes (IOPA)

$$IOPA = IOPB - \text{Income Taxes}$$
$$(16)$$

The other income concept, called *stockholders' profit* (SP), is defined narrowly as the income available to common stockholders. Again, both before- and after-tax variables are calculated.

Stockholder Profit before Taxes (SPB)

$$SPB = \text{Available for Common} + \text{Income Taxes}$$
$$(20) \qquad\qquad (16)$$

Stockholder Profit after Taxes (SPA)

$$SPA = \text{Available for Common}$$
$$(20)$$

Calculation of implicit interest (II). For the principal rate-of-return measure in this study, implicit interest on trade liabilities is estimated and included in the income concept. Because it is assumed that the costs of credit are included in the costs of material purchased on account, the average of beginning-of-year and end-of-year trade liabilities is estimated. Next, this average borrowed capital is multiplied by a short-term interest rate. The rate chosen is the 4–6–month prime commercial-paper rate. These calculations are summarized as follows:

$$TL = \text{Current Liabilities} - \text{Debt in Current Liabilities}$$
$$(5) \qquad\qquad (34)$$

$$ATL_t = \tfrac{1}{2}(TL_{t-1} + TL_t)$$

$$II_t = (CPR_t)\,(ATL_t).$$

For $t = 1960$ (for many firms balance sheet data for 1960 are not available):

$$II_t = (CPR_t)\,(TL_t)$$

where:

$TL = $ Trade Liabilities

$ATL_t = $ Average Trade Liabilities for year t

$CPR_t = $ Commercial Paper Rate for year t, in percentage

$II_t = $ Implicit Interest for year t.

Investment base definitions. The investment base concepts follow directly from the income definitions. When income is defined broadly to include income to all equity (OP), the base likewise is broad and is defined as *total assets* (A). An average of beginning-of-year and end-of-year assets is the denominator and is labeled *average assets* (AA).[3] The base for the narrow concept of income to stockholders is stockholders' equity (SE). The *average stockholders' equity* for each year (ASE) becomes the denominator in the calculation. These definitions are summarized as follows:

$$A = \text{Total Assets/Liabilities} - \text{Investments and Advances}$$
$$(6) \qquad\qquad \text{to Subsidiaries}$$
$$(31)$$

$$AA_t = \tfrac{1}{2}(A_t + A_{t-1})$$

$$SE = \text{Common Equity}$$
$$(11)$$

$$ASE_t = \tfrac{1}{2}(SE + SE_{t-1}).$$

For $t = 1960$:

$$AA_t = A_t$$

$$ASE_t = SE_t.$$

Rate-of-return calculations. The following summarizes the calculations of the six firm rate-of-return measures. These variables are subscripted with a t to indicate a separate computation of a rate of return for each year for each firm.

1.
$$ORB_t = \frac{OPB_t}{AA_t}$$

where:

$$ORB = \text{Operating Return before Taxes}$$

2.
$$ORA_t = \frac{OPA_t}{AA_t}$$

where:

$$ORA = \text{Operating Return after Taxes}$$

---

3. *Investments and advances to (unconsolidated) subsidiaries* is excluded from the investment base because their earnings are excluded in the numerator.

3.
$$IORB_t = \frac{IOPB_t}{AA_t}$$

where:

$IORB$ = Implicit Operating Return before Taxes

4.
$$IORA_t = \frac{IOPA_t}{AA_t}$$

where:

$IORA$ = Implicit Operating Return after Taxes

5.
$$SRB_t = \frac{SPB_t}{ASE_t}$$

where:

SRB = Stockholders' Return before Taxes

6.
$$SRA_t = \frac{SPA_t}{ASE_t}$$

where:

SRA = Stockholders' Return after Taxes.

Capital/output ratio definitions and calculations

Two forms of capital/output ratios are used. They differ in the definition of capital. In the first ratio, capital is defined as net plant or net capital assets; in the second, capital is defined as total assets. For both ratios, sales serves a a proxy for output. These ratios are called the fixed-capital/output ratio, denoted K/Q, and the asset/output ratio, denoted A/Q. The computations are summarized as follows:

$$K/Q_t = \frac{NP_t + NP_{t-1}}{2S_t}$$

where:

NP = Net Plant
(8)

S = Net Sales;
(12)

$$A/Q_t = \frac{AA_t}{S_t}$$

where:

AA = Average (firm) Assets as computed earlier

S = Net Sales.

(12)

1960–68 Period Firm Variables

All variables used in this study are period-average variables. No yearly variables are used. Thus, all the following variables in some way represent an average for the 1960–68 time period.

Average rate of return

The period-average rate of return for each firm is the mean (unweighted average) of each firm's nine yearly returns. This calculation is summarized as follows:

$$AR_i = \frac{1}{9} \sum_{t=60}^{68} R_{it}$$

where:

R_{it} = the general notation for all six (yearly) rate-of-return variables for firm i in year t.

AR_i = the general notation for all six period-average rate-of-return variables for firm i.

Definition and calculation of temporal risk

Two basic concepts of risk are used. The first concept of risk relates to the temporal uncertainty of earnings.[4] This type of risk, called temporal risk, is measured by each firm's *temporal standard deviation,* denoted TSD, and *temporal skewness,* noted TS. These moments of each firm's rate-of-return distribution are caluculated in two different ways. First, the period-average return is used as the expected value and the moments are then measured around these. Second, predicted yearly returns (from a simple time-series regression of each firm's returns) are used as the expected values. These risk variables measured around predicted values are denoted TSDP and TSP respectively. The computation of these risk variables is summarized as follows:

---

4. The other concept, spatial risk, is an industry concept; it is discussed in the section on industry variables.

Moments around period averages.

$$TSD_i = \left[\sum_{t=60}^{68} \frac{(R_{it}-AR_i)^2}{9} \right]^{1\!/\!2}$$

$$TS_i = \sum_{t=60}^{68} \frac{(R_{it}-AR_i)^3}{9(TSD_i)^3}$$

where:

R_{it} = the general notation for the six yearly rate-of-return variables for firm i in year t.

AR_i = the general notation for the six period-average rate-of-return variables for firm i.

Moments around predicted returns.

$$TSDP_i = \left[\sum_{t=60}^{68} \frac{(R_{it}-\hat{R}_{it})^2}{9} \right]^{1\!/\!2}$$

$$TSP_i = \sum_{t=60}^{68} \frac{(R_{it}-\hat{R}_{it})^3}{9(TSDP_i)^3}$$

where:

R_{it} = the general notation for the six yearly rate-of-return variables for firm i in year t.

$\hat{R}_{it}$ = the values for R_{it} which are predicted from a linear time series regression of the form: $R_{it} = a + bt$.

Definitions and calculations of other variables

Average firm size. The basic variable from which other forms of the size variable are calculated is the simple mean of the nine yearly values for average assets (AA_t) computed for rates of return. Period-average assets are denoted simply as A_i. This calculation is summarized as:

$$A_i = \frac{1}{9} \sum_{t=60}^{68} AA_{it}$$

where:

AA_{it} = the average beginning-of-year and end-of-year assets for firm i in year t. (See investment base calculation.)

Average capital/output ratios. Both measures of average capital/output ratios are simple means of the nine yearly values. The period-average values are denoted K/Q_i and A/Q_i for the fixed-capital/output ratio and asset/output ratio, respectively. These computations are summarized as:

$$K/Q_i = \frac{1}{9} \sum_{t=60}^{68} K/Q_{it}$$

$$A/Q_i = \frac{1}{9} \sum_{t=60}^{68} A/Q_{it}$$

where:

K/Q_{it} and A/Q_{it} are the yearly values for the ratio of fixed capital and total assets to sales (output).

Period growth rates. Period growth is measured as the percentage increase over the entire period. The total change in sales and total change in assets are divided by the beginning-of-period values. *Sales growth* is denoted as **SG** and *asset growth* is denoted as **AG**. These computations are summarized as:

$$SG_i = \frac{S_{68}-S_{60}}{S_{60}}$$

where:

S = Net Sales;
(12)

$$AG_i = \frac{A_{68}-A_{60}}{A_{60}}$$

where:

A = Total Assets/Liabilities − Investments and Advances
(6)   to Subsidiaries.
(31)

1960–68 Period Industry Variables

Industry variables are averages of each industry's member-firm variables. A weighted average is used only for one set of rate-of-return variables. In all other cases, unweighted averages are used.

Rate of return

Both an unweighted and weighted industry average rate of return are used in this study. Two steps are needed to calculate industry rates of return. First, the average return for each year is computed. Then these nine industry yearly values are averaged (always an unweighted average) to obtain the period industry average.

Unweighted industry averages. The computations of each year's unweighted industry average returns are summarized as:

$$UR_{jt} = \frac{1}{n} \sum_{i=1}^{n} R_{ijt}$$

where:

R_{ijt} is the general notation for all six firm rate-of-return variables for firm i in industry j for year t.

UR_{jt} is the general notation for all six unweighted industry rate-of-return variables for industry j in year t.

n is the number of firms in industry j.

The period-average industry return is the simple average of these nine yearly values. This computation is summarized as:

$$AUR_j = \frac{1}{9} \sum_{t=60}^{68} UR_{jt}$$

where:

UR_{jt} is the general notation for all six unweighted industry rate-of-return variables for industry j in year t.

AUR_j is the general notation for all six unweighted period-average industry rate-of-return variables for industry j.

Note: In the text of the study, the individual unweighted period-average industry rates of return are denoted simply as ORB_j, ORA_j, $IORB_j$, $IORA_j$, SRB_j, and SRA_j. The subscript j always indicates the variable is an industry variable.

Weighted industry averages. The computations of each year's weighted industry average return is summarized as:

$$WR_{jt} = \sum_{i=1}^{n} I_{ijt} \bigg/ \sum_{i=1}^{n} B_{ijt}$$

where:

I_{ijt} is the general notation for all six different income variables for firm i in industry j for year t.

B_{ijt} is the general notation for the two different investment bases for firm i in industry j for year t. See the rate-of-return calculations for the proper matching of bases with income concepts.

WR_{jt} is the general notation for all six weighted-average industry rate-of-return variables for industry j in year t.

n is the number of firms in industry j.

The weighted period-average industry rate of return is the simple average of these nine yearly values. This computation is summarized as:

$$AWR_j = \frac{1}{9} \sum_{t=60}^{68} WR_{jt}$$

where:

WR_{jt} is the general notation for all six weighted industry average rate-of-return variables for industry j in year t.

AWR_j is the general notation for all six weighted industry rate-of-return variables for industry j.

Note: In the text of the study the individual weighted period-average industry rates of return are denoted as $ORA_{\omega j}$, $ORB_{\omega j}$, $IORB_{\omega j}$, $IORA_{\omega j}$, $SRB_{\omega j}$, and $SRA_{\omega j}$. The subscript j always indicates the variable is an industry variable. The subscript ω is used to indicate the industry average is weighted. The unweighted average is without a subscript.

Industry spatial risk

The concept of spatial risk relates to the uncertainty of a potential entrant in predicting its average rate of return were it to enter an industry. Spatial, or intraindustry, risk is measured by second and third moments of firm period-average rates of return around the industry's period-average rate of return. These two risk variables, called *industry standard deviation,* denoted ISD, and *industry skewness,* denoted IS, are computed as follows:

$$ISD_j = \left[\sum_{i=1}^{n} \frac{(AR_{ij} - AUR_j)^2}{n} \right]^{1/2}$$

$$IS_j = \sum_{i=1}^{n} \frac{(AR_{ij} - AUR_j)^3}{n(ISD_j)^3}$$

where:

AR_{ij} is the general notation for all six period-average rate-of-return variables for firm i in industry j;

AUR_j is the general notation for all six unweighted period-average industry rates of return for industry j;

n is the number of firms in industry j.

Definitions and calculations of other variables

Average firm size. The industry average of firm period-average assets, denoted AA_j, is calculated as follows:

$$AA_j = \frac{1}{n} \sum_{i=1}^{n} A_{ij}$$

where:

A_{ij} is the period-average assets for firm i in industry j;

n is the number of firms in industry j.

Average capital/output ratios. The industry averages of firm period-average fixed capital/output and asset/output ratios, denoted AK/Q_j and AA/Q_j, respectively, are computed as follows:

$$AK/Q_j = \frac{1}{n} \sum_{i=1}^{n} K/Q_{ij}$$

$$AA/Q_j = \frac{1}{n} \sum_{i=1}^{n} A/Q_{ij}$$

where:

> K/Q_{ij} is the period-average fixed-capital/output ratio for firm i in industry j;
>
> A/Q_{ij} is the period-average asset/output ratio for firm i in industry j;
>
> n is the number of firms in industry j.

Average growth rates. The industry averages of member-firm asset-growth rates (AAG_j) and sales-growth rates (ASG_j) are calculated as follows:

$$AAG_j = \frac{1}{n} \sum_{i=1}^{n} AG_{ij}$$

$$ASG_j = \frac{1}{n} \sum_{i=1}^{n} SG_{ij}$$

where:

> AG_{ij} is the asset growth rate for firm i in industry j;
>
> SG_{ij} is the sales growth rate for firm i in industry j;
>
> n is the number of firms in industry j.

Relative variables. For all relative variables (profitability, size, and capital intensity) the calculations are made as follows:

Relative profitability (REL:AR)

$$REL{:}AR_{ij} = \frac{AR_{ij} - AUR_j}{AUR_j}$$

where:

> $REL{:}AR_{ij}$ is the general notation for all six relative period-average rate-of-return variables for firm i in industry j.
>
> Other variables as defined previously.

Relative size (REL:A)

$$REL{:}A_{ij} = \frac{A_{ij} - AA_j}{AA_j}$$

where:

$REL{:}A_{ij}$ is the relative asset size of firm i in industry j.

Other variables as defined previously.

Relative capital intensity ($REL{:}A/Q$, $REL{:}K/Q$)

$$REL{:}A/Q_{ij} = \frac{A/Q_{ij} - AA/Q_j}{AA/Q_j}$$

$$REL{:}K/Q_{ij} = \frac{K/Q_{ij} - AK/Q_j}{AK/Q_j}$$

where:

$REL{:}A/Q_{ij}$ and $REL{:}K/Q_{ij}$, respectively, are the relative ratios of assets to sales and fixed assets to sales for firm i in industry j.

Other variables as defined previously.

APPENDIX D

CURRENT-COST METHODOLOGY

The major objective of this appendix is to devise a methodology by which to estimate the relative discrepancy between profitability as accounted for on the basis of historical costs and profitability as accounted for on the basis of current costs. It is not the purpose of this methodology to derive precise measures of current-cost rates of return, but rather to determine whether the adjustment of performance measures for current costs alters observed patterns of profitability and changes the relation between performance and the structural variables, e.g., concentration. In other words, the thrust of the analysis is to determine the probable effect on the pattern of profitability (relative performance) rather than absolute levels of profitability.

Factors leading to distortions

With these objectives established, the need is to concentrate on the factors that will affect the pattern of industry profitability. For example, it would be expected that for most firms current-cost rates of return are lower than accounting rates of return. What factors will cause the adjustment for one firm (industry) to be significantly greater than for another? The following are suggested:

1. The relative asset growth of the firm or industry
2. The capital/output ratio of the firm or industry
3. The depreciation procedures followed by the firm or industry
4. The average useful life of a firm's fixed assets

Relative asset growth. The faster a firm or industry is growing, the lower the average age of its fixed assets. Because the age of fixed assets affects the magnitude of the adjustment to current costs (assuming rising prices of fixed assets), the newer the fixed assets the less their values are understated. Therefore, one would expect a greater adjustment for slow-growing (or declining) industries than for rapidly growing industries. In the methodology, then, the relative age of fixed assets becomes an important variable.

200

Capital intensity. Because it is the conventional treatment of fixed assets that gives rise to the major distortions in performance measures, the greater a firm's use of assets in production, the greater the relative adjustment. For example, the discrepancy for a retail store would be far less than that for a public utility.

Depreciation procedures. Depreciation policies affect the discrepancy between current- and historical-cost profitability measures. An accelerated depreciation policy would probably decrease the discrepancy between current- and historical-cost income flows but increase the discrepancy between asset values. The methodology, therefore, must deal with the impact of different depreciation policies on observed and current-cost rates of return.

Useful life. The last important factor affecting the discrepancy between current- and historical-cost rates of return is the average useful life of fixed assets. Other things being equal (e.g., growth rates), the longer the average useful life of a firm's fixed assets, the older the firm's assets and, therefore, the greater the discrepancy. Although it is the age of fixed asssets that, in large part, determines the relative discrepancy, asset growth and useful life are separately considered here as determinants of age directly and the discrepancy indirectly. In part, this separation of factors is useful conceptually. It is also necessary, however, because useful life determines the amount of depreciation to be taken each year in the determination of profit. The estimation of average useful life, therefore, is critical in this methodology.[1]

Identification of these factors as being the most critical in considering discrepancies between historical- and current-cost profitability forms the basis for the methodology developed below.

General Methodology and Concepts

The following theory and analysis follow those developed by Edwards and Bell in *The Theory and Measurement of Business Income.*[2] A detailed review of the concepts developed in this highly acclaimed book

1. At one point, I considered estimating average useful life as a ratio of actual gross plant to actual depreciation expense. This would have attempted to let the experience of each firm determine useful life. Unfortunately, that firms have different depreciation policies (and growth rates) is believed to cause a greater distortion in useful life estimates than does an alternative procedure. (See following discussion of methodology adopted.)

2. Edgar O. Edwards and Philip W. Bell, *Business Income* (Berkeley, Calif.: University of California Press, 1970).

is beyond the scope of this study. However, a few of the fundamental concepts are discussed. Edwards and Bell argue that accounting profits do not accurately portray the operating performance of the firm, for the reason that realized holding gains (and losses) are included. They introduce the concepts of current operating profit, realized business profit, and business profit (realized and realizable profits). Current operating profit "is by definition an increase in current purchasing power; it is the excess of the current purchasing power represented by the current value of output over the current purchasing power represented by the current value of input."[3] Current operating profit excludes all elements of holding gains and losses arising from changes in specific prices. The other two profit concepts include these holding gains. In realized business profits, only the realized holding gains are included, but in business profit the total realizable holding gains are included. In this study only current operating profits are used. However, the distinction between current operating profits and business profits is helpful in understanding the difference between current operating profits and accounting profits. A short example will illustrate.[4]

Suppose machinery costing $2,000 were purchased at the beginning of 1967. At this time, the price index for machinery stood at 120. Later, at the end of 1969, it was 180 and by the end of 1970, 204. The current cost of this machinery (new) at the beginning of 1970 is thus $3,000 ($\frac{180}{120} \times$ \$2,000); at the end of the year it is $3,400 ($\frac{204}{120} \times$ \$2,000). The current cost of using the machinery in 1970 (assuming straight-line) is computed by dividing the useful life into the average current-cost value during the year. If one assumes a 20-year life, then current-cost depreciation is $160 ($\frac{3,000 + 3,400}{2(20)}$).

Current operating profit is determined by subtracting the $160 from sales for the year. The excess ($60) of current-cost depreciation ($160) over historical-cost depreciation ($100) represents the realized cost savings during the year resulting from having purchased the machinery at a price lower than that prevailing when the services are received.[5] If actual sales for the year are $500 (automatically in current dollars), then current operating profit is $340 and realized business profit is $340 plus the

3. *Ibid.*, p. 124.

4. This example is adapted from *ibid.*, pp. 188–94.

5. Edwards and Bell choose to label these holding gains "cost savings." The services of the asset used up had a current value of $160, but cost the firm only $100. The difference is the cost savings realized through use.

realized holding gain of $60, or $400. The reader will note that realized business profit is the same (always) as accounting profits.

These concepts are summarized as follows:

Conventional Accounting Profit

Sales (at current prices)	$500
Less depreciation (at historic cost)	100
Accounting profit	$400

Current Operating Profit

Sales (at current prices)	$500
Less depreciation (at current cost)	160
Current operating profit	$340

Realized Business Profit

Current operating profit	$340
Realized cost savings (excess of current-cost over historic-cost depreciation)	60
Realized profit	$400

With these rather simple computations, a general methodology is established to derive estimates of current operating income considering the effects for fixed assets. It is argued that accounting income should not be used to measure firms' or industries' performance or the effect of monopoly power. The appropriate measure is current operating profit, which excludes all holding gains and losses.[6]

While the recognition of changes in fixed asset prices will affect profits, an equally important consideration remains with the adjustment of asset values to current costs. The reason, of course, is the concern with rates of return. Rates of return are, therefore, altered because of adjustments in both the numerator and the denominator.

Analysis is rather routine if useful life, date of acquisition, and current cost each year are known for each fixed asset. However, such is not the case. At best, only rough estimates of these necessary data can be made. The methodology for deriving estimates must be guided by the objectives set forth earlier. In view of these objectives the purpose is to derive estimates that reflect relative adjustments rather than absolute results. For example, the methodology developed below seeks to derive unbiased estimates of the relative ages of fixed assets rather than a precise measure of their average ages.

6. For a very illuminating discussion on the shortcomings of using accounting profit (or realized business profit) for management decisions, judgments of performance, and resource allocation, see Edwards and Bell, *Business Income*, pp. 220–32.

Detailed Methodology

The methodology is designed to adjust fixed assets for each firm to current cost for the period 1960–68 from data available on the Compustat Tapes. In addition to the Compustat data used in previous analyses, two additional variables are needed. For the longer, 19-year period of 1950–68, yearly capital expenditures (Variable No. 30) and gross plant balances (Variable No. 7) are needed. These data are available for 339 of the larger 768-firm panel.

Useful life

The estimation of useful life (L) is a critical step in the following methodology. A separate useful life estimate is made for each industry and is used for each firm in that industry. This life estimate is a weighted average of the useful lives of the two major classes of depreciable fixed assets—equipment (including machinery) and structures. Estimates for each of these two classes are obtained from the U.S. Treasury Department's 1964 industry useful-life guidelines[7] and are weighted by estimates of the ratios of equipment (and machinery) to structures for each industry.[8] The computation of useful life (L) is summarized as:

$$(1.1) \qquad L_j = \frac{1}{ER_j/LE_j + (1-ER_j)/LS}$$

where:

L_j = the weighted-average useful life of depreciable assets for industry j.

LE_j = the IRS estimate of average useful life of equipment for industry j.

LS = the IRS estimate of average useful life of structures. The value of 45 years is used for all structures in all industries.

ER_j = the estimate of the ratio of gross equipment to structures for industry j.

7. U.S., Treasury Department, Internal Revenue Service, *Depreciation Guidelines and Rules*, Revenue Procedure 62–21, Pubn. No. 456, Revised Aug. 1964 (Washington, D.C.: Government Printing Office, 1964), pp. 3–10.

8. Daniel S. Creamer of The Conference Board provided estimates of the ratio of gross book value of equipment and machinery to structure for each year from 1953 to 1965. The period-average equipment ratio (ER) is used in the calculation of useful life (L). The equipment ratios provided are for IRS three-digit industries. The equipment ratios are, therefore, used for all the four-digit industries in the IRS three-digit industry.

It is obvious the L is not a simple weighted average of the useful lives of equipment and structures. This follows from the use of the useful life estimate in the calculations of current-cost rates of return. First and foremost, L is used to estimate the amount of depreciation to be taken from revenue each year to obtain current operating profit. Second, estimated average useful life is used to estimate net depreciable assets (gross plant minus accumulated depreciation). Net fixed assets are used in the computation of total assets in the denominator of the rate-of-return measure. Instead of being an estimate of "average useful life," L is an estimate of the number of years it would take to fully depreciate (assuming straight-line deprecation) total gross plant.[9] In other words, L is the ratio of gross plant to depreciation expense calculated by assuming straight-line depreciation. A short example will clarify this.

Suppose a firm has 60 percent of its depreciable assets in machinery and equipment (ER = .60) and 40 percent (1 − ER = .40) in structures. Suppose total gross plant is $100, the average useful life of equipment is 10 years, and the average useful life of structures is 40 years. Of the $100 gross plant, it is estimated that $60 is equipment and $40 is structures. Assuming straight-line depreciation (and no salvage value), the yearly amounts of depreciation would be $6 for equipment ($\frac{\$60}{10 \text{ years}}$) and $1 for structures ($\frac{\$40}{40 \text{ years}}$). Total depreciation, given these assumptions, would then be $7; and the (weighted-average) rate of depreciation would be 7 percent of gross plant each year ($\frac{\$7}{\$100}$) . Hence, the weighted-average "useful life" would be the reciprocal of the weighted-average rate of depreciation, or 14.29 years. The calculation is summarized:

$$L = 14.29 = \frac{1}{.60/10 + (1-.60)/40}.$$

Therefore L is really not an average useful life because average useful life would be 22 years (10 years times 60 percent, plus 40 years times 40

9. "Gross Plant" on the Compustat tapes combines the total of structures, equipment, and land into a single figure. Separate figures are not readily available. This is the reason for the use of the equipment ratio. Although gross plant includes land, this inclusion is ignored in the methodology. This, however, would not materially alter the results because of the relatively small amount of land carried on the books of most firms. For example, the percentage of land to depreciable assets for all manufacturing was 2.3 percent in 1963 and ranged from 0.9 percent (Textile Mills) to 6.0 percent (Leather Products). See U.S., Treasury Department, Internal Revenue Service, *Statistics of Income—1963, Corporation Tax Returns* (Washington, D.C.: Government Printing Office, 1969), Table 3.

percent) instead of 14.29 years. In short, useful life (L) is defined in such a way that it can be used to calculate yearly depreciation expense.

Price indexes

To adjust historical costs of equipment (and machinery) and structures to current costs, a specific price index of these types of asset is needed. For machinery and equipment the Department of Commerce's GNP implicit deflator for producers' durable equipment is used; and for structures the implicit deflator for nonresidential structures is used. These two price indexes become one by weighting them by each industry's ratio of equipment to structures as follows:

(1.2) $$PI_{jt} = (EPI_t)(ER_j) + (SPI_t)(1 - ER_j)$$

where:

PI_{jt} = the price index for industry j in year t.

EPI_t = the GNP implicit deflator for producer's durable equipment for year t.

SPI_t = the GNP implicit deflator for nonresidential structures for year t.

ER_j = the period-average ratio of gross book value of equipment to structures for industry j.

An industry's price index for each year is used in the following methodology and is denoted PI_t. It should be remembered, however, that this price index is computed separately for each industry according to its ratio of equipment to structures.

Dates of acquisition and average age of 1959 plant

Because current-cost rates of return are calculated for the period 1960–68, the current cost of 1959 year-end assets is the starting point. (The denominator for 1960 rates of return is the average of 1959 assets and 1960 assets.) The first step in the computation of current costs for 1959 is to estimate the dates of acquisition and the average age of existing stock. This estimate is based on capital expenditures and the acquisition (through merger) of used assets for each firm.[10] Although a series of

---

10. Capital expenditures include both the current purchases of new *and* used equipment. When a firm purchases specific pieces of used equipment, the cost recorded on the books should be the purchase price. For the purposes of this methodology, if a firm purchased an asset for $10,000 in 1955, it makes no difference whether it

capital expenditures is available for each firm, acquisitions of used assets must be estimated from an analysis of the gross fixed asset account each year.

Retirements and used acquisitions. Because used acquisitions and retirements each year are computed by an analysis of the gross plant accounts and capital expenditures for that year, the two figures are net of each other. That is, in no year will there be both a used acquisition and a retirement. They are calculated as follows:

(2.1) $$R_n = K_n - (GP_n - GP_{n-1}); R_n \gtreqqless 0$$

where:

R = net retirements, i.e., gross retirements net of used acquisitions;

K = capital expenditures (Compustat Variable No. 30);

GP = gross plant (Compustat Variable No. 7);

n = year of reported event.

If $R_n < 0$, then $-R_n = UA_n$; or

(2.2) $$UA_n = (GP_n - GP_{n-1}) - K_n; UA_n > 0$$

where:

UA = used acquisitions.

Average age of capital expenditure. The next step is to estimate average age of the plant at 1959 year-end. The estimation is based on the assumption of a first-in, first-out flow of fixed assets. Step one is to accumulate the capital expenditures and used acquisitions beginning with 1959 for each previous year until this accumulation is equal to or greater than the gross plant balance of 1959. Thus, this procedure results in estimates of the dates of acquisition of all capital expenditures and used acquisitions which add up to the gross plant balance at 1959. This computation is summarized as follows:

(3.1) $$\sum_{i=0}^{k} (K_{59-i} + UA_{59-i}) \leq GP_{59}$$

---

was new or used. However, if a firm acquired used assets through a merger with another firm, the dollar amount carried to the firm's books would probably not be the purchase price but the *original* cost of the assets (debit to gross plant) along with the accumulated depreciation to date on those assets. In the following methodology, *used acquisitions* refers to only the used assets acquired through merger.

where:

$$k = \text{year accumulation equals or exceeds } GP_{59};$$

$$k \overset{<}{=} 59 - 50, \text{ i.e., 9.}$$

If this accumulation is not equal to or greater than GP_{59}, then the balance is assumed to have been acquired in $1950 - L^*/2$, where $L/2$ is rounded to the nearest integer [see (1.1) for definition of L].

$$(3.2) \qquad GP_{59} - \sum_{i=0}^{k} (K_{59-i} + UA_{59-i}) = BAL^b.$$

The year of acquisition of *BAL* is *b,* which equals $50 - L^*/2$ ($L/2$ rounded to nearest integer).

The subscripts of all variables are used to represent the year of the recorded event. A superscript is used to indicate the estimated date of original purchase or acquisition. For example, the balance is without a recorded date. Therefore the superscript *b* is used to indicate the computed date of purchase or acquisition.

Step two is to estimate average age. This requires two separate estimates: one just for capital expenditures and the second for both capital expenditures and used acquisitions. It is assumed that capital expenditures and used acquisitions occur at mid-year. Therefore, the capital expenditures in 1959 are one-half year old at the end of 1959. Likewise, the capital expenditures made in each previous year *n* are $1959 - n + .5$ years old at the end of 1959. Each year's capital expenditures are multiplied by this age index for each year. Should the situation exist where there is a balance (*BAL*), then the balance is multiplied by the age index $1959 - b + .5$. Next, products of capital expenditures (and the remaining balance should one exist), and the age indices are summed. This sum is then divided by the gross plant balance of 1959 less the accumulated used acquisitions from 1959 through $1959 - k,$ that is, the determined amount of *UA* in 1959 Gross Plant. The quotient (denoted *AK*) is the weighted-average age estimate of capital expenditures.

The computation of the age index (*AI*) is:

$$(3.3) \qquad AI_n{}^m = m - n + .5$$

where:

$$AI_n = \text{age index for year } n$$

$$m = \text{the year from which age is measured (1959).}$$

The computation of accumulated used acquisitions (AUA) is:

(3.4)
$$AUA = \sum_{i=0}^{k} UA_{59-i}$$

where:

AUA = accumulated used acquisitions from 59 through $59 - k$;

k = value of k found in (3.1).

Finally, the computation of average age of capital expenditures (AK) is:

(3.5)
$$AK_{59} = \frac{1}{GP_{59} - AUA} \left[\sum_{i=0}^{k} \left[(K_{59-i})(AI_{59-i}) \right] + BAL^b(AI_b{}^m) \right]$$

where:

AK_{59} = average age of capital expenditures which are determined to be included in the gross plant balance at year-end 1959.

Average age of entire plant. The next step is to estimate the average age of combined capital expenditures and used acquisitions. It is assumed that the average age of used acquisitions at the recorded date of acquisition (n) is the same as the average age of the firm's capital expenditures (AK) computed in (3.5). Therefore, used acquisitions are assumed to have been originally purchased new AK years earlier than the date of recorded acquisition (n) by the firm being studied.

The computation of the year of original acquisition (a) is:

(3.6)
$$a = n - AK*$$

where:

$AK*$ is AK rounded to nearest integer.

Therefore, the age index for used acquisitions is:

(3.7)
$$AI_a{}^m = m - a + .5.$$

$UA_n{}^a$ is interpreted as a used acquisition reported in year n but estimated to have been purchased originally (new) in year a. With each n, there is an associated a. At this point, a new series is generated called the *original purchase* (OP) series. This original purchase series represents each year's total of that year's capital expenditures and the used acquisitions estimated to have been purchased originally in that year.

The average age of the total gross plant is now computed on the basis of this *OP* series. Used acquisitions are now treated as new capital expenditures *AK** years earlier than recorded. For example, if a used acquisition is recorded in 1955, and the weighted-average age of capital expenditures [*AK* from (3.5)] is 4.58 years, then this used acquisition is treated as a "new" capital expenditure in 1950 (a = 1955−5). Thus it has an age of 1959 − 1950 + .5 years. The product of each year's original purchases and their respective age indices are summed and the total is divided by gross plant at the end of 1959. The quotient is the weighted-average age of the entire plant.

$$(3.8) \qquad AP_{59} = \frac{1}{GP_{59}} \left[\sum_{i=0}^{k} \left[(K_{59-i})(AI_{59-i}^{m}) \right] + BAL^{b}(AI_{b}^{m}) \right. \\ \left. + \sum_{i=0}^{k} \left[(UA_{59-i}^{a})(AI_{a}^{'m_a'}) \right] \right]$$

where:

AP_n = average age of plant.

Note: Later [$(AP_n)(GP_n)$] will be used to denote the value inside the large brackets.

Current cost of gross plant in 1959

The purchase date of each capital expenditure and the estimated dates for original purchase of used acquisitions and of *BAL* having been determined, it is easy to compute the current cost. Current cost as of 31 December 1959 of each original purchase is computed by multiplying the amount by the ratio of 1959 year-end price index to the price index at the date of original purchase.

The sum of each original purchase multiplied by these price-adjustment ratios becomes the estimated current cost of gross plant at 1959.

The current cost for each used acquisition, capital expenditure, or *BAL* is computed as:

$$(4.1) \qquad 1959CC_n^{\cdot} = \frac{OP_n{}^c (PI_{59} + PI_{60})}{2PI_c}$$

where:

$1959CC_n$ = the 1959 current cost for each original purchase in year n;

$OP_n{}^c$ = the original purchase (capital expenditure, used acquisition, or BAL) reported in year n with an estimated date of original purchase in year c;

n = year event recorded;

c = n, for capital expenditure (K);

c = b, for balance (BAL);

c = a, for used acquisitions (UA);

PI = composite price index, average for year.

The summation of current cost of each original purchase (OP) is the estimated current cost of gross plant.

(4.2)
$$1959 \; CCGP = \sum 1959 \; CC_n$$

where:

$1959 \; CCGP$ = 1959 current cost of gross plant.

Subsequent years' variables

Subsequent years' current-cost data and average-age estimates follow from previous results; the data generated are used and altered for each year.

Average age. The first computational step is to revise the estimate of average age for the plant at year-end. Essentially, the computation involves adding one year to the previous gross plant's age and adjusting this for the additions and retirements during the year. By adding the previous gross plant balance to the product of $(AP_{n-i}) \, (GP_{n-1})$ [see (3.8)], gross plant has been aged one year.

(5.1)
$$(AP_{n-1}) \, (GP_{n-1}) + (GP_{n-1}).$$

To this, add the weighted age of capital expenditures for the current year,

(5.2)
$$(K_n) \, (.5)$$

to get

(5.3)
$$(AP_{n-1}) \, (GP_{n-1}) + GP_{n-1} + K_n \, (.5).$$

Next, the weighted age of the retirements during the year is subtracted. Again, it is assumed retirements are on the first-in, first-out basis. Consequently it is important to retain the schedule of components (OP_n series) of the gross plant balance in each year, by amounts and date of original purchase. Retirements are the difference between capital expenditures and the change in gross plant during the year [see (2.1)].

The age of the retirement is simply the age of the oldest original purchase (OP_n) (new or used) included in the gross plant balance at the beginning of the year. The oldest layer (each year represents a layer) becomes the pool for retirements in successive years. Retirements come from each layer until it is exhausted; then the next year's layer is depleted. Thus, retirements in any year may be from more than one layer.

To complete the computation of average age each year, the product of the retirements and their age indices for each layer is subtracted from (5.3) above. Average age of gross plant is computed then by dividing this total by gross plant.

(5.4) $\qquad (AP_n)\,(GP_n) = (AP_{n-1})\,(GP_{n-1}) + GP_{n-1} + .5K_n - \Sigma R_n{}^r AI_r{}^m$

where:

$\qquad r =$ the determined date of original acquisition of the retirement in year n;

$\qquad AI_r{}^m =$ the age index for year r.

Average age of the plant is computed as:

(5.5) $\qquad\qquad\qquad AP_n = \dfrac{[(AP_n)\,(GP_n)]}{GP_n}.$

In case $R_n < 0$, then no retirements occur. The net acquisition of used plant is assumed to have the average age of the existing stock. Therefore, average age is computed by dividing (5.3) by the gross plant minus these used acquisitions.

(5.6) $\qquad\qquad AP_n = \dfrac{(AP_{n-1})\,(GP_{n-1}) + GP_{n-1} + .5K_n}{GP_n - UA_n}.$

Because the age of used acquisitions during the year is assumed to be equal to the average age of existing stock:

(5.7) $\qquad (AP_n)\,(GP_n) = (AP_{n-1})\,(GP_{n-1}) + GP_{n-1} + .5K_n + AP_n\,(UA_n{}^a).$

Note: $[(AP_n)\,(GP_n)]$ is computed because it is needed in the following year's computations.

Because the estimated age of original purchase for the used acquisitions is needed for current-cost computation and the reconstruction of plant balances, it is computed at this time. The used acquisitions in the current year n are assumed to have been originally purchased in year $n - AP*$, where AP is rounded to the nearest integer.

$$(5.8) \qquad\qquad a = n - AP_n*.$$

For all future computations, the used acquisition in the current year is treated as if it had been purchased originally in year a.

Current cost. In the computation of current cost each year, much of the data generated in the computation of average age is used. Furthermore, one will note that the procedures are very similar.

The first step is to multiply the previous year's current cost by the ratio of the current year's year-end price index to the previous year's year-end price index.

$$(6.1) \qquad\qquad CCGP_{n-1} \frac{(PI_n + PI_{n+1})}{(PI_{n-1} + PI_n)}.$$

The current cost (in year-end dollars) of capital expenditures during the year is added to this:

$$(6.2) \qquad\qquad CCK_n = \frac{K_n(PI_n + PI_{n+1})}{2PI_n}.$$

From this total is subtracted the current cost of retirements. The dates of the layers of these retirements are determined in the computation of average age. The associated price index is therefore identified. The current cost of retirements from each layer is:

$$(6.3) \qquad\qquad CCR_n{}^r = \frac{R_n{}^r (PI_n + PI_{n+1})}{2PI_r}$$

where:

$CCR_n{}^r$ = current cost of retirements in year n which were originally acquired in year r.

The current cost of gross plant is summarized as:

$$(6.4) \qquad CCGP_n = CCGP_{n-1} \frac{(PI_n + PI_{n+1})}{PI_{n-1} + PI_n} + CCK_n - CCR_n{}^r.$$

However, should there be net used acquisitions in the current year, the current cost of these must be added (instead of subtracting net retirement current cost). The current cost of used acquisitions is computed as:

$$(6.5) \qquad CCUA_{n^a} = (UA_{n^a}) \frac{(PI_n + PI_{n+1})}{2PI_a}$$

where:

$CCUA_{n^a}$ = current cost of used acquisitions in year n;

a = the estimated date of original purchase [see (5.8)].

Other variables generated

From these calculations, several other important variables are calculated in order to obtain rates of return.

Accumulated depreciation.

Current-Cost Accumulated Depreciation $(CCAD_n)$

$$(7.1) \qquad CCAD_n = (CCGP_n) \frac{(AP_n)}{L} ;$$

[see (1.1), (5.5), (5.6), (6.4)].

Historic-Cost Accumulated Depreciation $(HCAD_n)$

$$(7.2) \qquad HCAD_n = (GP_n) \frac{(AP_n)}{L} \text{ [see (7.1)]}$$

where:

GP_n is the gross plant as reported on the Compustat tapes.

Net plant.

Current Cost Net Plant $(CCNP_n)$

$$(7.3) \qquad CCNP_n = CCGP_n - CCAD_n \text{ [see (7.1)]}.$$

Historic Cost Net Plant $(HCNP_n)$

$$(7.4) \qquad HCNP = GP_n - HCAD_n \text{ [see (7.2)]}.$$

Depreciation expense.

Current Cost Depreciation $(CCDEP_n)$

(7.5) $$CCDEP_n = \frac{CCGP_{n-1} + CCGP_n}{2L} \text{ [see (7.1)]}.$$

Historic Cost Depreciation $(HCDEP_n)$

(7.6) $$HCDEP_n = \frac{GP_{n-1} + GP_n}{2L} \text{ [see (7.2)]}.$$

Income. The computation of each year's income figure, used as the numerator in the rate-of-return calculation, is similar to that used to generate implicit operating profit before taxes—previously denoted **IOPB** (see Appendix C). The only difference is that alternative depreciation figures are used.

Implicit Operating Profit $(IOPB_n)$

(8.1) $IOPB_n = \text{Operating Income}_n - \text{Depreciation}_n + II_n.$

where:

Operating Income is Variable 13 on the Compustat tapes;

Depreciation is Variable 14 on the Compustat tapes;

II is the Implicit Interest as calculated in Appendix C.

Implicit Current Operating Profit $(ICOP_n)$

(8.2) $ICOP_n = \text{Operating Income}_n - CCDEP_n + II_n.$

Implicit Historical Operating Profit $(IHOP_n)$

(8.3) $IHOP_n = \text{Operating Income}_n - HCDEP_n + II_n.$

Investment base. The investment base (total assets) is similar to that calculated for Implicit Operating Returns before Taxes on assets (**IORB**) in Appendix C.

Average Assets (AA) for *IORB*

(9.1) $A = \text{Total Assets/Liabilities} - \text{Investments and Advances to Subsidiaries}$

where:

> Total Assets is Variable 6 on the Compustat tapes.
>
> Investments, etc., is Variable 31 on the Compustat tapes.

(9.2) $$AA_n = \frac{A_n + A_{n-1}}{2}.$$

Average Current Assets (ACA) for $ICOP_n$

(9.3) $$CA = A - \text{Net Plant} + CCNP$$

where:

> Net Plant is Variable 8 on the Compustat tapes.

(9.4) $$ACA_n = \frac{CA_n + CA_{n-1}}{2}.$$

Average Historic Assets (AHA) for $IHOP_n$

(9.5) $$HA = A - \text{Net Plant} + HCNP$$

where:

> Net Plant is Variable 8 on the Compustat tapes.

(9.6) $$AHA_n = \frac{HA_n + HA_{n-1}}{2}.$$

Yearly rate-of-return variables.

Implicit Operating Return ($IORB$)

(10.1) $$IORB_n = \frac{IOPB_n}{AA_n}.$$

Implicit Current Operating Return ($ICOR$)

(10.2) $$ICOR_n = \frac{ICOP_n}{ACA_n}.$$

Implicit Historical Operating Return (*IHOR*)

(10.3)
$$IHOR_n = \frac{IHOP_n}{AHA_n}.$$

Period rate-of-return variables. Let R_{it} be the general notation for all three rate-of-return variables, and let AR_i denote the average return for firm $_i$. The period-average rate-of-return variables are labeled *IORB*, *ICOR*, and *IHOR* respectively. These calculations are summarized:

$$AR_i = \frac{1}{9} \sum_{t=60}^{68} R_{it}.$$

BIBLIOGRAPHY

BIBLIOGRAPHY

Books, Monographs, Reports

Accounting Principles Board, American Institute of Certified Public Accountants. *Basic Concepts and Accounting Principles Underlying Financial Statements of Business Enterprises*. Statement No. 4. New York: American Institute of Certified Public Accountants, October 1970.

————. *Accounting for Income Taxes*. Opinion No. 11. New York: American Institute of Certified Public Accountants, December 1967.

Accounting Research Division of American Institute of Certified Public Accountants. *Reporting the Financial Effects of Price-Level Changes*. Accounting Research Study No. 6. New York: American Institute of Certified Public Accountants, 1963, Appendix D, "Disclosing Effects of Price-Level Changes," pp. 169–218.

Alchian, Armen A., and Allen, William R. *Exchange and Production; Theory in Use*. Belmont, Calif.: Wadsworth, 1969.

Arnold, Thurman; Burns, Arthur R.; Levi, Edward H.; Mason, Edward S.; and Stocking, George W. "The Effectiveness of the Antitrust Laws." In *Monopoly Power and Economic Performance*, edited by Edwin Mansfield. New York: W. W. Norton and Co., 1964.

Bain, Joe S. *Barriers to New Competition*. Cambridge, Mass.: Harvard University Press, 1956.

————. *Industrial Organization*. 2d ed. New York: John Wiley and Sons, 1968.

Baumol, William J. *Business Behavior, Value and Growth*. Rev. ed. New York: Harcourt, Brace and World, 1967.

Brozen, Yale. "Significance of Profit Rate Data for Antitrust Policy." In *Public Policy toward Mergers*, edited by J. Fred Weston and Sam Peltzman. Pacific Palisades, Calif.: Goodyear Publishing Co., 1969, 110–27.

Chamberlin, Edward. *The Theory of Monopolistic Competition*. 7th ed. Cambridge, Mass.: Harvard University Press, 1956.

Chudson, Walter A. *The Pattern of Corporate Financial Structure*. New York: National Bureau of Economic Research, 1945.

Collins, Norman R., and Preston, Lee E. *Concentration and Price-Cost Margins in Manufacturing Industries*. Berkeley, Calif.: University of California Press, 1970.

Cootner, Paul H., and Holland, Daniel M. "Risk and Rate of Return," Massachusetts Institute of Technology, DSR, Project 9565. March 1963. Rev., February 1964. (Mimeographed.)

Cyert, R. M., and March, J. G. *A Behavioral Theory of the Firm*. Englewood Cliffs, N.J.: Prentice-Hall, 1963.

Edwards, Edgar O., and Bell, Philip W. *The Theory and Measurement of Business Income*. Berkeley, Calif.: University of California Press, 1970.

Fama, Eugene F., and Miller, Merton H. *The Theory of Finance.* New York: Holt, Rinehart and Winston, 1972.

Friedman, Milton. *Capitalism and Freedom.* Chicago: University of Chicago Press, Phoenix Books, 1962.

Goldberger, Arthur S. *Econometric Theory.* New York: John Wiley and Sons, 1964.

Hall, Marshall, and Weiss, Leonard. "Appendix to Firm Size and Profitability." n.d. (Mimeographed.)

Hicks, J. R. *Value and Capital.* 2d ed. Oxford: Clarendon Press, 1946.

Johnston, J. *Econometric Methods.* New York: McGraw-Hill Book Co., 1963.

Nelson, Ralph L. *Concentration in the Manufacturing Industries in the United States.* Economic Census Studies No. 2. New Haven, Conn.: Yale University Press, 1963.

Robinson, Joan. *The Economics of Imperfect Competition.* London: Macmillan and Co., 1933.

Rosenbluth, Gideon "Measures of Concentration." In *Business Concentration and Price Policy.* National Bureau of Economic Research. Princeton, N.J.: Princeton University Press, 1955.

Scherer, F. M. *Industrial Market Structure and Economic Performance.* Chicago, Ill.: Rand McNally and Co., 1970.

Schor, Stanley S. "The Capital-Product Ratio and Size of Establishment for Manufacturing Industries." Unpublished Ph.D. dissertation. University of Pennsylvania, 1952.

Schumpeter, Joseph A. *Capitalism, Socialism, and Democracy.* 3d ed. New York: Harper Bros., 1950.

Shepherd, William G. *Market Power and Economic Welfare.* New York: Random House, 1970.

Sherman, Howard J. *Profits in the United States.* Ithaca, N.Y.: Cornell University Press, 1968.

_____. *Macrodynamic Economics: Growth, Employment, and Prices.* New York: Appleton-Century-Crofts, 1964.

Smith, Adam. *The Wealth of Nations.* Modern Library ed. New York: Random House, n.d.

Steindl, Joseph. *Small and Big Business; Economic Problems of the Size of Firms.* Oxford, England: Basil Blackwell, 1947.

Stekler, H. O. *Profitability and Size of Firm.* Berkeley, Calif.: Institute of Business and Economic Research, University of California Printing Dept., 1963.

Stigler, George J. *Capital and Rates of Return in Manufacturing Industries.* Princeton, N.J.: Princeton University Press, 1963.

_____. *The Organization of Industry.* Homewood, Ill.: Richard D. Irwin, Inc., 1968.

Vernon, John M. *Market Structure and Industrial Performance: A Review of Statistical Findings.* Boston: Allyn & Bacon, Inc., 1972.

Williamson, Oliver. *The Economics of Discretionary Behavior: Managerial Objectives in a Theory of the Firm.* Englewood Cliffs, N.J.: Prentice-Hall, Inc., 1964.

Winn, Daryl. "Profitability and Industry Concentration." Working Paper No. 7. Bureau of Business Research, Graduate School of Business Administration, The University of Michigan, 1970. (Multilith.)

General References

Dun and Bradstreet. *Million Dollar Directory, 1968 and 1971.* New York.

Fortune Magazine. *Plant and Product Directory of the 1,000 Largest U.S. Manufacturing Corporations,* 1963–64 and 1965–66. New York: Time, Inc.

News Front. *News Front Directory of 7,500 Leading U.S. Manufacturers.* New York: News Front, 1961.

News Front. *25,000 Leading U.S. Corporations.* New York: News Front, 1970.

Standard and Poor's. *Register.* New York: Standard and Poor's Corp.

Standard and Poor's *Compustat Information Manual.*

Government Documents

U.S. Congress. Joint Economic Committee. *Postwar Movement of Prices and Wages in Manufacturing Industries,* by Harold M. Levinson. Joint Committee Print, Study Paper No. 21. Washington, D.C.: Government Printing Office, January 1960.

U.S. Congress. Senate. "A Bill to Supplement the Antitrust Laws, and to Protect Trade and Commerce against Oligopoly Power and, for Other Purposes." S. 1167. 93rd Cong., 1st sess., 1973. *Congressional Record,* March 12, 1973.

U.S. Congress. Senate. Committee on the Judiciary. Statements of Richard B. Heflebower in *Economic Concentration. Hearings* before the Subcommittee on Antitrust and Monopoly, 88th Cong., 2d sess., 1964. "Part 2: Mergers and Other Factors Affecting Industry Concentration."

U.S. Congress. Senate. White House Task Force on Antitrust Policy. Phil C. Neal, Chairman. "Task Force Report on Antitrust Policy." *Congressional Record.* May 27, 1969.

U.S. Congress. Senate. White House Task Force on Productivity and Competition. George J. Stigler, Chairman. "The Stigler Report on Antitrust Policy and Enforcement." *Congressional Record.* June 12, 1969.

U.S. Congress. Senate. Committee on the Judiciary, Subcommittee on Antitrust and Monopoly. Report prepared by the Bureau of the Census. *Concentration Ratios in Manufacturing Industry, 1963.* Part I and Part II. Washington, D.C.: Government Printing Office, 1966 and 1967.

U.S. Federal Trade Commission. *Economic Report on the Influences of Market Structure on the Profit Performance of Food Manufacturing Companies.* Washington, D.C.: Superintendent of Documents, September 1969.

U.S. Federal Trade Commission, and Securities and Exchange Commission. *Quarterly Financial Report for Manufacturing Corporations.*

U.S. Securities and Exchange Commission. *Directory of Companies Filing Annual Reports with the Securities and Exchange Commission.* Washington, D.C.: Government Printing Office.

U.S. Treasury Department, Internal Revenue Service. *Depreciation Guidelines and Rules.* Revenue Procedure 62–21, Publication No. 456. Rev. August 1964. Washington, D.C.: Government Printing Office, 1964.

U.S. Treasury Department, Internal Revenue Service. *Statistics of Income—1966, Corporation Income Tax Returns.* Washington, D.C.: Government Printing Office, 1970.

U.S. Treasury Department, Internal Revenue Service. *Statistics of Income—1963, Corporation Income Tax Returns.* Washington, D.C.: Government Printing Office, 1969.

Journal Articles

Adelman, M. A. "The Measurement of Industrial Concentration." *Review of Economics and Statistics* 33 (Nov. 1951): 269–96.

Alexander, Sidney S. "The Effect of Size of Manufacturing Corporation on the Distribution of the Rate of Return." *Review of Economics and Statistics* 31 (Aug. 1949): 229–35.

Arditti, Fred. "Risk and the Required Return on Equity." *Journal of Finance* 22 (Mar. 1967): 19–36.

Bailey, Duncan, and Boyle, Stanley E. "The Optimal Measure of Concentration." *Journal of the American Statistical Association* 66 (Dec. 1971): 702–6.

Bain, Joe S. "Corrigendum." *Quarterly Journal of Economics* 65 (Nov. 1951): 602.

_____. "The Profit Rate as a Measure of Monopoly Power." *Quarterly Journal of Economics* 55 (Feb. 1941): 271–93.

_____. "Relation of Profit Rate to Industry Concentration: American Manufacturing, 1936–1940." *Quarterly Journal of Economics* 65 (Aug. 1951): 293–324.

Baker, Samuel H. "Risk, Leverage and Profitability: An Industry Analysis." *Review of Economics and Statistics* 55 (Nov. 1973): 503–7.

Brozen, Yale. "Barriers Facilitate Entry." *Antitrust Bulletin* 14 (Winter 1969): 851–54.

_____. "Concentration and Structural and Market Disequilibria." *Antitrust Bulletin* 16 (Summer 1971): 241–48.

_____. "The Antitrust Task Force Deconcentration Recommendation." *Journal of Law and Economics* 13 (Oct. 1970): 279–92.

_____. "Bain's Concentration and Rates of Return Revisited." *Journal of Law and Economics* 14 (Oct. 1971): 351–69.

_____. "The Persistence of 'High Rates of Return' in High-Stable Concentration Industries." *Journal of Law and Economics* 14 (Oct. 1971): 501–12.

Caves, R. E., and Yamey, B. S. "Risk and Corporate Rates of Return: Comment." *Quarterly Journal of Economics* 85 (Aug. 1971): 513–17.

Collins, Norman R., and Preston, Lee E. "Price-Cost Margins and Industry Structure." *Review of Economics and Statistics* 51 (Aug. 1969): 271–86.

Comanor, William S., and Wilson, Thomas A. "Advertising and the Advantages of Size." *American Economic Review* 59 (May 1969): 87–98.

_____. "Advertising Market Structure and Performance." *Review of Economics and Statistics* 69 (Nov. 1967): 423–40.

_____. "On Advertising and Profitability." *Review of Economics and Statistics* 53 (Nov. 1971): 408–10.

Conrad, Gordon R., and Plotkin, Irving H. "Risk/Return: U.S. Industry Pattern." *Harvard Business Review* 46 (Mar.–Apr. 1968): 90–99.

Cootner, Paul H., and Holland, Daniel M. "Rate of Return and Business Risk." *Bell Journal of Economics and Management Science* 1 (Autumn 1970): 211–26.

Davis, Hiram S. "Relation of Capital-Output Ratio to Firm Size in American Manufacturing: Some Additional Evidence." *Review of Economics and Statistics* 38 (Aug. 1956): 286–93.

Dyckman, T. R., and Stekler, H. O. "Firm Size and Variability." *Journal of Industrial Economics* 13 (June 1965): 214–18.

Felton, John Richard. "Concentration, Conditions of Entry, and Profit Rates." *Mississippi Valley Journal of Business and Economics* 1 (Spring 1966): 1–13.

Fisher, I. N., and Hall, G. R. "Risk and Corporate Rates of Return." *Quarterly Journal of Economics* 83 (Feb. 1969): 79–92.

_____. "Risk and Corporate Rates of Return: Reply." *Quarterly Journal of Economics* 85 (Aug. 1971): 518–22.

Friedman, Milton, and Savage, L. J. "The Utility Analysis of Choices Involving Risk." *Journal of Political Economy* 56 (Aug. 1948): 279–304.

Fuchs, Victor R. "Integration, Concentration, and Profits in Manufacturing Industries." *Quarterly Journal of Economics* 75 (May 1961): 278–91.

George, K. D. "Concentration, Barriers to Entry and Rates of Return." *Review of Economics and Statistics* 50 (May 1968): 273–75.

Gupta, Manak C. "The Effect of Size, Growth, and Industry on the Financial Structure of Manufacturing Companies." *Journal of Finance* 24 (June 1969): 517–29.

Hall, Marshall, and Weiss, Leonard. "Firm Size and Profitability." *Review of Economics and Statistics* 49 (Aug. 1967): 319–31.

Hall, Marshall, and Tideman, Nicolaus. "Measures of Concentration." *Journal of the American Statistical Association* 62 (Mar. 1967): 162–68.

Henning, John A. "Marginal Concentration Ratios: Some Statistical Implications—Comment." *Southern Economic Journal* 36 (Oct. 1969): 196–98.

Hymer, Stephen, and Pashigian, P. "Firm Size and Rate of Growth." *Journal of Political Economy* 70 (Dec. 1962): 556–69.

Jarrett, Jeffrey E. "Risk Comparisons between Public Utilities and Non-Regulated Industries." *Mississippi Valley Journal of Business and Economics* 6 (Winter 1970–71): 1–9.

Kamerschen, David R. "Market Growth and Industry Concentration." *Journal of the American Statistical Association* 63 (Mar. 1968): 228–41.

_____. "The Determination of Profit Rates in 'Oligopolistic Industries.'" *Journal of Business* 42 (July 1969): 293–301.

Kilpatrick, Robert W. "The Choice among Alternative Measures of Industrial Concentration." *Review of Economics and Statistics* 49 (May 1967): 258–60.

_____. "Stigler on the Relationship between Industry Profit Rates and Market Concentration." *Journal of Political Economy* 76 (Mar.–June, 1968): 479–88.

Lanzillotti, Robert F. "Pricing Objectives in Large Companies." *American Economic Review* 48 (Dec. 1958): 921–40.

Leibenstein, H. "Allocative Efficiency and 'X-Efficiency.'" *American Economic Review* 56 (June 1966): 392–415.

Lintner, J. "Effect of Corporate Taxation on Real Investment." *American Economic Review* 44 (May 1954): 520–34.

MacAvoy, Paul W.; McKie, James.; and Preston, Lee E. "High and Stable Concentration Levels, Profitability, and Public Policy: A Response." *Journal of Law and Economics* 14 (Oct. 1971): 493–99.

Mann, H. Michael. "The Interaction of Barriers and Concentration: A Reply." *Journal of Industrial Economics* 19 (July 1971): 291–93.

_____. "A Note on Barriers to Entry and Long Run Profitability." *Antitrust Bulletin* 14 (Winter, 1969): 845–49.

_____. "Seller Concentration, Barriers to Entry, and Rates of Return in Thirty Industries, 1950–1960." *Review of Economics and Statistics* 48 (Aug. 1966): 296–307.

_____, and Meehan, James W., Jr. "Concentration and Profitability: An Examination of a Recent Study." *Antitrust Bulletin* 14 (Summer 1969): 385–95.

Marcus, Matityahu. "Size of Establishment and the Capital-Output Ratio: An Empirical Investigation." *Southern Economic Journal* 32 (July 1965): 53–62.

_____. "Profitability and Size of Firm: Some Further Evidence." *Review of Economics and Statistics* 51 (Feb. 1969): 104–7.

Miller, Richard A. "Market Structure and Industrial Performance: Relation of Profit Rates to Concentration, Advertising Intensity and Diversity." *Journal of Industrial Economics* 17 (Apr. 1969): 104–18.

_____. "Marginal Concentration Ratios as Market Structure Variables." *Review of Economics and Statistics* 53 (Aug. 1971): 289–93.

_____. "Marginal Concentration Ratios: Some Statistical Implications—Reply." *Southern Economic Journal* 36 (Oct. 1969): 199–201.

_____. "Marginal Concentration Ratios and Industrial Profit Rates: Some Empirical Results of Oligopoly Behavior." *Southern Economic Journal* 34 (Oct. 1967): 259–67.

Moroney, John R., and Duggar, Jan W. "Size of Firm and Capital-Output Ratios: A Comparative Study in U.S. Manufacturing." *MSU Business Topics* 15 (Summer 1967): 16–23.

_____. "Vertical Integration and Capital-Output Ratios in U.S. Manufacturing Industry." *Quarterly Review of Economics and Business* 7 (Summer 1967): 23–27.

Nelson, Ralph L. "Market Growth, Company Diversification and Product Concentration, 1947–1954." *Journal of the American Statistical Association* 55 (Dec. 1960): 640–49.

Osborn, Richards C. "Concentration and Profitability of Small Manufacturing Corporations." *Quarterly Review of Economics and Business* 10 (Summer 1970): 15–26.

Qualls, David. "Concentration, Barriers to Entry, and Long Run Economic Profit Margins." *Journal of Industrial Economics* 20 (Apr. 1972): 146–58.

Rhoades, S. A. "Concentration, Barriers to Entry, and Rates of Return Revisited." *Journal of Industrial Economics* 20 (Apr. 1972): 193–95.

_____. "Concentration, Barriers and Rates of Return: A Note." *Journal of Industrial Economics* 18 (Nov. 1970): 82–88.

Shepherd, W. G. "The Elements of Market Structure." *Review of Economics and Statistics* 54 (Feb. 1972): 25–37.

_____. "Trends of Concentration in American Manufacturing Industries, 1947–1958." *Review of Economics and Statistics* 66 (May 1964): 200–12.

Sherman, Roger, and Tollison, Robert. "Technology, Profit Risk, and Assessments of Market Performance." *Quarterly Journal of Economics* 86 (Aug. 1972): 449–62.

Stekler, H. O. "The Variability of Profitability with Size of Firm, 1947–1958." *Journal of the American Statistical Association* 59 (Dec. 1964): 1183–93.

Stigler, George J. "A Theory of Oligopoly." *Journal of Political Economy* 72 (Feb. 1964): 44–61.

Weiss, Leonard W. "Average Concentration Ratios and Industrial Performance." *Journal of Industrial Economics* 11 (July 1963): 237–54.

_____. "Concentration and Labor Earnings." *American Economic Review* 56 (Mar. 1966): 96–117.

Wenders, John T. "Profits and Antitrust Policy: The Question of Disequilibrium." *Antitrust Bulletin* 16 (Summer 1971): 249–56.

Winn, Daryl N., and Leabo, Dick A. "Rates of Return, Concentration and Growth—Question of Disequilibrium." *Journal of Law and Economics* 17 (Apr. 1974): 97–115.